Have you ever gotten trapped in a parallel state of consciousness,

somewhere between sleeping and wakefulness, unable to breathe for the

pressure on your chest, heart palpitating, Out of Body, paralyzed,

unable to move?

Have you ever awakened from a surreal dream state,

vocal cords frozen, unable to call out for help,

even to someone lying right beside you?

Have you ever had the sensation of floating out of your physical body,

sinking or falling, weightless, adrift ...

and what or who is that presence in the room?

This is no small thing, not necessarily the ramblings of someone experiencing a psychotic break. But that's exactly what it sounds like and how it feels ... Until after the sigh of relief that "it" is over, and the shallow breath of fear inhaled, waiting ... wondering ... will I survive the next one? Will this ever stop? If any of this sounds familiar in any way, know, I have been there, I am there, we all are there, whether we realize it or not. When I'd had enough of the dismissive suspicion after confiding in trusted friends and professionals, the vacant stare, the rise of the left brow ... I started doing my homework, and as extensive a research project as I could bear. Not so much about what I "found" but what I "lost." I lost a knee-jerk reaction to falling into fear of the unknown because it became known. I rose into spiritual confidence through committed discipline and daily practice.

In this book, I share my findings.

SLEEPLESS

Transcend the Fear
of
Sleep Paralysis

JAI

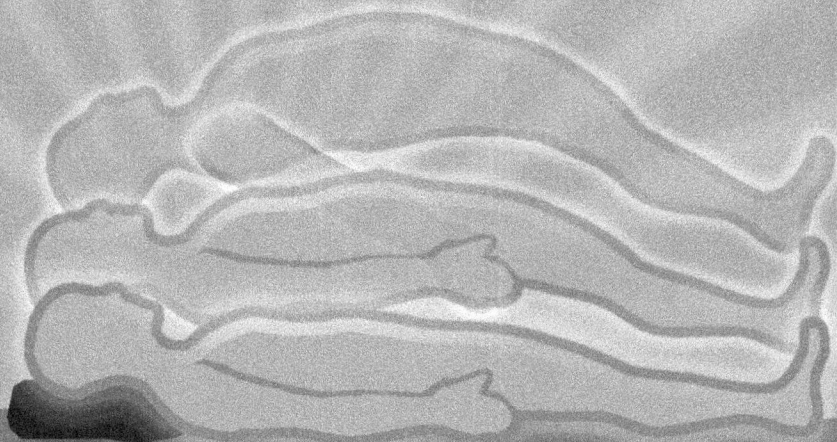

SLEEPLESS

Transcend the Fear
of
Sleep Paralysis

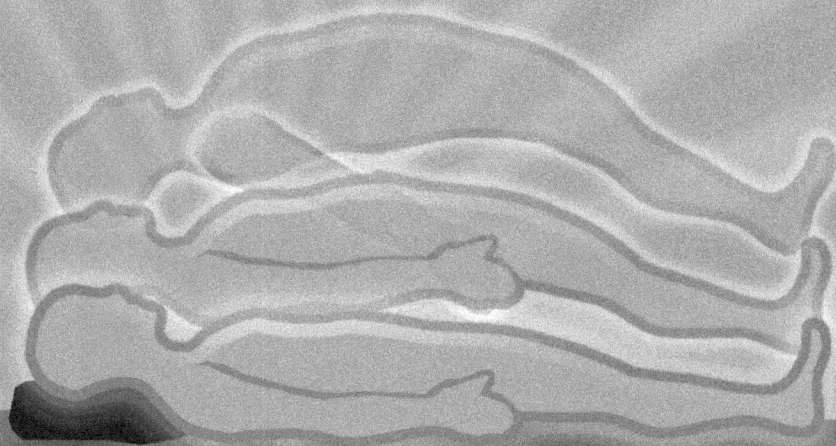

SLEEPLESS; Transcend the Fear of Sleep Paralysis
By JAI.

Copyright © 2019 by JAI (Dream Universal Media)

ISBN-13: 978-1-7324068-4-1

Edited by: Timothy Rodd

Disclaimer:

The materials contained in this text, and related recordings, are provided for general information only and do not constitute medical or psychological professional advice. The author nor the publisher accepts responsibility for any loss which may arise from inappropriate reliance on information contained in this text.

The contents of this book and the recordings of the meditations herein are protected by copyright under international conventions, and the reproduction or retransmission of the contents of this text and related recordings and artwork is prohibited without the prior written consent of the author.

The content of this text and related recordings, including all music, all text, all downloads, all music samples, and all other material, are owned or controlled by *dream universal media* and their content and technology providers. ALL RIGHTS RESERVED. Unauthorized duplication or distribution of this content is strictly prohibited.

A Note of Caution:

If you are experiencing thoughts of harming yourself or others, or seized by overwhelming emotions, attempting Mystical Meditation that involves Self-Inquiry, or the witnessing of the mental process through meditation and contemplation, is NOT advised as it may cause these feelings to intensify. You are encouraged to seek the immediate help of a licensed therapist or healthcare practitioner.

The information in this text is for informational purposes only and not intended to diagnose, treat, cure, or prevent any disease. If you are experiencing symptoms of depression or a physical problem, it is advised that you see medical and psychological professionals for evaluation.

Consecration

May the words of my mouth and the meditations of my heart be acceptable to The Most High, Creator of all the worlds. I pray that my will and Thy Will become as One. I write from that Oneness.

I offer this book in the Name of the One Holy, True, and Eternal God, Lord of all the worlds and Timeless realms, in all of their physical and non-physical appearances. We seek to know the Oneness of The Divine and not be distracted by the phenomena of creation and the divisive labels that seek to define what cannot be defined. I bear witness to the truth of Timeless Wisdom delivered by the prophets, apostles, messengers, saints, angels, guardians, and servants of The Divine Light.

My soul is grateful for the Protection, Love, and Guidance of The Comforter, The Holy Spirit. I accept that The Faces that have been shown us, as Manifestations of The Creator, known and unknown, seen and unseen, were, and are, among us … never departed. In the ebb and flow of The Return, we prepare ourselves for our rightful place among the surrendered, the worthy.

I offer this journal from no position of authority. I am but a traveler, a student, a seeker, lifting my pen and voice to express praise, and thanks to The Almighty, The Most High, for the blessing of this opportunity to share this journey with you.

I have learned
so much from God
that I can no longer
call myself
a Christian, a Hindu, a Muslim,
a Buddhist, a Jew.
The truth has shared so much of itself
with me
that I can no longer call myself
a man, a woman, an angel,
or even a pure Soul.
Love has
befriended Hafiz so completely,
it has turned to ash
and freed me
of every concept and image
my mind has ever known.

~ Hafiz ~

Dedication

I thank The Most High for that first trip to the other side for evidence that there is no "veil" between worlds. You showed me that the realm of Maya was just the tip of the iceberg. You smiled Transcendence upon me from one dimension into the next. Thank you for opening the portal to the Mystic and showing me that this is not all there is. You showed me that death is only a figment of the collective imagination. You taught me that people really can change. You've shown me a higher Love.

I thank my mother, Dorothy Raushanna Hassain, the sunshine of my life, for teaching me that there is no such thing as a one-dimensional world. Her life still breathes through me, and all of the lives she so graciously touched. She was one of the most powerful Natural Mystics I have ever known. I am so grateful to her for all of the love she brought to my life. She was my biggest fan and often my only fan … and I was and am hers. She was a warrior … a peacemaker … a counselor … a healer … a real, live angel. I thank The God every day for ever having known her.

I give thanks to my ancestors, who remembered me before I was the thought that is me, who delivered me to my understanding, who speak from their watery and earthly graves from the realm of the Timeless to remind me there is no such thing as death. You are the vibration of an ancient drum beating itself into Ultimate relevance, telling true stories time wrote in the Ether of their erasure. The Spirit of cultures of origin occupied, set aside, and buried under the Earth from which a new world rises, snatching Light back from thieves and raiders, grave robbers, and soul traders. Scientists, still unsure of what the magic means, can only wonder as it surfaces in dreams of clandestine things that rise like the Phoenix to be known again.

This Magick cannot be burned down with a library. It will not be mocked. It breathes a sacred breath that cannot be choked out or gunned down with silver bullets. It is airborne and cannot be buried, disguised, or replaced with lies. It flows through the bloodline of the body of consciousness that is waking up from this dream. The mouthless whispers emerge from a mosaic of inspired visions of prophetic graffiti, inscribed upon the walls of what will not be forgotten. Voices ride the whirlwinds of the unborn realm into the eye of the cyclone, that place of stillness and silence and Light.

Acknowledgments

Many thanks to Timothy Rodd for opening your Third Eye wide enough to see a finish line I almost lost sight of, and for tirelessly helping me cross it. Thank you for sharing your energy and refusing to stop just short of the journey's victory. I may have given up had you not been inspired to see that and become an intervention in my life. I know my mom loves that you helped me share this story of healing. Thank you for graphic design, cover art, and all of your editing work.

Thank you, Richard Allen, for pulling me out of the perfect storm. I give thanks for the braided twists and turns of fate and circumstance the Universe delivered to my doorstep that caused our paths to cross. Your spiritual strength and guidance helped me to bear the unbearable. Thank you for being the angel that tore Nicholas and me away from the grip of the reaper. The Natural Mystic is alive and well in your heart of hearts.

Matthias Swaby – I thank you for your prayers. Your life is a testament to the power of God over life and death. I thank God for you and for the spiritual intervention that performed a profound healing in my life. I can never repay you for your bravery, persistence, and courage, fearlessly confronting demons with the touch of an angel of God. Your humble manner and your chosen surrendered life are a soul's inspiration. I am blessed to have been welcomed into your spiritual family.

Arthur Hakalani Pacheco – Mahalo! I miss you! Thank you for teaching me more about death than I ever wanted to know. I will always remember your radiant smile, your melodic laughter, and looking forward to current stories of your dramatic inter-dimensional journeying … each with a wild metaphysical twist, pouring out more Light and Love than anyone could contain all at once. Thank you for sharing your ethereal world, welcoming us into it, and teaching us that it has always been our home. You made such a graceful dance of living in the Light and singing the blues at the same time.

Nicholas … Thank you for lending your beautiful voice to the Dream Universal Guided Meditation recordings. The vibration of your voice brought a powerful healing spirit to the meditation. Thank you for believing in me and pushing me to reach higher.

Night Shift Editing Team – Thank you all for your energy, time, and diligence. The devil is in the details. Thank you for following it through to the last breath of exorcising that beast.

The Light Meditation

Written by JAI
Tim Rodd: Narration, Copy Editing, Post Production
Levi Chen: Chinese Harp or Zither
Rahmon Muhammad: Sound Engineer
Sebastian Robertson: Sound Engineer

Many thanks to prolific composer, producer, visionary musician, and performing artist … the heart and soul of Yin Yang Records and Liquid Gardens, Levi Chen. Dream Universal extends immense appreciation, love, and light for your participation in our healing Mystical Meditation journeys. The East meets West meets the Cosmos, ethereal soundscapes of Meditation of my Soul, featuring the interplay of ambient electric guitar textures and the traditional Gu Zheng, Chinese harp, formed a sound that perfectly complements our catalog of healing meditations.

SLEEPLESS

Transcend the Fear of Sleep Paralysis

Table of Contents

Consecration

Acknowledgments

WHAT IS SLEEP PARALYSIS?   01

What is Sleep Paralysis?   02

Manifestations of Sleep Paralysis   14

States of Consciousness Associated with Sleep Paralysis   23

The Nightmare: Fuseli Painting - Sleep Paralysis   29

The Chakra System

    36

Meditation Posture Diagram   40

Preparation for Chakra Visualization Exercise

    41

Targeted Chakra Visualization Exercise to Strengthen Your Defense   42
    System - Lower Portal Visualization

Targeting Individuals through the Lower Portal   47

Targeted Chakra Visualization Exercise to Strengthen Your Defense   51
    System- Upper Portal Visualization

Self-Inquiry Meditation   59

Clinical Interpretations of Sleep Paralysis   66

The Danger of Body/Mind Identification and Sleep Paralysis   70

APPENDIX ONE - The Body System   73

The Body System Diagram 74

The Body System 75

- The Light Body/Subtle Body/Auric Body 75

- The Mental Self 77

- The Emotional Self 78

- The Physical Self 78

- The Soul/The Ether/The True Self 80

The Aura in Psychic Self-Defense Sleep Paralysis 82

Aura Diagrams:

- Healthy Aura 89

- Polluted Aura 90

- Aura Under Psychic Attack 91

- Light Sphere of Protection 92

- Refuge: The Merkaba Vehicle of Light 93

APPENDIX TWO - The I AM & Non-Physical 95
    Existence (NPE)

The Meaning of The I AM 96

Protect the I AM 100

I AM Consciousness Rising 103

Diagram –Who are you? 109

The Ego Under Attack 110

APPENDIX THREE - PLANES OF EXISTENCE 115

Planes of Existence Diagram 116

Planes of Existence 117

- 0 – Unknowable 117

- 7 – Realm of Divinity 119

- 6 – Archetypal Realm   120
- 5 – Etheric Realm   121
- 4 – Astral Realm   122
- 3 – Mental Realm   124
- 2 – Emotional Realm   125
- 1 – Physical Realm   126

Manifestation: As Above So Below   130

WHAT CAUSES SLEEP PARALYSIS?   137

Adapted sections are shared here from my book, FEARLESS: PSYCHIC SELF-DEFENSE, Transcending the Fear of Spiritual Warfare. They are specifically conformed for their relevance to the experience of Sleep Paralysis.

Signs of Natural Psychic Abilities   138

Spiritual Warfare   146

Signs of Positive Mysticism   149

Signs of Negative Mysticism   152

Spiritual Emergencies   159

- Spiritual Emergencies Induced by Spiritual Practice   159
- Group Karma   160
- Spontaneous Kundalini Awakening   162
- Yoga Samadhi and Sleep Paralysis Events   165
- The Danger of Cultural Appropriation   170

Global Experience of Sleep Paralysis Diagram   171

Regions of the World and Names for Sleep Paralysis and Associated   172
    Entities

Experiences/Symptoms in Common and Reported Causes   175
    or Triggers of Sleep Paralysis

Reported Causes or Triggers of Sleep Paralysis   185

How Non-Physical Beings Shapeshift and Appear to Us   187

APPENDIX FOUR - FACELESS: The Sacred Relationship   189
    THE ARCHETYPE OF THE UNDEAD

The Archetype of The Undead   190

GAINING CONTROL OVER SLEEP PARALYSIS EVENTS 207

Gaining Control Over Sleep Paralysis Event   208
Protection Practices to Study and Incorporate into your Spiritual   219
    Discipline
Nothing to Prove   223
Methods of Spiritual Protection   226
The Power of Prayer Intervention and Faith   242
The Phenomenon of Weaponized Prayer   252
The Power of Repetitive Prayer   263
    -    The Om Diagram   267
    -    The Sacred Om, Ohm, AUM   268
    -    The Power of "HU"   275

APPENDIX FIVE - FACELESS: The Sacred Relationship   281
    THE ARCHETYPE OF THE INTERCEDING SPIRIT
    (HOLY SPIRIT)

The Archetype of The Interceding Holy Spirit   282

APPENDIX SIX - Meditation is the Bridge Between   301
    Worlds of Consciousness

Meditation is the Bridge Between Worlds of Consciousness   302

The Sacred Self   306

Basic Guidelines for Meditation   308

Journaling   313

APPENDIX SEVEN - The Light Meditation   317

The Light Meditation   318

The Light Meditation Transcript   319

Epilogue   332

Becoming One with Sacred Space as Pure Consciousness   343

About the Author   346

Meditation Download Instructions   348

Works Cited   349

Recommended Reading   350

APPENDICES ONE - SEVEN are presented within the contextual flow on these subjects, provide easy access, and avoid disrupting the continuity of related, relevant materials, shared here from other cited books.

Material shared from THE TIMELESS NOW: Healing from Loss and Grief, FEARLESS: PSYCHIC SELF-DEFENSE, and FACELESS: THE SACRED RELATIONSHIP, by Jai, because of its relevance to the subject of this book.

APPENDIX ONE - The Body System

APPENDIX TWO - The I AM & Non-Physical Existence (NPE)

APPENDIX THREE - Planes of Existence

APPENDIX FOUR - FACELESS: THE SACRED RELATIONSHIP - The Archetype Of The Undead

APPENDIX FIVE - FACELESS: THE SACRED RELATIONSHIP - The Interceding Spirit (Holy Spirit)

APPENDIX SIX - Meditation is the Bridge Between Worlds of Consciousness

APPENDIX SEVEN - The Light Meditation

You are invited to join SLEEPLESS: Transcend the Fear of Sleep Paralysis, a Facebook support group designed specifically as an expanded study guide. This subject matter cannot be contained in any single text. This group serves as a resourceful interactive site, offering healing and inspiration. In times of overwhelm, seek professional help and support from trusted family, friends, and wise spiritual counsel.

What is Sleep Paralysis?

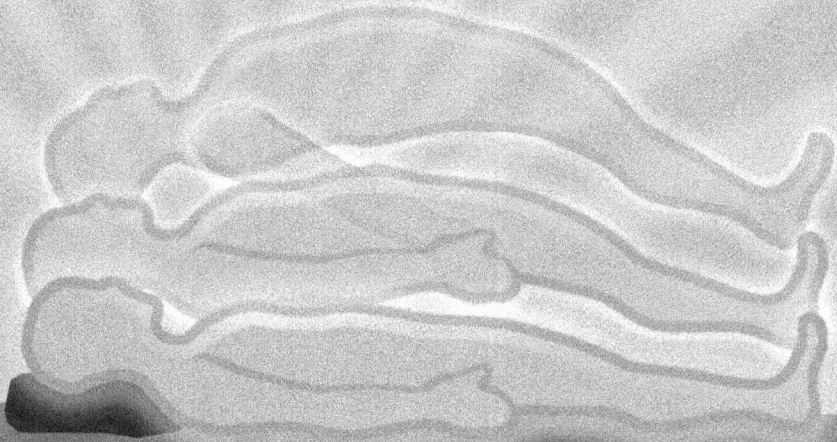

What is Sleep Paralysis?

Imagine … Somewhere in-between dreams … between awake and asleep … somewhere in between rapid eye movement and painfully rapid, thunderous, reverberating heart palpitations, one last shallow breath frozen in a compressed throat, failing to sound an outcry for help. On the bed, in the silent darkness, lies a body, cold, clammy, and rigid … seized and defenseless, caught in the clutches of some ominous, threatening, invisible force … blanketed by the heavy, grey aura of death's first moments. SILENCE screaming through complete awareness of what is happening … again … a million soundless questions flood a mind, frozen in fear and stuck inside of a horror movie after the music changes and gets creepy. Time stands still. It is difficult to determine how long a Sleep Paralysis event lasts. After it is over, it feels like its duration could have been a few seconds, a few minutes, but it feels like a few hours or a lifetime.

Imagine waking up from what appeared to begin as a night of peaceful sleep, unable to move, speak, react, defend yourself, or call for help … even to someone in the same room or bed. Imagine being afraid of the dark, afraid to go to sleep, afraid to sleep alone, afraid to confide in anyone what is going on, afraid of being ridiculed, afraid to even know what the truth of it is … every time, wondering …

- What is happening to me?

- Why is this happening to me?

- How long will this one last?

- Will it last forever?

- Can I break this spell?

- Am I dying?

- Am I dead, and I just don't know it?

- WHAT or WHO is the presence I feel in the room?

- Who …? What is the evil is in this room?

- Who … What evil is trying to get inside of me?

- Who … What evil is moving inside of me?

- Whose voice is taunting me?

- What are those shadows?

- Why is my mouth sealed shut?

- Why can't I move?

- Why can't I scream for help?

- What is holding me down?

- Why can't I remember what I'm supposed to say and do to make it stop?

- How long was I "out?" … "gone?"

The unrelenting, ever-hovering anticipation of the terror lurking in unseen shadows can pave the way for a full array of psychological and physical ailments and syndromes, the most common of which initially presents as sleep disorders. Some people who experience this enigmatic condition are fortunate enough to have the counsel of medical professionals who do not knee-jerk to a prescription pad for anti-depressants and sleeping pills as a solution for every malady. If, after seeking help, no physical or psychological cause is found, isn't it reasonable to explore other possible causes? Shouldn't it at least make one *wonder* if something *else* is going on? … beginning with the question, "What is that threatening presence in the room that many feel during a Sleep Paralysis Event? Why do the victims of such

S.P. events invariably complain of feeling "attacked by something evil and not of this world?"

The first time I experienced a Sleep Paralysis event, I didn't know what a psychic attack was. I had never heard mention of the term. My mother intervened when she heard "choking" sounds from my room in the middle of the night. She told me that when she entered the room, she found that nothing of me was touching the bed, except the back of my head and my heels. I was frozen in an arched position. What I remember is that I was hovering over my physical body. I was looking down at it, and I could not release myself from the force that pulled me out of it and prevented me from getting back in. It felt as though my Life Force was being sucked out of my chest area around my heart and Solar Plexus region. I could not figure out how I was being pulled out.

There was an acute and chilling awareness of 'self' as a non-physical reality. All I knew is that I could not get back in. I remember there being an awareness that if I could not get back in my body, it would die. That was when terror seized me. My mother had to shake me back to consciousness aggressively, but I knew that I had not been unconscious, not awake, nor asleep. My body of consciousness had spontaneously separated from my physical body. The two were connected but moving further and further apart, threatening to break the energetic silver cord that connects them.

I had no context for what was happening. That was the beginning of my journey and study of the mystical path. I learned that there are many realms of consciousness with distinctive properties. I learned that there is more than one way of being "attacked" by someone with a grudge, seeking to manipulate others against their will, and cause them harm. I knew that this drama didn't fall out of a vacuum.

I knew that there was a physical and non-physical point of origin of this strange, violent energy. I knew the intention was malevolent.

I instinctively knew there was nothing physically wrong with me and that what happened was beyond any level of common understanding and experience. I knew that whatever it was or wasn't, it was of a spiritual, otherworldly nature. I knew it was beyond the realm of cause and effect, Time and Space, good and incredible evil, matter, and whatever its antithesis would be. To have had the literal life-force snatched from my physical body and left helplessly struggling to get back 'in' as it gasped for air ... compressed and choking ... dying. It was beyond anything I'd ever imagined even possible.

Every possible physical cause was considered and ruled out. That was the beginning of my journey through the netherworlds. I lost friends. I lost family. I lost jobs. I lost the ability to communicate candidly with everyone I knew at the time. I lost the ability to sleep without fear of it happening again. It became a solitary hell, with even apparently unrelated aspects of my life forever impacted by this bizarre "secret" that would have had me branded insane, by anyone that I'd trust to confide in. It was not possible to foresee when it would happen again ... if, perhaps, it had gone away for good ... how living with it would compromise the experience of ever being able to live a "normal" life.

Years later, dazed from another sleepless night, trying to feel "normal," I was wandering through the Woodland Hills swap meet near my home. I strolled past a booth that was elegantly decorated with exquisite celestial art, unusual to see at an open market in Los Angeles. Mystical symbols danced in reflections on the cubicle wall, illuminated by the light of a single lamp with a base sculpted in the form of an angel. Smoke clouds of sage, frankincense, and myrrh circled around the mysterious European lady seated in a wicker fan back chair in the corner. The song of the streams of water flowing over the rocks and amethyst crystals of a decorative fountain rose to meet and mingle with exotic reed flute music.

I don't remember her name. I remember her floral-patterned flowing chiffon belted caftan. She was much older than me at the time. She leaned forward, arm braced on a cafe table draped with a colorful cloth that was painted with the same strange symbols on the wall, her cards, and her books.   Her pensive stare dissolved into a confused frown line … our eyes met with her asking, "Why would? … How could ANY body do something like that to you? Whispering under her breath,"… so young … so *innocent*?" She looked at me, shaking her head with an empathic sorrow that penetrated to the core of my being … as though she saw a picture of my whole life pouring out from behind my perplexed eyes and feigned smile.

With an outstretched hand, she motioned for me to step inside and have a seat in a chair on the other side of her table. I remember laughing to myself, shaking my head "no" and smirking, saying, "I don't have any money for you." I had noted the decorative bookcase behind her with items that resembled things I'd seen in movies … cards, coins, a sage wand burning, stones, and crystals. I kept walking. She called out to me, "Why? … How? … could ANY body do something like that to you … again whispering … so young … so innocent? Come! *You* need a reading! I can help you. You MUST know exactly what I am talking about. Oh my God … What must your life be like?

Her blue eyes clouded over with tears. "Hmmmm," I thought. "She still has a future in the film industry … very authentic …" I kept in mind that Hollywood is the land full of tear-filled eyes from an eye drop bottle, longing for stardom. She told me in a snarly voice that she didn't want my money and that I couldn't afford her anyway. She told me she wanted to teach me how to do what she does. She offered, "I can teach you how to save yourself. You have no choice but to learn. The portal is *you*. You already *know* how to do what I do. I want to be the one who makes you remember. You have no choice."

My response was "normal," considering her persistence … "Look, lady, *please,* I am not interested in whatever it is you are peddling." Unless you have the perfect purse, I can fill up with the take-home pay from my new job that I'm looking for … I'm going to just keep on walking," *trying not to be rude.* She followed me down the aisle. I was nervous. She was dressed like pictures I'd seen of a hippie past her prime, yet effervescent with a sparkle, an energy, a mystical elegance that flowed with her colorful, sheer scarf and wrap … piercing eyes dancing around too-wide pupils … narrowed and squinting with obvious concern … *fear*, perhaps? … *horror*? I said again what I was sure would turn her away, "I really have no money," with a silent, "…for you." She offered to "read" me for free, and that if I would agree to it, she would be so *thrilled* to teach me (or make me remember) for free.

I was disarmed by money not being a factor. I said to myself … "Oh, so what!" and sank into the comfortable portal/time bubble that was a rattan gliding chair … and disappeared into her stories about my life, even before I was born, known and unknown to me. She knew about the Sleep Paralysis I suffered from and told me that it was not a physical condition but the manifestation of what is known as a psychic attack. I had no place for any of it to land, HOWEVER … It just so happened that I was going through a hellish family feud and had angered an entire family of powerful mystics. WELL! That was the first clue that I had no choice but to learn about what I was living at the effect of. I had no idea that anyone could actually project an energy that could, in any way, affect another person, place, thing, or situation … not to mention the idea of shifting or projecting an entire alter reality. I knew there was something about the encounter that was no coincidence and that there was something about her that was real. How could she know so much about a perfect stranger?

After a long list of manifestations that she forecasted had come true ... I went back to find her. I didn't understand how any of this could be happening. I didn't believe in it. I wanted to know more. She had left without a trace that she had ever been there. Nobody knew her or where she had gone. I never saw her again, but she had planted a seed that cracked open and pushed its way through to the surface, to the Light ... that, many years later, grew into a flowering, fruit-bearing tree. After life had become terrifying and unbearable enough, I began to study the science of metaphysics. Maybe I ultimately went too far. Maybe not. Had I not gone too far, how else could I have eventually known what "too far" looks and feels like ... not to mention the price to be paid for the practice of spiritual indiscretions and line crossings.

The next day, I was in a Sunset Blvd. diner, and an elderly lady walked over to my table, after stopping short at the exit and spinning around to make eye contact with me. She was dressed reminiscent of elegant vintage Hollywood. She headed straight to my booth with an "I'm on a mission look." She criticized my driving ... scolded me for driving too fast and recklessly. She described my car, which was parked in a structure a block away. A far-away look passed over her eyes ... she began to describe what she was seeing in what she called a "vision." "The hood is up. Steam is pouring out. So much rain ... can't see ... loud music (radio) ... too loud. You're alive, but I don't see you in the car." "Get your son! He is far away. He is in danger." She left her tattered business card on my table and told me we'd be having coffee at her cottage-styled home up the hill from the Chateau Marmont. This was all way too much for one week, even in La La Land, where everything is an illusion anyway. I told her I'd had enough of the woo-woo for one lifetime, and that I didn't believe in it.

After my encounter with the lady at the Woodland Hills Swap Meet, this all was just too much to ignore … especially after the next day, I found myself standing outside my car on the street she described, in a torrential rainstorm. Late for work, I had been driving too fast for the sudden change in weather conditions and hit an oil slick. My car hydroplaned and slammed into the car in front of me, which sped away into the distance. That simply doesn't happen. A rear-end collision is always the fault of the driver who hit the car in front, and nobody speeds away to handle their own damage without compensation from the driver at fault. There must have been another story there. How did I end up outside of the car? The sky had opened up and obstructed my vision. I could not see a car's length ahead of me. The car in front of me had no brake lights or tail lights. My car received the most damage. On impact, I completely freaked out, screaming uncontrollably. I jumped out of the car to assess the damage, so hysterical that I left the keys in the ignition and the car running. On reflex, I locked the door, locking myself out of the car, screaming in the rain. I saw the entire scene in my mind from a bird's eye view and reflected upon the vision the lady in the diner had seen. The hood was up, steam pouring out, and the music was blasting what she had described as her least favorite genre (she told me it was distracting) … the car was locked with me outside of it. I immediately began making arrangements to remove my son from a situation that turned out to be just in time to avoid the danger she had seen in her vision.

I was so shaken, that after I got the catastrophe all sorted out, I dug up the business card she had left on the table at the restaurant. She invited me to her Vintage-Hollywood styled hillside home that looked like a little gingerbread house. She began filling in all of the details about the magickal world of what I once called "woo-woo" and believed to be so ridiculous. She told me everything she knew about Sleep Paralysis. She said I had no choice but to understand what it was and learn how to protect myself. She never charged me a cent. She told me of her retired aspirations to continue her Hollywood success story. She said those dreams were eclipsed by her passion for all things mystical. Several months went by, and then, one day, I showed up for coffee again, and she was gone. She told me from the beginning that it was just her style. She told me that her energy builds and builds and that the only way she could avoid being overwhelmed by it was to move and start over and over again.

Years of curiosity and denial passed, with my share of periodic bouts of Sleep Paralysis. The most dramatic was an apparition of a fiery skull that appeared in the ceiling corner of the bedroom, with a terrifying laugh reminiscent of Vincent Price, one Halloween Night. With the volume of the wicked laughter, my ethereal body had risen higher and higher out of my physical body to the point of separation. I was unable to get back in. I witnessed it dying, not knowing what would happen to "me" next. "Something" mysteriously awakened a person on the other side of the house by grabbing her foot, shaking her awake, and pulling off her covers. She passed her bathroom in the master bedroom and entered the hallway looking for a bathroom. She said that when she passed my room, she heard me "choking" and found me nearly unconscious. She shook me awake, and at that point, I knew I had to find a solution to whatever this was. I'd had enough!

That was the point at which I made a commitment to find out what was really going on and find a way to "fix" it. I studied for years and was blessed with experienced and knowledgeable teachers and resource information.

I learned:

- In REM (rapid eye movement), dream-state images have a surreal quality. Visions of images that appear to be present in the room are called "hypnagogic hallucinations." There are a variety of psychological and physical conditions that can cause the manifestation of these para somatic symptoms, such as narcolepsy, sleep apnea, migraines, anxiety, and a variety of sleep disturbances, including Post Traumatic Stress Disorder (PTSD), insomnia, and sleepwalking.

- A qualified medical specialist should not be ruled out in determining the cause of the phenomenon of Sleep Paralysis, because there really are physical and/or psychological conditions that manifest in symptoms identical to those that suggest spiritual/psychic/paranormal activity.

- Sleep Paralysis is often a spontaneous, activation, or initiatory rite of passage … the opening of a portal, and a bridge of consciousness between planes of existence. It is the point at which we discover that we have no choice but to embrace the reality that there is more than one reality. You may find yourself at war with violating forces so powerful that they can render you helpless. You witness yourself passing in and out of death-like states, being pulled into commanding, energetic vortices so subtle, they are not perceivable by ordinary senses. Particularly disturbing is the dog-whistle effect that causes you to perceive and suffer an S.P. Event as someone lays beside you, unaware.

- There are non-physical energies, entities, and angelic or demonic activity, sometimes associated with Sleep Paralysis. An attack can be triggered by spiritual practices and environments of your own or others. It can be as random as being in the wrong place at the wrong time. It may not even have anything personally to do with you or the astral residue of others. There may be no apparent cause. It is important to understand how to manage this phenomenon without succumbing to fear because those in-between states of sleep and conscious wakefulness can leave one feeling vulnerable and defenseless.

During my initial independent studies, which spanned many years, the only person I could really talk to was my mother. She advised me to do whatever I had to do to end the "nightmares." She understood to some degree because she had her own "woo-woo" story to tell after a Near Death Experience she had when giving birth to me. She was the first to teach me that the transmigration of the human soul is far more complex an experience than she had ever taught me in theological terms.

Then, one day, it happened to her. I remember her first experience of Sleep Paralysis … after being so "understanding" about my many years of fears and complaints about the experience. I ended up finding out that she had not been as "understanding" of my issue with Sleep Paralysis as she'd led me to believe.

My mom had never really given me "the look" … you know … the one that would shadow even a trusted friend's face when I'd gamble to share my terrifying experiences … that look that whispers, "you're barking mad." That look that says, "Uh-oh … no more doing lunch with youuuuu!" She was the only one I knew who wouldn't do that.

Several years later, we were living in Hawaii. One night she ran out of her room with a look on her face like she had seen a ghost. She was a brave and feisty person and didn't scare easily, so I knew there was something terribly wrong. She sat next to me, barely breathing, hardly moving. I kept asking, "What's wrong?" She kept saying, faintly … "Nothing …" After a while, she asked me to recount the experiences I'd had in the past with the phenomenon I know now to be, Sleep Paralysis.

As I described again the dreaded details of the experience, her eyes widened in shock. She began to apologize to me for "thinking I was crazy." She insisted that it *did* sound crazy, but that now she knew that it wasn't … that it was quite real.

In shock, hugging her, I exclaimed … "Oh NO!!! They got you too! … I know! I know! It's scary, but it's okay. You're okay! Oh no! They got you too! I'm so sorry that happened to you! Don't be afraid …" I had shared with her unwelcomed stories of the Menehunes, Kahunas, and certainly the Press Down Ghost I had learned about in my studies. These were ancient and contemporary legends of old and new mystical Hawaii and the nonphysical beings and energies that graced the Hawaiian Islands. I was amazed at how similar the experiences I'd heard about the 'press down ghosts' paralleled my own astral attacks.

My mom was so sweet … she had tears in her eyes when she told me, "If I had only known, I could have helped you … but it just sounded crazy. But it's not crazy. It is very real! I am so, so sorry!" The moral of my having shared this particular story is to assure you that if you are experiencing bouts with Sleep Paralysis, even your most loving and trusted confidants, no matter how well-intended they may be, may file these attacks away under the category of "crazy." Quietly and fearlessly do your own research and understand what this condition is, what it isn't, and why it is specifically occurring in *your* life.

Manifestations of Sleep Paralysis

Medical and spiritual professionals assured me that the Sleep Paralysis Events I suffered were not linked to a physical cause or sleep disorder. I ruled out issues relating to disrupted sleep patterns, diet, exercise, mental health challenges, alcohol or drug abuse, and emotional disorders. I worried that if these unsolicited experiences were not of a physical cause, the possibility of a Spiritual Emergency must be met with well-informed methods to regain control over my life after concluding that my experiences were consistent with what is known as a "psychic attack." It was then that I began to gather information that turned out to be a part of my research for this book.

Accounts of manifestations of Sleep Paralysis consistently include:

- a sensation of weightlessness, drifting, sinking or falling, rising or floating, uncontrollably;

- a sensation of paralysis completely overwhelming the physical body and causing waves of pressure in the chest area or the feeling of being held down, conscious but helpless, and unable to speak or move, perhaps with the exception of the eyes. Some report feeling choked, breathless, or feeling smothered. There may also be a strange vacuuming sensation … sucking or pulling the Life Force out through the chest and solar plexus area;

- a feeling of the spirit, soul, or non-physical body of consciousness disengaging from or being pulled out of the physical body, and not being able to get back in.

- a panicked feeling of impending doom or of possibly dying;

- an episode may introduce with an awareness of the sound of whirling wind, whispers, the echoing sound of a train thundering down the tracks, and auditory sensations of being underwater;

- hearing buzzing or ringing in the ears with no apparent physical source;

- pulses and waves of a current with an electrical quality, overwhelming the physical body and leaving it in a weakened, defenseless state;

- profound full-body vibration;

- transitional stages of experiencing sensations of floating, swaying, futile flailing about, desperate involuntary jerking, jolting, shuddering, lurching movements that may resemble a seizure, even though there is no movement of the physical body possible. In an attempt of the mind to defend or regain control of the physical body, we are challenged to resist this powerful, immobilizing force;

- convulsing, stiffening, tensing, contractions, or muscular spasms;

- an overwhelming condition called "scissor lock" that occurs when the subject is fully conscious. The physical body may lose all control, convulse, stiffen, and be rendered completely unable to move;

- tingling sensations over the entire body may occur at the point of the separation of the etheric body from the physical body, and upon attempts at or after successful re-entry. The skin may take on a cool, effervescent feeling. The physical body is lying in a death-like state, while the non-physical body, after having been expelled, is still in the realm of experiencing;

- a sensation of choking and a seizing of the vocal cords, restricting airway passages. The paralysis in the throat region hinders attempts to call out for help. This struggle may be perceived as frantic, with accompanying guttural or gagging sounds;

- the physical eyes may be closed, though the eyes of the non-physical body are open and able to see the vision as it continues to unfold on both sides of the veil of consciousness;

- seeing and hearing things that are not apparently there, feeling a non-physical "evil" or threatening presence in the room. An apparition like that can parallel the experience of clinical "hallucinations." It is reasonable to rule that possibility out before jumping to conclusions and classifying it as paranormal activity;

- occurring as a dream continuing into a perceived waking state, consistent with what is known as a Lucid Dream. The open eyes of conscious awareness may witness dream imagery spilling over as visions, into the actual sleeping area, in various states of density. There may be an accompanying hyper-vigilant state that causes the unsettling feeling of a disturbing energy present in the room. Vivid images can appear as holograms or as translucent ghostly apparitions, but more often than not, there is nothing to see … only a strong presence to feel;

- reports, among diverse cultures, of entities of varied elemental presentations sitting down on the victim's chest. The Chinese used to call the experience of Sleep Paralysis, "GuiYa," which means "ghost pressure." In Hawaii, it is called the "press down ghost." In the Caribbean, they are called duppies. They are called by many names; Wetiko, Archon, Shapeshifter, Skin Walker, Incubus, Succubus, Jinni (Jinn, Djinn), Reptilian, and many others;

- experiencing a drop in body temperature or the temperature of the room;

- seeing varied presentations of moving shadows.

<u>Effective spontaneous actions to take at the onset of a Sleep Paralysis Event:</u>

- Identify unique "precursors" to these events and exercise the precaution expressed in the adage "an ounce of prevention is worth a pound of cure." Reset the energies of your environment to conform to a higher frequency using modern and ancient remedies for malefic, discordant energies before a crisis arises is preferable to stomping out brush fires as they erupt.

- Resist the compulsion to panic and try to pull one's entire body out of the state of paralysis and try to move just one finger. If you can manage to move just one finger, one toe (the big toe), the eyes, or the tongue, consciousness can be pulled back into the physical body, breaking the energetic grip of the attack. We may feel a full-body surge of energy with an electrical quality, gradually releasing the binding grip of the paralyzed state, allowing the return of full control over the physical body, and restoring full consciousness.

- Repeat a mantra or prayer that empowers your fearless spirit, whether it can be intoned aloud or not.

- Some remarkable individuals report being able to pull themselves out of these episodes at will. I have heard reports of "Inception" style "dream within a dream" experiences, in which consciousness was lost and regained in a dream, transcending one dream state, and awakening into another, then into fully conscious wakefulness. A safe landing place between levels of consciousness is a constructed buffer for the impact of each transition. I have heard of individuals who slip out of the physical body during paralysis state and are able to engage in astral travel.

- The meditation practice of Anapanasati (Mindfulness of Breathing) is helpful to keep from panicking. Intone and repeat in your mind your strongest 'power mantra' and prayer until you can feel its vibration at the center of Thought.

- Disassociate from the physical body. Practice remembrance of the True Self in a non-physical context through a consistent meditation regimen (Self-Inquiry).

Common Post Sleep Paralysis Attack Symptoms:

There is a certain type of pain specific to the aftermath of a Sleep Paralysis Event that is difficult to describe. It starts with the awareness that one has had some type of psychically phenomenal, paranormal experience that is difficult to accept, even in the context of a horror film. There is a special brand of secrecy it is shrouded in because it is an awkward conversation to have, often with unpleasant consequences. There is often no one to confide in, not even a professional to help or advise.

Some of the after effects include, but are not limited to:

- debilitating fear and helplessness;

- uncontrollable crying, rage, depression, helplessness;

- hyperventilation;

- light-headed, dizzy, vertigo;

- chills and/or rushes of fever;

- cold, clammy skin;

- dry mouth;

- pale complexion;

- skin feels bruised all over;

- skin too sensitive to touch;

- eyes hypersensitive to light;

- hypersensitivity to sound;

- the sensation of the rawness of skin like a steam burn or sunburn;

- throbbing, pulsing, painful sensation of full body fascia;

- tension, aching, stiffness, and weakness in joints and muscles;

- distortions in hearing (echo chamber);

- a racing heartbeat, pressure on the chest, and upper body;

- chest pain and pressure;

- waves of nausea;

- vomiting;

- swelling in the abdominal cavity;

- unusual sensations and/or movement in the abdominal cavity;

- mental confusion, exhaustion;

- shivering, trembling, muscle twitches, and cramps;

- symptoms associated with lack of sleep;

- feelings of being violated;

- extremely anxious states of hypervigilance;

- panic attacks;

- insomnia and sleep disorders;

- extreme states of chronic, clinical depression;

- preoccupation with avoidance/distraction/coping behaviors.

<u>Practices and spontaneous experiences associated with Sleep Paralysis:</u>

- Lucid Dreaming;

- Remote Viewing;

- Astral Travel;

- Intentional or spontaneous Out of Body Experiences;

- Certain types of deep meditation;

- Self-hypnosis and being hypnotized by another;

- Reiki and other methods of energy healing, remote or direct;

- Certain types of Yoga practice;

- Anesthesia;

- Drug use and/or abuse;

- Plant medicine ceremony practices and rituals;

- Sacred spiritual practices that were never meant to be treated like a ride in an amusement park or for entertainment purposes;

- Cultural appropriation of mystical practices and traditions without instruction, supervision, or permission;

- Rites and rituals associated with secret orders and societies;

- Projections of energy with intention from a person or group of people;

- Advanced levels of spiritual/mystical intense study and practice;

- Extremely emotional states of mind (anger, passion, envy, jealousy, shock, grief);

- Incidents consistent with accounts of alien contact or abduction experiences;

- The sensations involved with Sleep Paralysis can be indicators of the first stage of a spirit "walk-in" experience. A spirit "walk-in" happens when a disembodied being (spirit) literally "walks in" and takes sole or shared occupancy of a particular physical body vessel;

- The initial related feelings can be a precursor of an attempted possession by a being that may or may not be a malevolent entity;

- Near Death Experience, the physical body is exited and re-entered;

- Initial stages of a full spiritual awakening or a terrifying Spiritual Emergency.

Sleep Paralysis is a very real problem that many people report suffering, regardless of whether or not they are engaged in mystical practices and studies, whether or not they are the victim of a psychic attack, and whether or not they even know what it is. If the full spectrum of manifestation were understood, fear would diminish, and it would be robbed of its shock value. Many who suffer this mysterious phenomenon are children, who are often accused of having an over-active imagination. It sends out a message of judgment, as though there is something wrong with a person who experiences a naturally occurring manifestation when viewed from a multi-dimensional perspective.

I have experienced this phenomenon many times before. It can be terrifying. Reports of Sleep Paralysis generally come from people who already have evidence to support their belief that they are experiencing a psychic or spiritual attack. Often, we believe we are aware of who the attacker is. It is not wise to feel too sure of knowing who it is because we could be wrong. It is more important to know with certainty that the body lying there that we can't get back into is not who we really are. We are the consciousness that observes it. Often these attacks are coming from a source you would never suspect of tapping into the secret arts on a power trip, not understanding that such violations will eventually boomerang and result in their own downfall. They may not be coming from a physical source at all. Many people suffer these attacks in secret because they don't want people to call them crazy, even though "crazy" typically does not operate that way. Whether or not the source of this phenomenon is physical or non-physical, there are recommendations that will help with managing these episodes.

It is more commonly the ego self that is targeted by the generic, run-of-the-mill, mischievous practitioner of secret arts, closet conjurer, the caster of an evil eye, Sahir (witch), the 'throw a rock and hide their hand' kind of coward. In particularly unique "attack" scenarios that I have experienced, it was not my ego self "I" (physical self) that was under attack. It was my Essential "I," (non-physical Self) I AM presence, the "I in I" that was fighting for survival. They were trying to kill me. I did not understand then that my Essential, True Self is indestructible. I did not have a conscious clue what was really happening to me or how any of what I was experiencing was even possible. All that could help me was to awaken to the I AM of my Essential Self and learn how to fearlessly remain in That ... *stay* there ... where I felt safe. It is permanent and unchanging. It is eternal. It is unbreakable. It is imperishable. All that saved me was my connection to That ... who I really am and the Ultimate I AM, the Original Flame, from which we all arise as sparks. All we have to call upon is the Manifestation of the Absolute I, The Source of all, and seek refuge there, in the Realm of Divinity. No evil can enter there.

States of Consciousness Associated with Sleep Paralysis

The I AM is the True Self, the unconditioned state of conscious awareness. The sensations associated with the onset of a Sleep Paralysis Event (SPE) are not unlike the initial sensations of a Near Death Experience (NDE) and can parallel the first phases of an intentional or spontaneous Out of Body Experience (OBE), and/or Astral Projection and Travel. They can even manifest as precursors to experiences of Clairvoyance, Clairaudience, Telekinesis, Channeling as a medium, Remote (energy) Healing, Remote Viewing, Lucid Dreaming, and many more. They are part and parcel to, and often, the *goal* of many mystical practices.

The next level of this play of consciousness may involve not having a "goal" at all. There is more to experience when we are able to pay more attention to our actual 'be'ing than our incessant 'do'ing, as we release our attachment to any expected outcome. When we access the freedom of continual becoming, as a field of consciousness, we become available to energies that can trigger a complete "awakening" or Self-Realization experience. Such an experience can activate a wide spectrum of manifestations that may appear to be consistent with a Spiritual Emergency.

When we consider higher planes of possibility, symptoms common to the phenomenon of Sleep Paralysis can be viewed as indicators of evolving consciousness if we choose to see it that way. Many of the sensations that can spontaneously present in Sleep Paralysis events are associated with any activity that can produce an altered state of consciousness. We exist as a braided, circular tightrope of consciousness and manifestation, intertwined in the most intimate embrace, the sacred union of the electromagnetic field of energy that we are, and the physical vessel that is the container of it. Our many bodies, from the subtlest to gross matter, are distinguished from one another by the rate of their vibration. When they begin to interact with one another, engaging and disengaging, an apparent energetic effect may present, as the same sensations at the onset of a Sleep Paralysis Event.

Some study their entire lives to be able to master the experience of navigating consciousness outside of the human body. Practices that involve exiting the body can be risky. It is not advisable to attempt it without knowledgeable guidance because it essentially leaves a vacancy available to another occupier. Nature abhors a vacuum. When out of body, whether it is spontaneous or intentional, it is important to be surrounded by the Light of our most powerful prayer for the protection of both the physical and non-physical bodies, for both are vulnerable.

In the study and practice of any activity that could cause an astral projection, it is generally understood that the etheric "silver cord" that connects at the physical navel will always be there to pull or lead them back to the warm body they call "home." The silver cord extends as far out as the practitioner fearlessly chooses to travel. The fear factor can hinder the experience of reaching a level of mastery of intentionally induced or naturally occurring states of detaching from and returning to the physical body. In our consideration of the positive implications of the OBE or Out of Body Experience, we must include:

- The evolution from homo sapien to homo projection. That suggests that we have the natural capability of projecting outside of our physical bodies;

- Cultivation of the ability to cure illness by healing the body matrix energetically;

- Moving into a multi-dimensional awareness that sparks the understanding of the scientific studies affirming that consciousness can manifest and animate artificial limbs, avatars, robotics, and forms of artificial intelligence;

- The formless Self existed *before* the physical form. That fact explains the phenomenon of phantom limbs of amputees who continue to feel sensation in a limb that is no longer a part of their physical body. We are not bodies having out of body experiences … we are fields of consciousness having an "In the Body Experience." Awareness can exist and function without the physical body as a point of reference. Implications of the exploding of fixed definitions of past, present, and future tenses opening and navigating through portals of Time;

- Considering the Laws of Cause and Effect, ask the question, "If we have *observed* the effect of a cause, is it possible we have *changed* a fate or destiny, for having *witnessed* possible and probable outcomes?" The answer is YES;

- Accept the challenge of harnessing the energy of this and related spontaneous phenomena, regardless of its source and cause, and reducing it to a controlled laboratory experiment;

- Accept that the understanding of such phenomena can offer the benefit of freeing us from imposed scientific interpretations, as well as mystical or religious dogma and manipulations. We are then free to interpret our reality according to our own experiential belief system;

- Resistance to any hypothesis that who we really are ceases at the time of physical death;

- Refine our understanding that we are all connected and embrace a quantum sense of the Oneness of all;

- Acceptance of our innate mystical nature and capacity to sense and interact with subtle energies, presences, and realities;

- Change our personal perception of "ownership" of and self-identification as a mere body. We are more than what we see in a mirror. We are the awareness that emanated that.

The primary objective of this study is to expand our knowledge base and raise our frequency to be able to disengage from the grip of any entity or force that seeks to violate our spiritual sovereignty. At certain points, I feel like someone asked me, "What time is it?" … and I proceeded to tell them how to build a clock. For some who have never experienced Sleep Paralysis, it may even have bored you. Perhaps you had judged it as some weird thing that could not possibly have anything to do with you like I thought before it happened to me. Well, the night is young. If not you, someone you cherish may be enveloped in a horror story beyond your capacity to understand it. You may be the only person they trust with the barring of their soul. Maybe you will treat them with empathy and respect, sharing your knowledge of this torture that comes and goes, uninvited, unexpected in the night. You may be able to help rescue them, or one day yourself, from one of the most out-of-control feelings one can imagine.

I present an invitation to come out of the shadows of superstition and fear to examine the personal and social implications of embracing this phenomenon as a "normal" gift and the manifestation of our mystical, multi-dimensional beings. What if we see it from a position of power rather than disempowerment? What if we chose to recognize the potential for it to give us the desire to find meaning in our eternal lives? What if we allow it to reveal how much being ethical really matters, as we consider cause and effect and the consequences of our choices and actions? What if this realization caused us to upgrade the quality of our ambitions from pure materialism and vanity to altruistic goals that seek to make a difference that will outlive our bodies? More than anything … What if everybody knew this?

We might want to refine our personal values and form a more humane society, showing greater concern for all beings, and taking responsibility for environmental and planetary awareness of the consequences of our actions and inactions. What if we own our power as more than flesh and bone and create the change we are capable of creating, beginning with the deepest level of our Self? The most powerful way of achieving these selfless goals is to connect and resonate with the 'Most High' Frequency ... with The God of our highest understanding. If we choose to, we have the authority to rebuke fear of the known, the unknown, and the unknowable. All of the myriad manifestations of quantum consciousness will become a welcome partner dancing across the stage of time and Timeless, as Light and shadow, as Ether and matter.

When an attacker attacks, generally, he or she is not attacking the Essential Self. They are attacking the illusory self, the "me-ness" of our own perceptions of self. As awareness rises out of shallow, one-dimensional perceptions, and we choose to remain in the I AM formless consciousness, fear subsides, and the attack begins to unravel. An attacker's motives and weapons are fear-based and feed upon our fear for strength. If we are lost in the hallucination of identifying as the most impermanent, fragile manifestation of ourselves, the physical body, we are defenseless. If we shift to identify with the True Self, formless and eternal, we are free to ride the waves of a higher frequency, one that scrambles the frequency of the attacker.

If these 'attacks' were just physical, that would be bad enough, but some are not just physical. It is disturbing how committed some are to hard positions of denial of that fact when it is also historically known to possibly have non-physical, even paranormal causes. Why are the "experiencers" of this horror mocked, demonized, victim blamed, and dismissed as having had a purely physical or psychological episode, when it is *commonly* illustrated with images depicting the involvement of malevolent psychic/etheric/spiritual energies, entities, and phenomena? The following is a popular work of art associated with Sleep Paralysis, eerily consistent with visions and apparitions some have reported. These experiences commonly occur and are addressed globally in traditions of diverse cultures. So, how is it so casually written off as folklore, superstition, psychosis, and something that should be kept a secret?

The Nightmare

John Henry Fuseli

THE NIGHTMARE: FUSELI PAINTING
"One of the most unexplored regions of art is dreams." – Fuseli

This version of John Henry Fuseli's famed painting, "The Nightmare," is housed at the Detroit Institute of the Arts. It was first shown at the Royal Academy of London in 1782. What is known as an incubus/demon/jinn crouches on the chest of the victim. "Nightmare" is well-known to be associated with the phenomenon of Sleep Paralysis. It depicts these "visitations" or attacks in disturbing imagery, consistent with Fuseli's sleeping visions, waking dreams, and astral crime scenes. In this painting, a female is subjugated, oppressed by a male-ish monster, pressing the life out of her, seizing her breath, and smiling at her demise. The little fiendish monster sitting on her chest has inspired poetry and consideration that intentions are sexually suggestive, as though it was a part of the motive for what appears to be a murder.

In Fuseli's rendering of images portraying a type of attack associated with Sleep Paralysis, he affirms that it can be connected to the work of demons, in this case, specifically incubi. An incubus is a masculine-gendered entity who seeks to initiate sexual activity with a sleeping woman, according to traditional folklore. Its female manifestation is called a succubus. When the species of an entity called a jinn is involved, there is more of a likelihood of gender fluidity, appearing and appealing to either sex.

Samuel Johnson, in his book, "A Dictionary of the English Language," offers the definition of Sleep Paralysis as a "nightmare," a common term used in reference to bad dreams. "Mara," is a Sanskrit word associated with Buddhist concepts of death, rebirth, desire, and the embodiment of forces and energies that seek to thwart enlightenment. A "mare" or "mara" is a malevolent entity, a manifestation of a stalking, predatory, wicked spirit that eats Light within the parallels of the dreamer's consciousness. They smother, choke, torture, and press crushing weight down upon the chests of humans while they sleep, seeking to inflict harm upon their victims in order to push them to extreme emotional states. Heightened levels of intense fear can trigger the fight/flight response causing the subject to produce a torrential rush of potent, hormonal, adrenalin-cortisol charged, ethereal substance. This organic, grade-A energy supply is called "loosh."

The term loosh identifies a natural bioenergetic substance radiated by animals and humans caught in the throes of intense mental, physical, emotional, and spiritual pain. Intense emotion arises from abuse and trauma scenarios involving cruelty, brutality, violence, torture, pain, grief, stress, and particularly extreme states of *fear* and anger. It is believed by some that this energy can be harvested for various purposes, to the extent that highly controversial pseudoscientific research and experimentation involving constructing devices used as 'accumulators' sought to determine the ability to collect the energy.

Determinations were made that extreme levels of psychic suffering can stimulate the production and emission of this powerful Life Force energy that is characteristically likened to Kundalini energy from ancient Indian traditions, and Qi of traditional Chinese medicine. Positive stimuli are also powerful energy sources, such as that induced by spontaneous heightened states of excitement, passion, sexual arousal, and orgasm, through associations with industries that peddle sex and porn. Extreme states of elation are also linked to dramatic outbursts of fans at music concerts and highly competitive sports events, particularly those that are aggressive or violent in nature.

The reason certain hyperdimensional beings *project* energies of an electrical quality known to trigger Sleep Paralysis is to harvest the negative loosh to feed upon and use as a vital nutrient. These negative entities have a strong incentive to be connoisseurs of top-of-the-line organic, grade-A energy because they are invested in cultivating and "collecting" it for their sustenance. We are not dealing with what we know to be a normal appetite, which should concern us as we are at the bottom of their food chain.

The energy these beings and entities seek to extract from humans curiously parallels a massless, omnipresent substance … a mysterious, yet measurable force, characteristically resembling descriptions of loosh energy, that is called "orgone." Orgone refers to a pseudo-scientific, bioenergetic, ethereal, radiant energy used to channel the energy of healings, and clearing electromagnetic energy fields because it is an essential expression of physical and psychological health. It is known by many names among diverse cultures, healing traditions, and mystical paths. The fact that orgone is associated with sexuality suggests that it shares certain characteristics with Kundalini energy in the way that it operates, and is believed by some to be a living, interactive energy.

That would make it make more sense that the focal point of manipulations of the energetic system is the First or Root Chakra (sexual energy center), where the seat of the Kundalini energy is located. The revitalizing properties of that energy, whatever you want to call it, is a coveted natural resource. The study of our own multi-dimensional body system is one of the first steps to protecting ourselves from attack, as long as we remember that we are more than our chakras. We *are* all of the planes, domains, dimensions, and realms.

Phenomenal aspects of Sleep Paralysis warrant being studied in great depth, more than most other phenomena. I have observed that its elements can be precursors to experiences that are not necessarily a Spiritual Emergency. There is a powerful charge associated with it, a sort of electrical surge of kinetic energy that seems to be a catalyst, triggering a wide spectrum of paranormal experiences and mysterious phenomena. It is not always the curse it feels like, but instead may be evidence of coveted spiritual gifts. It may well be a *Mark* of the Natural Mystic.

Sleep Paralysis can be one of the first manifestations of special abilities in intentional mystical and spiritual practice, scientific studies of human consciousness, and spontaneous spiritual awakenings. As bizarre as these episodes can be, it may *feel* like a "Spiritual Emergency," but turn out to be a life-changing gift of spiritual transcendence.

Any altered state of consciousness, whether induced, projected, or spontaneous, can trigger the onset of Sleep Paralysis. Because the origin may be from beyond Time and Space, our 'Laws' of Cause and Effect may seem to be mocked, creating the illusion of events having no apparent cause or source. There are documented accounts of terrifying encounters with what was described as "the devil," some starting with telepathically audible voices warning of an impending attack. Full body paralysis ensues … electrical vibrations spark between the fascia and outer skin … something squeezes the life, the breath, out of compressed lungs. The presence of an energetic evil permeates the room, triggering unprecedented states of extreme fear and physical sensations that defy description. It was not my direct experience, but some have even reported being raped.

Why is it that after numerous trips to medical and psychological practitioners, people are prescribed antidepressants, sleeping pills, anti-anxiety drugs, offered antipsychotics, and questioned about psychedelic drug use and all manner of chemical and drug addiction? I have heard that remedies have even led to referrals for surgery … For WHAT? … To remove these stealthy, wayfaring, invisible shapeshifters from the subtle realms of consciousness?

Everything that I was given as a "remedy" only served to trigger more profoundly uncontrollable attacks. This is one of the reasons East must meet West in matters of health care. Why are so many people made to suffer a prescription bottle on a nightstand by the bed, and be made to believe that the cause of their suffering can *only* be physical or psychological? At what point do we call the Padre, or the Raqi, or the Shaman, for an exorcism of the real cause?

The body/mind approach seems to me to be rooted in the practice of Western medicine, though I notice a shift over recent years into deepening respect for a broader spectrum of holistic healing. I have lived in and among many cultures around the world, and most do not seem confused or dismissive about there being *something* else going on that does not point to a purely physical cause for this phenomenon, even though there are many physical manifestations. 10th century Persian medical texts have accounts of Sleep Paralysis. Over time researchers from diverse perspectives have supporting documentation of paranormal interference as a factor in Sleep Paralysis. As far back as 1664, a Dutch physician classified a medical observation of a 50-year-old woman as suffering from "Night-Mare," with symptoms consistent with Sleep Paralysis … leading up to the 19th century when the diagnosis was first termed "Sleep Palsy," then "Sleep Paralysis.

The fact is there are serious physical conditions that manifest the same symptoms. That is why I would never advise *any*one to ignore that possibility. By all means, consult everyone … then, if that doesn't work, meditate on whether or not to call Father Merrin (The Exorcist).

Why is it that when someone confides in people they trust enough to talk to, that "I am experiencing vicious psychic attacks at the hands of a malevolent occultist or a terrifying energy or entity," … it is met with suspicion, fear, and judgment? Why are these reports met with a level of suspicion that threatens imminent intervention (if there is even a modicum of true concern or respect)? More often than not, avoidance games ensue, and associations become awkward, and eventually abandoned. Where does this word "woo-woo" come from, as it relates to real-life situations that compromise the lives and very souls of these so-called "loved" ones, secretly suffering these relentless assaults?

How *dare* anyone suggest that the *only* credible cause for these self-reenacting horror stories is purely physical, or only experienced by crazy people. The last time I checked, crazy just doesn't operate that way. If someone is "crazy" to that degree, there would be other manifestations besides these occasional nocturnal romps with demons. This is real!!!

Basic Human Chakra System

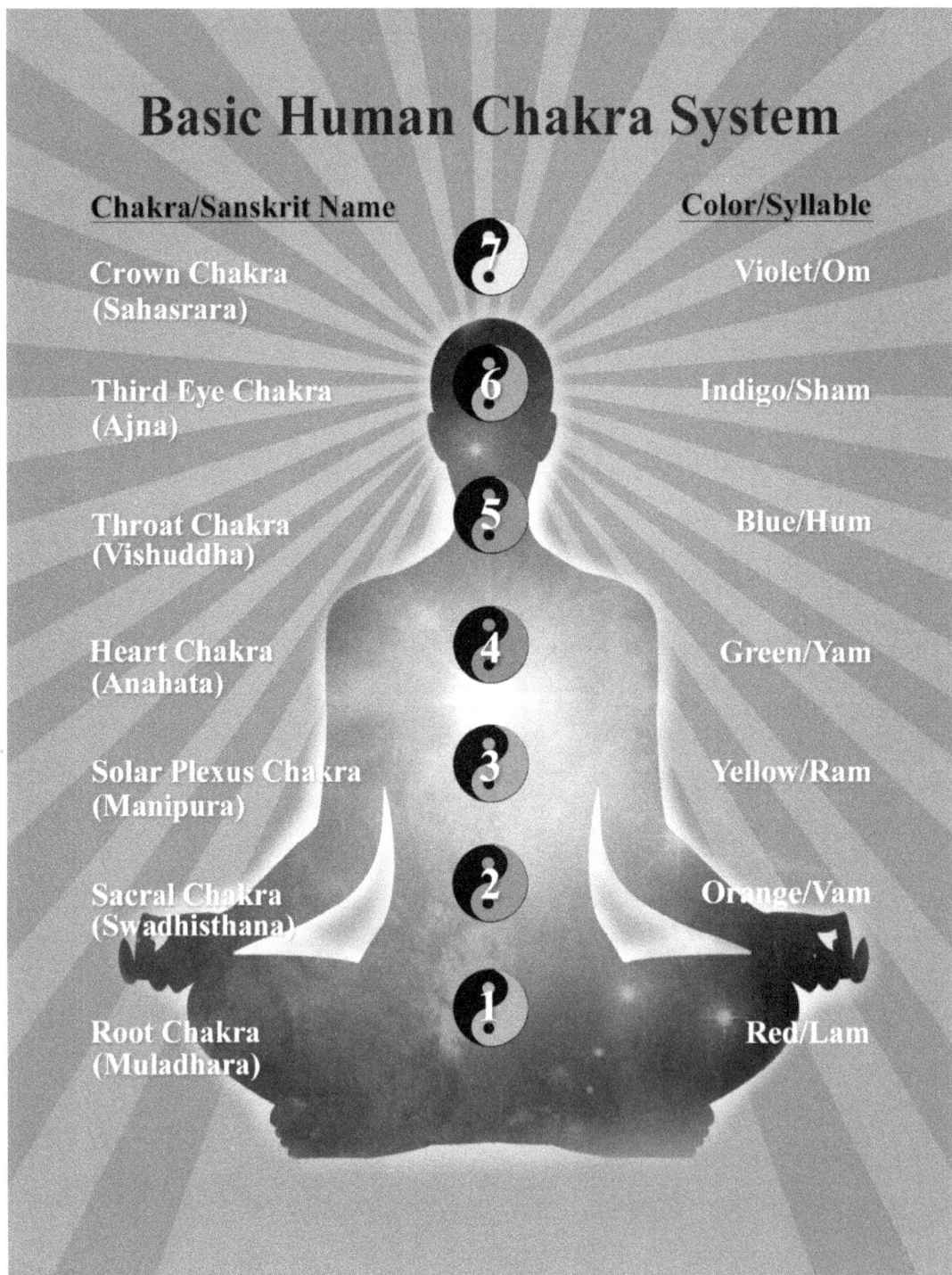

Chakra/Sanskrit Name	Color/Syllable
Crown Chakra (Sahasrara)	Violet/Om
Third Eye Chakra (Ajna)	Indigo/Sham
Throat Chakra (Vishuddha)	Blue/Hum
Heart Chakra (Anahata)	Green/Yam
Solar Plexus Chakra (Manipura)	Yellow/Ram
Sacral Chakra (Swadhisthana)	Orange/Vam
Root Chakra (Muladhara)	Red/Lam

The vortices of the body's energy centers (Chakras) are illustrated as a Yin Yang to demonstrate their polarities and the balance that needs to be maintained.

We must concentrate our energies on understanding the function of the Chakra System and study methods of clearing blockages that can have a negative effect on our physical, mental, emotional, and spiritual health. A strong and balanced Chakra System will make one less vulnerable to the negative energies that constitute a psychic attack. There are many styles of meditation that are specifically helpful in maintaining optimum health of the chakras. A meditation for each of the chakras has been provided here to increase the flow of positive energy to each chakra and eliminate the magnetic, negative energy that can cause physical, emotional, mental, and spiritual harm.

The word chakra is derived from the Sanskrit word "chakram," which means "wheel." This term refers to a network of seven major funnel or cone-shaped energy vortex centers in the "subtle body." They are believed to be about six inches in diameter, extending one inch out from the physical body. The wider opening is on the outside of the back and front of the physical body, with the small tip being located inside our body near the spine, connecting the two. They are located vertically, from the base of the spine up through the top of the head. They move energy in and out in a spiraling motion and function to inhale and exhale vital energy, based on the direction of their spin. Each center relates to particular states of mind, connecting to the experiences of the physical body, as well as the energy that surrounds it.

Chakras are considered the intake organs for energies from our external environment. Due to blockages, the Chi or Ki energy cannot flow freely, resulting in physical, mental, emotional, and spiritual disease. Chi is the "breath" or "wind" and vital Life Force in all things. Any obstruction or weakness of the Chi force can result in vital physical organs not receiving needed energy and can cause a deterioration of our health on all levels.

There are colors associated with each of the chakras. Meditating on a particular chakra and visualizing its corresponding color is known to stimulate the energy of that chakra. Sound vibration can also affect the chakras. Each chakra has a corresponding tone. Certain meditation practices are designed to clear energetic obstructions and blockages of the Chakra System by raising our Kundalini energy force. The objective of some meditation and Yoga practices is to cause the Kundalini to rise to the level of the Crown Chakra, resulting in spiritual enlightenment, transcendence, and emergence from Time and Space. There are exercises that we can incorporate into our regular spiritual discipline, which will keep the energy of the Chakra System fine-tuned, clean, and strong.

There are as many varied descriptions of the function of the chakras as there are belief systems. There is a multitude of variances of correspondences relating to every aspect of the Chakra System, based on the tradition of who is describing them. This is in no way intended to be a thorough explanation of any particular tradition. It is an overview of how chakras relate to meditation and other spiritual practices.

This visualization exercise is helpful when making a deeper energetic connection at the more profound levels of meditation. Your meditation is more powerful when you bring a question or issue into it, determining which chakra directly corresponds with that subject matter. Ask for a healing to take place in your life.

Before engaging in any meditation, observe recommended basic protocol regarding personal hygiene and the cleanliness and ambiance of your setting. Sit in a private, quiet, comfortable place with soft lighting. Avoid meditating in complete darkness, and never meditate under fluorescent or CFL lighting. Facing the East is energetically best. Touch the tips of your index fingers and thumbs together.

Touch your tongue to the roof of your mouth, and clench your butt muscles tight to facilitate the most effective channeling of energy. If you are not able to sit in a full or modified Lotus position, be mindful of your posture and sit up in a comfortable chair.

Meditate on the area of each of the chakras and visualize its corresponding color, spinning clockwise. Breathe that color in through your nostrils and exhale it out of your mouth as you visualize a circle of that color that you are creating with your breath. This exercise will help clarify your issues and reveal answers to your questions.

Meditation Posture

Yoga-Union of Mind, Body, Spirit, seeking Union with the
  Divine One

Mudra-Hand gesture that directs the flow of energy to body
  during meditation

Lotus Position-seated (appropriate for you), back straight,
  legs crossed, hands resting on knees, palms up, index fingers
  and thumbs touching, mindful natural breathing.

Uttarabodhi (Sanskrit) Hand Mudra
*Thumbs touching and index fingers touching (pointed
down), all other fingers intertwined at the Solar
Plexus level.*

. Inspires sense of inner unity and alignment with Divine Source.
. Enlightenment, insight, inspiration.
. Calms the mind, reduces stress levels, improves concentration.
. Dispels fear, realization to fear nothing or nobody except God.
. Problem solving, decision making.
. Improves self-confidence, realization of the Higher Self.
. Refreshes the body system and recharges it with energy.
. Shield for the body and mind from negative forces.

Preparation for Chakra Visualization Exercises

- A protection prayer and mantra should precede all meditations on the Crown Chakra. Speak the breath of the prayer/mantra into a clean cloth to be placed over the Crown Chakra.

- In all of these meditative exercises, with deep concentration, hold your focus on the color spinning clockwise in the vortex of each chakra. Fix your attention on the question or issue you have taken into your meditation to clear, cleanse, or heal.

- To perform a *banishing* of negative energies, the vortex should initially be visualized as spinning in a *counter*-clockwise direction, using the *mindful* breath as the animator of motion. For cleansing or healing energies to be issued *in*, the direction must be reversed to spin in a clockwise motion.

- After completing your meditation, as with all meditation practices, it is important to ground yourself before you resume your everyday activities, especially before you drive or perform any activity that would require alert, grounded concentration. If you feel light-headed or unfocused after your meditation, there are many ways to ground yourself. Bring yourself back to alertness by washing your face and hands with cold water, eating a serving of fruit, drinking a glass of cool or cold water, taking a brisk walk barefoot on the ground, playing music, dancing, or exercising.

- There is a visualization that is commonly used for grounding that works well. Visualize your physical self standing with your bare feet planted firmly on the ground or the floor, as close to ground level as possible. Imagine yourself sending roots, like those of a tree, down into the Earth. Inhale through your nostrils as you visualize pulling the Earth energy up through your roots. As you exhale, your roots are pushing deeper into the Earth. After several minutes you will return to your previous state of alertness.

Targeted Chakras Visualization Exercise to Strengthen your Defense System – Lower Portals Visualization

Targeted Chakras:

Just as there is a Yin and Yang energy to all of creation, this polarity also exists in energetic reference to our chakras. I will not refer to one as good and the other bad. Both sides exist for a reason, and neither can exist without the other. One is the domain of our gifts, and the other the domain of our challenges. They engage in the elegant dance of creation as each side flips like a coin and becomes its own polar opposite. The ideal perspective is not to entertain an attachment or aversion to either side. They are as Shadow and Light. Accept them both as necessary energies to navigate the seas of this life in perfect balance. Just know that these energies can be used either for or against us. Knowledge is power.

The First or Root Chakra is located between the legs at the sacral-coccyx joint and is referred to by some as the sexual center along with the Second Chakra. It is strongly associated with our physical reality, our will to live, and is a generator of the energies of physical vitality. It is connected to the Earth element and is believed to be associated with the sense of smell. Kundalini is a Sanskrit term for the primal energy that sleeps, coiled like a snake at the base of the spine in the area of the Root Chakra. It is the source of latent concentrated power, strength, and profound will. The uncoiling of the Kundalini is the manifestation and realization of optimum human potential by revitalizing and transforming all of the chakras as it rises in a manner that can spark enlightenment. The Root Chakra has a shadow side when it is out of balance and can open the door to entity possession scenarios. Care is to be exercised in meditations that concentrate on the clearing of this area. The unleashing of a spontaneous Kundalini release before one is prepared for the rush of energy associated with the raising of it is something that some have not survived intact.

A Spontaneous Kundalini Release is considered a Spiritual Emergency and can have extreme and unpredictable consequences. The process of raising the Kundalini force is a gradual one, and when done in a prescribed manner can be a transformative experience. It could also be the gateway and portal of a targeted, potential "host," through which attacking entities may use to accomplish a complete possession. These practices are to be studied with a knowledgeable and experienced teacher that you feel comfortable with and whom you feel you can trust.

*Focus on the energy of the Root Chakra and visualize **red light** whirling in a clockwise motion, gaining momentum with the intensity of your focused visualization and depth of breath.*

Speak to it. Say,
"I release this issue to The Great Spirit and ask for a healing to take place in my life."

The Second Chakra (The Navel Chakra) is located just above the pubic bone on the back and front of the body. It is the seat of our emotions and is approximately located at the center of the sacrum. The Second Chakra is associated with the water element and is connected to feelings of sexual passion, danger, health, energy, and hate. Some believe this chakra is associated with the sense of taste. It generates energy for the immune system and the sexual organs. As vital as it is to keep this very important chakra in optimum health, it is nearly animalistic to function only from the level of its intense, primal energy.

An obstruction or imbalance can manifest in unbridled sensual indulgences, carnal, emotionless, even violent, or obsessive, compulsive behaviors. This kind of damage can reach back into a childhood wrought with extremes of restriction, taboos, repression, and false or negative judgmental information regarding the sexual function. Damage can also occur as a result of the breach of boundaries through sexual abuse.

*Focus on the energy of the Second Chakra and visualize **orange light** whirling in a clockwise motion, gaining momentum with the intensity of your focused visualization and depth of breath.*

Speak to it. Say,
"I release this issue to The Great Spirit and ask for a healing to take place in my life."

The Third Chakra or Solar Plexus Chakra is located in the Solar Plexus or upper abdominal area of our body. It is related to the element of fire and the principals of sight and light. It supplies energy to the stomach, gallbladder, liver, spleen, pancreas, and nervous system. As its name suggests, this chakra pulls from the energy of the Sun, distributing vital Life Force to all of the other centers. The spiritual planes provide a source of essential energy whether or not we tap into it during meditation. This chakra is associated with feelings of desire and acquisition. It is very sensitive to external stimuli. It is associated with our intuition we call "gut" feelings, and directs how we connect with others.

For this reason, it is a chakra we should concern ourselves with about protection against those who seek to energetically *invade* and deplete our energy reserves to do us harm. The Third Chakra can serve as an effective point of entry, providing a portal through which energy can be absorbed and transmitted.

Absorption of negative energies in this area is damaging to our overall health and well-being and are associated with a psychic or spiritual attack.

It is advisable to do prayers for protection focusing on the Third (Solar Plexus) and Seventh (Crown) Chakra area before entering into meditation. Visualize a large, heavy, metal vault door that you may, at will, close and lock against those who may, either intentionally or unintentionally, drain or poison your energy. During times you feel unusually exhausted and depleted, you may be experiencing an invading entity or force stemming from the influence of your own emotional state or an energetic influence from another. Simply shut and lock the impenetrable vault door to your Solar Plexus Chakra with intense protection prayers, enabling an energetic force field around you that will shield you from any attack.

*Focus on the energy of the Solar Plexus Chakra and visualize **yellow** or **golden light**, whirling in a clockwise motion, gaining momentum with the intensity of your focused visualization and depth of breath.*

Speak to it. Say,
"I release this issue to The Great Spirit and ask for a healing to take place in my life."

The objective of socio-cultural constructs that seek to lock us into the lowest energetic realms of our existence is to keep us from ascending to our optimum potential and make us slaves to whatever the current agenda is. If we were to cross the threshold, The Fourth – Heart Chakra, and raise our energies all the way up through that vital energetic channel, we would not be so easy to manipulate. We would be a force to be reckoned with.

Targeted Chakras

Crown Chakra

7

Third Eye Chakra

6

Throat Chakra

5

Heart Chakra

4

Upper Chakras

- -

Solar Plexus Chakra

3

Lower Chakras

Sacral Chakra

2

Root Chakra

1

Kundalini

Targeting Individuals Through the Lower Portals

How we get targeted for even the most random of attacks is to be perceived as lacking in self-esteem from the perspective of the True Self, living low-vibrational, Lower Chakra lifestyles, which turns a human into an energy factory to satisfy the insatiable appetite of demons. Primary targets are:

- people with a highly reactive mind, who are not in charge of their own thoughts, desires, cravings, and emotions, particularly in extreme levels of adrenalin-laced excitement (sports, music, and entertainment events);

- people who are inclined to indulge thought-forms and behaviors hurtful to self and others, of unbridled sexual fantasy and violence, uncontrollable anger with a tendency toward aggression, cruelty, sadism, and bloodshed;

- people who are highly reactive, responsive to every twitch of the crotch, driven in a low vibrational, predatory, covetous, animalistic way, guided by only one sense, sight. These people can't entertain a single thought one notch above the First Chakra, as they spin on extreme love/hate, attachment/aversion drama;

- people who will not take responsibility for the state of their own energy in a quest for Self-Realization. They are too lazy, indifferent, or arrogant to do the personal shadow work required to raise their frequency through study and spiritual/mystical practice and discipline;

- people who are resistant to entering the Realm of Divinity through prayer, meditation, contemplation, surrender … the very place these entities cannot enter, to secure a sure win in this dangerous game of hide and seek;

- people with obsessive/compulsive craving drama and insatiable appetites for immediate sensual gratification in habitual, neurotic, uncontrollable, irrational behaviors. These behaviors may manifest as uncontrollable addiction to drugs, alcohol, sex, porn, food, and consumerism, among other things, leaving the victim trapped in the 'hungry ghost' hell of unfulfilled longing;

- people whose level of "desire" and blind ambition is so over the top that even the success, belongings, and lifestyles of friends, family, and even strangers, are coveted and targeted with what is known as the Evil Eye (Ayn), and Envy (Hassad);

- people who are highly competitive, steeped in the toxic energy of jealousy, envy, blind ambition, intellectual snobbery, and hatred;

- people who are held in bondage to their attachments, clinging, hoarding, selfishness, oblivious to any sense of obligation to reach out and help others;

- fans (fanatics) of varied types, who engage in irrational celebrity worship that can create energetic attachments and alignments with virtual strangers, with no consideration for the unholy spiritual pacts they may be tapping into the frequency of;

- narcissists who cause harm, seeking to exalt themselves over others with the Satanic mindset of, "I am better than you!" through egoic, hateful, violent mindsets projected upon others based on class, gender, race, skin color, physical characteristics, religious beliefs, ethnicity, and further judgments of perceived "otherness" and differences;

- people who harbor toxic, vile, and odious vanity-based identity fixations that seek to harm others of targeted social and cultural diversities;

- people who entertain their egos with the spinning of drama, cruel bullying behavior ... people who hurt people, lacking compassion, empathy, and remorse;

- people with involvements in, or identifications with, the hypnosis of political or religious fervor, laced with dualistic obsessions of crime/punishment, saint/sinner scenarios, targeting and harming others.

These people are the most likely to make themselves available as viable energy sources and literal portals, resulting in complete occupation and sometimes voluntary possession pacts with entities that will ultimately take them over. Voluntary possession scenarios occur when we fall into a "trap" of agreement and make energetic contracts with demons;

This is not a game. This is our *lives* and the *quality* of life we must be wise enough to choose. If this is a checklist, we must all line up for a cure. Much of this negative energy is just a side-effect of being human. So many of us are victims of cultural conditioning, binding generational curses, energetic influences we are unaware of, and poor lifestyle choices that result in the bondage that binds us to low vibrational thoughts, behaviors, attachments, and addictions. These are only a few of the causes that can result in our getting locked in the spin of our three lowest energy vortices, suffering the physical, mental, emotional, and spiritual consequences for refusing to do the self-work that it takes to raise that energy up beyond the reach of our physical reality. We are Divinely blessed with the gift of Free Will. We are free to choose. We are not exempted from the consequences of our choices.

If we live our lives from our lowest three chakras, it throws off the entire Chakra System, which will result in physical, mental, emotional, and spiritual illness. That's bad enough. But to consider the possibility our energy is being manipulated and harvested, whether it sounds crazy to you or not, it could clarify the urgency of understanding that, whoever or whatever they are, their interest in humans could be beyond pure mischief. We could be a source of nutrition for these vampiric parasites, some with bodies, some maybe not. A wide variety of these negative entities and forces have the ability to influence and drain the vortices of our subtle body and energy fields of elements of our Life Force to use for their own sustenance. Some are able to project frequencies that trigger emotional states that cause us to generate and emit either positive or negative "loosh" that they collect to restore their supply. The stirring and brewing of these states can extend from intrapersonal relationships to mass manipulations involving systems of advanced technology, social programming, and techniques of mind control.

It deepened my perspective on how important it is to our overall well-being and survival, to understand and study how, but particularly WHY, these negative forces operate the way they do, the interference they cause, and the pain they are capable of causing … particularly if we are inclined to give in to the reactive mind. The most potent of all the emotions they are able to arouse and feed upon is fear. One way to become less attractive to such predators is to raise our frequency and become everything they just don't have an appetite for, and ultimately, simply bore them … disengage from the cravings, desires, and impulses that make us a magnet that attracts their attention.

Targeted Chakras Visualization Exercise to
Strengthen your Defense System – Upper Portals Visualization

Imagine living our lives, not ignoring the lower chakras but raising their energy all the way up the center channel, as our body system is intelligently designed to do. Understand the nature of the upper chakras, and understand why we must not get trapped in the lower three. It is the undoing of all that is good in this world.

***The Fourth (Heart)* Chakra** (The Bridge) is located in the heart area and is associated with the realm of emotions and sensations of love, compassion, warmth, empathy, and the pleasure center, balanced by will. It distributes energy to the heart, circulatory system, and upper back. This chakra is believed to be associated with the element of air and the sense of touch. It is the mid-point of the seven chakras, with three above and three below. It is the point where the spiritual and physical planes are bridged, determining the potential for transcendence. On that bridge is the seat of the Divine One.

When the energy of the Heart Chakra is balanced and healthy, it flows with love and compassion, forgiveness and nurturing, healing, and acceptance. A closed or blocked Heart Chakra can give way to grief, anger, jealousy, fear of betrayal, abandonment issues, and emotionally crippling hatred of self and others. This tends to be the chakra that is most often obstructed or badly damaged due to emotional disappointment, trauma, anger, and an inability to forgive. Often people have experienced suffering so emotionally devastating that forgiveness is not easy, nor seemingly possible, without some manner of spiritual intervention.

It is important to concentrate on this area and send healing energy through meditation, visualization, and contemplation on the Divine. Affirm that nothing is greater than The Creator. Affirm that nothing is more healing than the contemplation of The Creator and that nothing is abler to facilitate a more powerful transformation. Forgiveness is the most powerful cure for blockages in the Heart Chakra center. No one is perfect. If we are so vain to expect forgiveness from others for our own imperfections, and not be willing to forgive others and ourselves, we cause ourselves abysmal emotional pain and suffering. To open wide the receptive portals of intuition and discernment, the Heart Chakra must allow for the unobstructed flow of positive energy. Meditation is one of the most effective ways to restore balance.

*Focus on the energy of the Heart Chakra and visualize **green light** whirling in a clockwise motion, gaining momentum with the intensity of your focused visualization and depth of breath.*

Speak to it. Say,
"I release this issue to The Great Spirit and ask for a healing to take place in my life."

The Fifth (Throat) Chakra is located in the front and back of the throat. It supplies energy to the bronchi, thyroid, lungs, and alimentary canal. This chakra is believed to be associated with the element of Ether and governs the principle of sound related to the sense of hearing. In situations of attempted entry by a negative energy or entity that has been projected with malefic intent, the point where the back of the neck and spine meet is a major focal point of entry, as well as the intersection point for either powerful healing or great harm. It is called the **_Zeal Point_** (see diagram below). Protect and cleanse this area with sage, frankincense, myrrh, salt, strong meditative energy, recitation of a mantra, and repetitive prayer.

The veils between the worlds become thin when engaging in Mystical Meditation, and nothing should be taken for granted or written off as a coincidence. It is sometimes difficult to distinguish reasonable concern from paranoid delusion. That is why the faculties of spiritual discernment should be fine-tuned in every possible manner to ensure that we do not find ourselves vulnerable to attack. At the same time, we should ensure that we do not attack ourselves with our own ungrounded, unreasonable fears.

The Law of Attraction affirms that we speak things into and out of existence with the vibratory power of the spoken word. Silenced, unexpressed, or disregarded speech becomes the innermost cry of the voiceless. The result is the energetic obstruction of the Fifth Chakra, making any attempts at authentic communication a challenge.

The rebound effect of the power of the spoken word has inspired many common proverbs and quotes. It is said that before your words leave your mouth, you are their master. After they leave your mouth, you become their slave. The creative power of the spoken word is tried and true. The great poet, Hafiz, is quoted, "The words you speak become the house you live in."

*Focus on the energy of the Throat Chakra and visualize **blue light** whirling in a clockwise motion, gaining momentum with the intensity of your focused visualization and depth of breath.*

Speak to it. Say,
"I release this issue to The Great Spirit and ask for a healing to take place in my life."

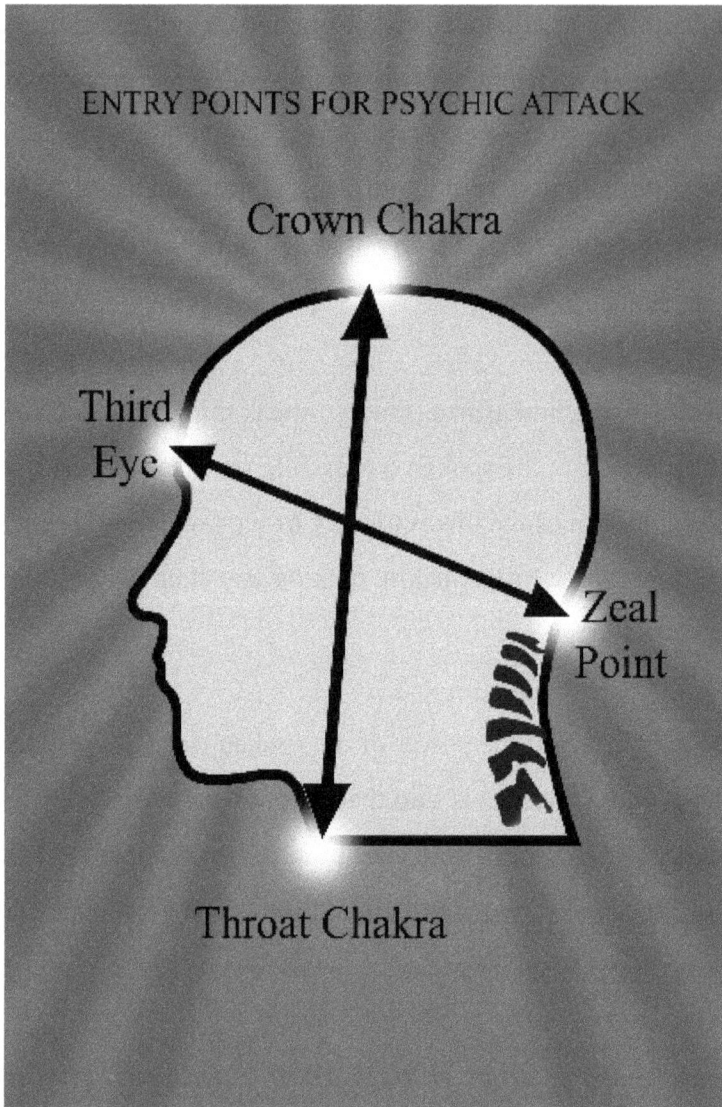

ENTRY POINTS FOR PSYCHIC ATTACK

Crown Chakra

Third Eye

Zeal Point

Throat Chakra

The area approximately at the point where the base of the skull and the spine meet, is a significant entry point to manipulative energies and entities, as are the Crown and Solar Plexus Chakras.

The Sixth (Third Eye) Chakra is located on the forehead, at the mid-point between and just above the brow line. It is believed to be the eye through which the astral body is able to see. It has been referred to as the "Psychic Eye," as it is considered to be the portal through which psychic energies are received and transmitted. It is the window through which we may view the astral and higher planes if we dare to enter and journey there. The Sixth Chakra is associated with the "Sixth Sense," Ether, Light, and the *never* sleeping eye of the I AM Consciousness, the veil between worlds, the bridge between dreams. Its energies, from tradition to tradition, in ancient and contemporary spirituality, are identified in many ways.

When we turn within and journey through the innermost planes of existence, we strip ourselves of our ego and our Self-limiting identifications, which allows us to let go of our fear of the loss of our personhood. Through Third Eye vision, we are able to see our essential nonphysical being, as well as that of others. We can access energies that are less available to us as we view ourselves only in a physical context. It is associated with paranormal experiences of all kinds. That includes but is not limited to, Clairvoyance, Clairaudience, Psychometry, Telekinesis, Energy Healing, Telepathy, Prophecy, Dreamtime, Out of Body Experiences (OBE), Insight, Foresight, the powers of the Mystic Seer, Higher Self, the gift of viewing the subtle energies of chakras and auras, even visions into the Timeless Realms, beyond past, present, and future. Some of the highest states of consciousness are associated with the Third Eye. It is the ever-watchful eye of the Natural Mystic, inducing states of a place in consciousness known by many names in various traditions; Samadhi, Turiya, Nirvana, Fanaa, Zazen, Dhyana, Moksha, Satori, Bliss, Jhana and others. It is also an entry point through which invasive negative energies may gain access into the depths of our psyche and do incredible harm.

The Sixth Chakra is associated with the flow of energy to the pituitary, lower brain, left eye, ears, nose, and nervous system. It also facilitates transcendence to higher planes of consciousness and controls the many levels of concentration realized through Mystical Meditation. It affects inner and outer realities to the extent that it commands the whole of the personality. The positive energy of the Sixth Chakra (Third Eye) is maintained by deep levels of meditation, visualization, and embracing the spirit of compassion, forgiveness, and empathy. Sound and aromatherapy contribute to the health of this sensitive chakra.

In the study of Psychic Self-Defense, the Third Eye is profoundly significant. It orchestrates the energetic fusion of all of the lower chakras. The rush of energy emanating from the First Chakra pushes its way up through the ambition and willfulness of the Second Chakra; the fiery spirit of the Third Chakra; the compassionate spirit of the Fourth Chakra; the vibration and resonant incantations of the Fifth Chakra, speaking into the manifestation of the desires that emanate from the First Chakra; to rest comfortably in the seat of the soul's vision, the Sixth (Third Eye) Chakra; touching Divine Will at the Crown, the Seventh Chakra. This pure magic is accompanied by a profound responsibility for the consequences of their manifestations, focusing on the nature of conscious and subconscious intention. For every pebble cast into the vast sea of Karma, the ripple effect reverberates beyond that, into the unknowable, and boomerangs right back into our lives and the lives we affect.

For this reason, among others, it is important to be mindful of the company we keep. We could be keeping company with someone who is incurring horrible Karma for whatever reason. Read the energy of the people you allow in your life on a regular basis, and trust your intuition. If you have no power or influence to help the person or change the person or the group of people, it is important to understand the phenomenon of Group Karma. It is wise to distance ourselves from such negative energies whenever possible. It is always possible. Not doing so is like sitting on the lap of someone that owes a debt he or she cannot pay and consequently has a contract or price on their head. That puts you in just as much jeopardy as the person committing the Karma incurring offense. A determination such as this is to be made without exacting judgment because no one is perfect. We each go through what we must go through, at whatever juncture of our lives, to move us toward our eventual Self-Realization. Understanding this, we have the right and the responsibility to choose our associates wisely from among people with spiritual integrity.

*Focus on the energy of the Third Eye Chakra and visualize **purple light** whirling in a clockwise motion, gaining momentum with the intensity of your focused visualization and depth of breath.*

Speak to it. Say,
"I release this issue to The Great Spirit and ask for a healing to take place in my life."

<u>The Seventh (Crown) Chakra</u> is located at the top of the head and has the highest rate of vibration of all the chakras. It supplies energy to our right eye and our upper brain. It is associated with the experience of direct contact with Divinity. The Crown Chakra is the doorway to the Sacred and should be protected and honored as such. It is guarded best through prayer, meditation, and ritual contemplation on The Divine One. When performing any sacred spiritual work, most mystical traditions advise that a head covering be worn to shield the Crown Chakra, symbolically deflecting energies that are not of Divine Source. It is a symbolic gesture to acknowledge that it is a sacred point of entry that is not open to welcoming any energies other than those, very specifically, of The Divine.

The Crown Chakra is the portal between the worlds. It is the gateway, on either side, for energies and entities from other planes of existence that may seek to manipulate, influence, and even inhabit or possess one's physical being. It is very important in protection exercises, and before meditation and prayer, to concentrate on this area to enforce that nothing enters there except that which is of pure Divine Light.

It is not advisable to seek to host or channel any entity other than the Pure Energy and Light of The God of our highest understanding, for it can be a very dangerous practice. We are not perfect. Our abilities to discern the quality and origin of what energies we allow to enter us in this fashion may not be as informed as we may think, even if we have ascended to extremely high levels of consciousness. To avoid making the mistake of leaving the Crown Chakra open and available as a doorway to receive energy through meditation or other spiritual practices, we must perform a thorough banishing of unwanted energies and entities and implement the strongest forms of spiritual protection.

Perform the Light Meditation in this text. Visualize a sphere of pure, white/silver Light, the color of soft lightning, just above your head. This sphere of Light is charged with strong prayers and positive affirmations of unwavering faith. Visualize it showering its beautiful Light in an energetic rain that covers your entire being in a clockwise, circular pattern, forming a glowing, egg-shaped, protective aura all around the physical self as a shield, as illustrated in the aura graphics. Affirm that no weapon formed against you will prosper.

*Focus on the energy of the Crown Chakra and visualize **white light the color of a soft white lightening** whirling in a clockwise motion, gaining momentum with the intensity of your focused visualization and depth of breath.*

Speak to it. Say,
"I release this issue to The Great Spirit and ask for a healing to take place in my life."

Self-Inquiry Meditation

A Course in Miracles teaches that "The self that needs protecting is not real." All mystical paths teach, "We are not our bodies. We are not our thoughts. We are not our feelings. We are not our fears. The True Self is more than that." Between provocation and reaction to the triggering, there is a breath, empty of ego. A single breath is an opportunity, a processor of thought and thought-form, a moment between being and "nothing." In that space is our power to choose our response. In our response lies our growth and our freedom."

For me, the transcendence of fear of hyperdimensional interferences began with Vipassana, India's ancient meditation technique. Vipassana translates from Sanskrit to basically mean "insight" or "Prajna" – insight into the true nature of reality. It is as a veil lifted to allow seeing the essential nature of things as they really are, with lucidity and clarity of mind. The objective of the Vipassana meditation practice is to free one's self from the bondage of suffering by cultivating perspectives that transcend the body/mind attachment to responding emotionally to every sensation that would cause the experience of fear. That was one level.

Another powerful perspective I have found is to know the True Self, remain "*as*" the True Self, and know that our animating personal breath is a Breath shared with us of the Divine One … and our connection to the Ultimate Self. The ultimate epiphany of consciousness comes in the knowledge that these beings cannot enter the Realm of Divinity as we are able to. We follow that Breath to its Source. There is our refuge.

I do not know how to keep this perspective secular in this expression, even though I do not promote or denounce the "religious" beliefs of anyone. I see the "True Self" as being the animating life-force, entrusted to us by the Creator of this shell, that houses who we really are. I also see the word "God" (as Creator) being recklessly used as a divisive thought-form, even ascribed basic characteristics of common 'personhood,' bearing the potential for incredible suffering and destruction.

The purpose of this text is not to tell anyone what to believe in. But in battling hyperdimensional forces such as the ones that may be present in phenomenal experiences associated with Sleep Paralysis, we must know that we are not alone. Within the context of our inherent Oneness with The Creator Being of our Highest understanding, we are absorbed into Timeless Light. Whatever That is … We are That, holding fast to the knowledge that we did not create ourselves … that What created us has the Ultimate Power to protect and sustain us. Our True Essence is not from here, not from the Plane of our physical dwelling. That is why God "concepts" are consigned to the Realm of the Unknowable, as referenced on many sacred mystical paths, because it is pure vanity and shirk to claim to "know" the Unknowable.

I know nothing. I AM nothing. And I *still* say, "My prayers and my sacrifices, my life, as well as my death are all of, and belonging to That Realmless Realm and That Unknowable One, Whom I experience … Who knows the "I" in me … Who is The Breath that permeates, animates, this reed flute that I AM … so whom shall I fear? I do not seek Oneness. I AM Oneness. Symptoms fade … fear, terror, panic, apprehension of impending attack subsides, dissipates … into that 97% of all there is … whatever That is. Only 3% of reality can show up in a mirror. Only 3% of all creation is visible to the average human eye. Into Self-Illuminating Triple Darkness, from whence we emerged, we return. Where ego dissolves, the lower-case "i" becomes the upper-case "I" humbled into embracing that One Love, the "I in I," the I AM, in surrender to the remembrance of That.

A particular meditation works for me as an effective deterrent for managing fears of lower Astral Realm traffic and its sometimes-harmful agendas. It is a practice called Self-Inquiry (Self-Enquiry) that I was introduced to through the meditation techniques of Non-Dual, Advaita, and Zen philosophies, particularly that of Sri Ramana Maharshi, The Sage of Arunachala. This acclaimed Indian guru/mystic (30 December 1879 – 14 April 1950) instructs that in the practice of Self-Inquiry, one focuses on "abiding as the Self" … the True Self … reaching the point of Ultimate Self-ness with one repetitive question, "WHO AM I?"

No meditation practice I know of more directly addresses the phenomenon of Sleep Paralysis than that one. The false projections and fake identities that sought to incorrectly define our being, fade with the awareness of what I AM *'not'* … *not* this body … *not* this mind … *not* this fear … *not* alone. The meditation is complete when the meditator disappears … disappears to egoic branding and labeling … disappears to perspectives and desires of the lower self … disappears to everything that one is *not*. What is left? That is who we *are*. That is the answer.

The word "ego" has many interpretations. It can refer to personal self-worth, self-confidence, or in a psychological context may refer to the mediator between the subconscious and conscious mind, a manifestation of person-ality and individuated body/mind identification. We must become the knowing of the difference between "me" and "I," or we are nothing but a walking corpse on the pathway to a hole in the ground. When we ask ourselves, "Who am I?" we must know we can't find "I" in the mirror. The True Self, the "I," the "I in I," the I AM, nonphysical awareness/consciousness that is unique to our being, yet not unique to all things … That is who we truly are. When we find ourselves on the outside of the body vehicle looking at it, voluntarily or involuntarily, for whatever reason, we must know that the cold, inanimate duppy is not who we are. When trapped in the terrifying grip of a Sleep Paralysis Event, it is more important than ever to remember that ... We are more than that! We are One with That Which manifested it.

In the process of an "attack," when one may feel ejected from the physical body, self-perception is invaluable. We may look down upon that helpless body lying there and know that it is not who we really are. Body/mind identification in mystical practice is an obstacle. It is a product of the ever-busy ego, constructing and reconstructing, remodeling, repurposing, rewiring, and redefining the Self as some AI-bot drone that is here to live, consume, die, and just do what it is told. Obey! These conditioned priorities get placed on the back burner of a life-disrupting phenomenon that nobody really understands. Who we really are is *not* powerless or helpless. Self-Inquiry specifically triggers identification as the True Self, as the principal means to transcend the illusion of body/mind self-classification and abide as pure Self-awareness, surrendering to the experience of Oneness with the Unknowable.

At the age of 16, Sri Ramana Maharshi had a "death experience" which paralleled the symptoms and manifestations of a classic Sleep Paralysis Event. The experience of that 'episode' left his body "rigid with the sudden fear of death," struck by what he called "a flash of excitement" or "heat". He became aware of a "current" or "force" that seemed to "possess" him. He witnessed himself as the True "I" or "Self" and observed himself as having dissolved into Oneness with the Supreme Being. His devotees communicate, he held that he ultimately realized that "the body dies, but that the "current" or "force" remains alive." As the observer, or witness, inquiring within, *"Who is the seer?"* He saw the seer disappear, revealing that which is Eternal." This+ is the foundation of the Self-Inquiry meditation that extends beyond releasing the fear of the shadows that life naturally casts to the release of the fear of death itself. One asks in meditation and contemplation, as did

Sri Ramana, "What is it that dies?" … Then, identifies the "current" or "force" as the Realized Self.

The introspective question "Who am I?" does not use any specific object as a focal point, rather it observes the transcendence of body/mind identifications to Zero-Point Existence. I have heard it said that this question is not asked to "answer the question." It serves to dissolve the questioner.

- The Self-Inquiry method is an interrogation that makes the mind enter into a state of void.

- Repetition of the Yogic/Vedantic negation, "Neti, Neti. (Not this, nor that)" begins to peel back the layers of labels and conditioning that blind us to who we really are. "I am not this body. I am not this mind. I am not this reflection in the mirror. I am not this story I am telling myself of who I am. I am not …"

- We become the witness to the emergence of the True Self (with no concepts, no conditioning, no attributes, no story, no mind, no form, no past, no future, no time, no attachments, no aversions).

- We become transpersonal consciousness, aware of the Pure Awareness … beyond duality, beyond intellect, beyond agenda, beyond memories, beyond gender, beyond linear thinking, beyond rationale, neither this nor that … the unknowable … The Unknowable.

- The object of the meditation (the "I") becomes the ultimate revelation.

- The Ultimate Self cannot be known by means of our mundane manner of thinking. With the acceptance of that, a kind of *surrender* presents itself to a once loud, busy, distracted, delusional mind, and brings a Self-centered peace of mind and contentment.

- The elimination of all that was believed to be known allows space for revelation to rising up from the Silence.

- Only by eliminating what is known (our thoughts, perceptions, and emotions) is it possible to reveal to the linear mind the Ultimate "I," the I in I, the Eternal Now.

- We immerse and dissolve ourselves into the knowingness that becomes increasingly visceral and profound in this revelation of our own True Nature, who we really are.

- The question itself is born from *Stillness,* and it is also fed from the *Silence* that is home to our mind and our inner being.

- The question rises up from the spaciousness to name the Nameless, to define the Undefinable, as just That ... Undefinable.

- As our realization of the True Self reveals our Oneness with Divine Existence, we disappear to the fear, and become unavailable to the attacker. We seek refuge where they cannot enter, in the Realm of Divinity, our True Origin and Home.

- What appears to be a void is seen as Self-illuminating Triple Darkness, latent Light, the spontaneous immeasurable awareness of who we really are. The question "Who am I?" exists within us in a dormant state and emanates to manifest the harmony of our entire complex being. This harmony ignites the flame of Self-Realization and recognition of our union and relationship with Divine Existence.

- Again, the question, *"Who am I?"* is not meant to get an answer, and it is not rhetorical either. *It is meant to dissolve the questioner.*

- Upon what feels like the 'death bed' of the paralyzed questioner, the question arises, "Who am I?" The answer frees the bound and gagged sufferer of identity. The True Self, That observes, answers, "I AM!" The spell, the paralysis of false identifications, is broken. Release any question other than, Who am I?

The Inquiry MUST begin … Who is the body in that bed that "I" am hovering above? How is it that all that would animate it is still with "me," floating here, in some bizarre nonphysical state of being? My thoughts are with "me." My emotions, what I would call the "soul" of my being … It is all with "me," the "I" that observes the inanimate body encased in the names, words, labels, evaluations, and judgments that made it feel "real." So, who is that body, the one I've seen in all of my mirrors, in transitional phases of its existence? Who am I? The beginning of Self-Inquiry. Who am I? Which one is my True Self? Identification only as the physical "self" is the most dangerous of the deceptions of Maya, the illusory Realm of Existence. In Maya, the nonphysical is visible as it vibrates at a lower rate of speed … slowed down enough to trick a Timeless, imperishable, formless being into believing that its defining reality is only what can be seen with ordinary vision.

Clinical Interpretations of Sleep Paralysis

Sleep Paralysis is a condition that occurs in the transitional state (Alpha) between awakened or conscious (Beta) while falling into deep REM (rapid-eye-movement) sleep called hypnagogia, or upon awakening, hypnopompia. A presentation of what is called "atonia" collapses the muscles in such weakness that movement of any sort is impossible. When a person awakens in such a state, the fear alone can produce a (Beta brainwave) Fight/Flight emergency response in the brain. "Fight" is not possible because of the physical paralysis state, leaving the body defenseless. "Flight" is not possible because a chemical in the brain that restrains movement in dream state suppresses the ability to act upon activities occurring in (Theta) dream state.

Even more paradoxical is the 'unconscious' (Delta) state, which some experience in deep, non-dreaming sleep, just above the level of being 'brain-dead.' This state is associated with access to the Collective Unconscious and even to the level of consciousness of the Realm of Divinity. The ultimate goal would be to experience the Realm of Divinity (the Unknowable) at any and all levels of consciousness. It is believed to present in a fetus in the final stages of pregnancy, in the earlier months of infancy, and reemerges in the final stages of consciousness during the 'death' process. The brain produces low-frequency Delta waves during disassociated states of profoundly deep meditation, mystical, and spiritual practice, as consciousness splits from the *perceived* self into states of non-physical awareness. Some believe they are the source of empathy, deeply penetrating and hypnotic, like the vibration of a drumbeat.

Brain Wave Patterns

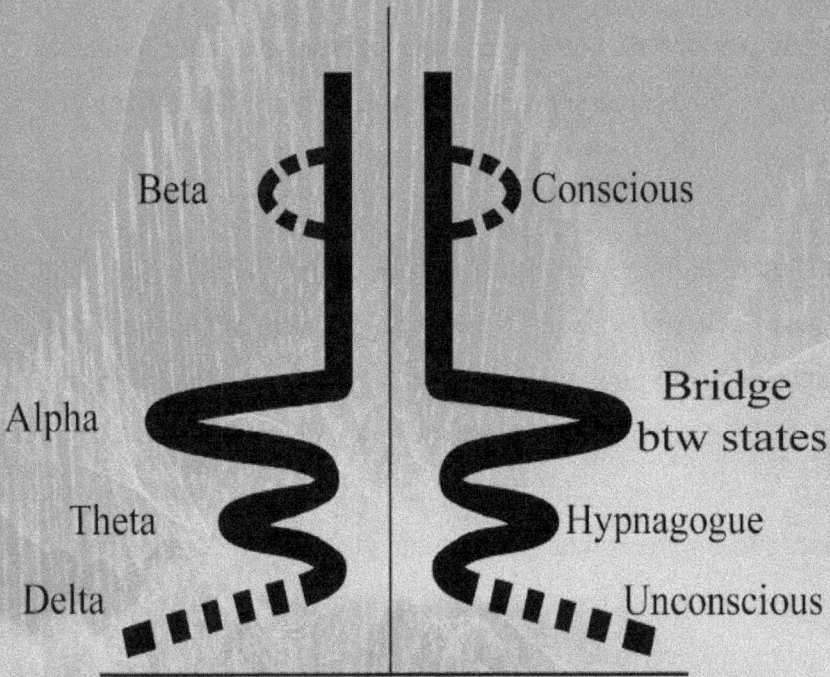

Beta   Conscious

Alpha   Bridge btw states

Theta   Hypnagogue

Delta   Unconscious

Beta Waves (14-30 Hz) Focus, Cognition, Attentiveness

Higher levels associated with disease, anxiety, separation, Fight or flight

Alpha Waves (8-13.9 Hz) Increased Serotonin, relaxation, increased learning, mild trance like state

Meditation, access of sunbonscious mind,state before falling asleep or waking up

Theta Waves (4-7.9 Hz) REM Sleep, creativity

Increased emotions, incresed learning, emotional changes

Deep Medtation, trance,access to unconscious mind

Delta Waves (1-3.9 Hz) Dreamless sleep, release of human growth hormones

Trance-like, non-physical state,loss of body awareness

Access to collective unconscious mind

The Yin and Yang of brainwaves affirm that there are two sides of the brainwave frequency "benefit/detriment" scenario … largely depending on the activity one seeks to be engaged in. In Tesla quotes referencing "energy, frequency, and vibration," it is clear that not only can these factors manifest in paranormal experiences, but they can also be responsible for frequency (personality) clashes among people and other beings of discordant or incompatible frequencies.

There is definitely an electrical current and quality to the vibrational sensations of a Sleep Paralysis Event, experienced by some as a current of electricity running through their chest and upper body, along with an energetic pressure pushing and pulling at the same time. Often there are sound effects like buzzing or deep, echoing, muffled or rumbling sounds, rushing waves of energy and pulsation from the sound of bursts and gusts of wind, trains barreling down tracks, or a stillness that feels palpable. It often has the pulse of a heartbeat. But is it the rhythm of a heartbeat? That's a deep meditation!

After significant research on the subject, not to mention my own personal experiences, it is clear this phenomenon is very serious and far more common than most people realize. Even though it occurs on the threshold of the Dreamtime experience as what may appear as a physical condition, some argue that it may be associated with psychic attacks in spiritual warfare. It is risky to settle for a one-dimensional, dry, clinical version of an explanation for Sleep Paralysis. Although it is presented in this text as more of a spiritual phenomenon, many physical causes cannot be ruled out and may require consultation with a medical professional. If you research the subject, you will find two conflicting bodies of opinion to explain it, and some offer no explanation for it at all. Whatever the cause or source, this condition can be terrifying.

Sleep disorders may occur when the victim becomes anxious, fearful, and worried about "the next time" to the extent that sleep is avoided. The fear and lack of sleep only compounds the problem and makes one even more vulnerable. If you are experiencing bouts of Sleep Paralysis, do not become so overwhelmed by fear that you forget the powerful spirit that you are. We must own the fact that there is something non-physical about us that cannot be touched by anything but the like energies of the Creator that loved us … from Self, into individuated existent. When spiritual study and practice affect the energetic force field we emit and are enveloped in, it can rob Sleep Paralysis of the only power it has over us … becoming the focal point of our attention.

The Danger of Body/Mind Identification and Sleep Paralysis

In my book, FACELESS: THE SACRED RELATIONSHIP, I speak of the cultural and traditional implications of body/mind identification as it relates to Sleep Paralysis. It is important to engage in Self-Inquiry to contemplate on which of the bodies is the real YOU. When we look in the mirror, we may or may not love the image that we see. In many ways, we possess the power to alter the image of the body vehicle. We generally care for that image in the same manner that one cares for a car. We clean it. We maintain its mechanical functions. We sometimes cosmetically alter it to suit our subjective standards of beauty. We take care in how we fuel it. We drive it with caution. We protect and insure it. But with a car, we don't often lose our focus in remembering the difference between the vehicle and the driver.

As with a car, some of us are attached to the beauty of our car more than the mechanics or practicality, even the safety of it. Then on the day that abuse and careless handling returns a consequence, the original beauty that attracted us to it in the first place is gone, along with our attachment to the original perception of its beauty.

We are misinformed to hate age, death, and infirmity. It is easy to be seduced into that type of thinking. But, what is worse is the fact that we let "images" define us and represent who we really are. The I AM, the Eternal Spirit that we are, breaks mirrors and renders labels, judgments, and superficial identifications empty and void of power over us. We are embracing the purification of being stripped down to raw awareness to heal the damage the ego is capable of attracting.

I was left with no choice but to submit myself to stand at the crossroad where all that is sacred intersects with this field of consciousness that I AM. I had to become identified with my formless, Eternal Self, the I AM my Higher Self, just to survive. I had to embrace my Higher Self as an indestructible, untouchable part of me. I had to accept that I am is only the *witness* … not the *victim,* of the incessant drama conjured by mischievous phenomena and the patchwork quilt of illusions. Our transcendence from the shadows of a victim complex is to see this drama for what it really is. It is a looped reality show … a play called Leela … occurring on a stage called Maya, the illusory world we cling to as reality.

From the perspective of the Higher Self "witnessing" a psychic attack, the attacker is disarmed by the intended victim's realization of the True Self, the I AM. The Self-Inquiry ensues. Who is under attack? Who is the "I" that I defend? I rest my faith in that perspective, knowing that just as surely as I am the witness of this body of identity, I once believed my "self" to be, The Ultimate "I" witnesses me and intervenes in my affairs. It watches over my Realized Self, protecting, guiding, and defending as the shared Essence of who I AM. A force stronger than fear conquers Spiritual Emergencies as extreme as Sleep Paralysis and related phenomena. That force is knowledge, beginning with the knowledge of Self. That force is the connection between our own Divinity and the Divinity of the Creator.

The most disturbing thing about Sleep Paralysis is the fact that it strikes just as we drift off to sleep when we are most vulnerable to attack. That is why keeping a detailed journal is important. The triggers must be studied. The complex phases of it must be studied. The more that is known about this phenomenon, the less threatened we will feel. With training, practice, and experience, we discover that we are more powerful than that which we choose to fear.

As an interesting spiritual exercise, look in the mirror, then draw close to the image we see. The eyes are the mirrors and portals of the soul. We make eye contact with the reflection of our eyes and look deep within. We study them. We venture behind them. We see the beautiful spirit that is the *driver* of the vehicle, rather than being overly preoccupied with the vehicle. We make sure that the driver receives a higher level of attention than the vehicle. There are references throughout this book to "Body System" with its complex circuitry of energetic awareness. It is important to be able to visualize this system, even though an illustration can only render an abstract interpretation of the seen and the unseeable.

I included several appendices from other books I have written to share related material and provide effortless cross-referencing. The appendix that follows this section is an overview of the many aspects of our "body," in approximations that do not reflect an exact location.

APPENDIX ONE

The Body System

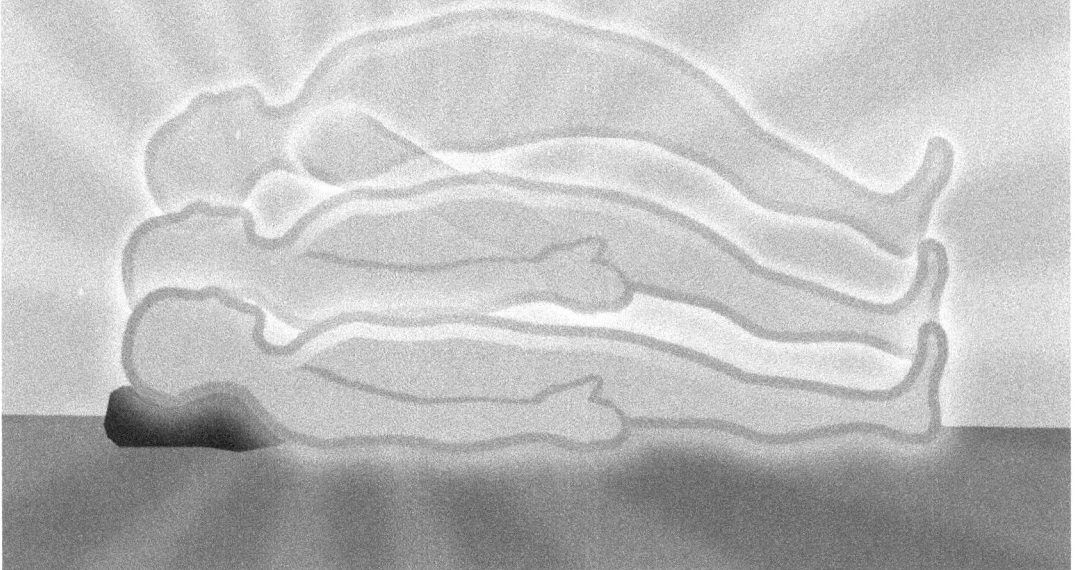

The Body System

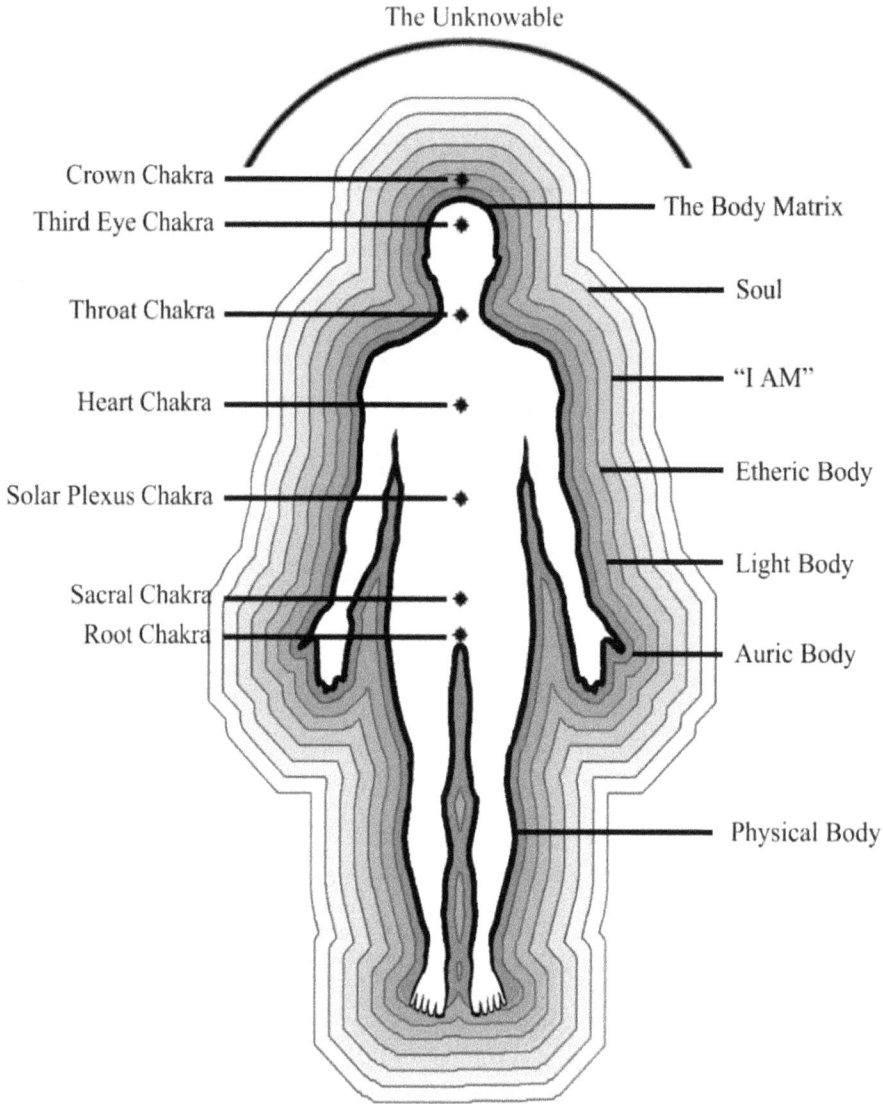

The Unknowable

Crown Chakra

Third Eye Chakra — The Body Matrix

Throat Chakra — Soul

"I AM"

Heart Chakra — Etheric Body

Solar Plexus Chakra — Light Body

Sacral Chakra

Root Chakra — Auric Body

Physical Body

The multifaceted body matrix is a system that knows no boundaries or borders.
They are interconnected and can make a dominant manifestation for their own
time and purpose, even while still connected to the physical body.

This diagram is a representation/approximation and in no way indicates
actual or exact locations of the "bodies" of the Body System.

The Body System

The ability to recognize all aspects of our True Being, particularly our energetic frequencies, is important. We continually evolve into a perfect vessel for the Spirit of the Natural Mystic ... That Sacred Indwelling Presence, a Spark from The Original Flame. Our Mystical Meditation discipline begins with our decision to become a desirable container through which The Creator chooses Its Expression. This process involves every aspect of our being; spiritual, mental, emotional, and physical. We are not one body. We are many bodies, variously layered in many forms, rising, fusing into Oneness, seeking balance and union. We must give each aspect of our many selves their own domain of significance in our lives. Our many bodies must be cleansed and healed with Light and Love to repel anyone or anything of a non-resonant frequency, energy, or vibration. We must be firmly assured that we are not the limited, finite, perishable body we see in the mirror. It is the same one that invariably turns up in various states of decomposition and gets closed up in a casket or reduced to ashes in an urn. We are more than that.

The Light Body/Subtle Body/Auric Body

The soundest advice I can offer in approaching mystical studies is, *Know The God* and acknowledge our relationship with The God with our every breath. Be conscious that we have come into this incarnation, unblessed with a sense of separation from the Light that emanated the Essence of our being, with the responsibility and challenge of recognizing our Oneness with That Ultimate Light, the Source, The God. Through this consciousness of Oneness with Source, we realize our True Self as our Ultimate Identity and are able to rise into blissful union. The Eternal Light, the Unknowable Soul that we are, is all that we have and all we will ever need to be. We must see ourselves in the big picture that extends beyond our physical form, from that pinpoint Light at the core of our beingness, shining through this Earthly form, radiantly cloaked in rainbow colors. We may call that

Light, our coat of many colors, our aura. It is indeed a protective field of energy, but only with the recognition of its Source.

I cannot imagine a more chaotic, empty, and lonely life than the feeling of separation from The Source, The God. In my references to "The God," I speak of the Love from which we all emerged. I say "The" God to distinguish The Creator God from lesser gods, for there are many. Our sacred connection with The God transcends Earth plane precepts and concepts. It is a particularly important consideration as it relates to the incessant thought-form of personification of The God ... ascribing attributes of personhood, rather than allowing for the Unknowable qualities of Divinity ... inclusive in perspective, rather than divisive and exclusive.

Before blindly embracing any spiritual practice served up by mortal beings, we must consider the source, consider the Cause and Effect, and consider the consequences. We place ourselves in grave spiritual danger when we assign Powers of Divinity to anything, any entity, or any person (with or without a body) by petitioning for protection or favors. We must yield to The Greatest of Spirits, That Which Created all. We need no intercessor or interpreter. We are One with That. Allow the Frequency. The subtlest body is The God Essence that we are. There is something Divine about us.

The body that hovers above the impending corpse lying on the bed, choking out, struggling for one breath to confirm life ... is *not* our True Self. As it is permitted, go in and allow it to take that breath. Reanimate and resume the egoic identity until it is time to be called into Ultimate Reality ... but we must never ever forget who we really are.

The Mental Self

The mental process plays a major role in making meditation work as we fortify the Light body to become a powerful warrior, fearless on the battlefields of the mind's relentless struggle to make things permanent that are not. It is within the higher frequencies that our strongest meditations and prayers for healing occur. The first thing we must understand is who we really are. We are not our minds. We are not our bodies. Who we really are is what observes the mind and all of its myriad changes. It is within the hidden chambers of our minds that we may access and process the knowledge of who we really are.

We must exert an effort to reprogram the conscious and subconscious negative messages we give ourselves. These are conditioned, programmed belief systems that we may not even be aware of, sabotaging our best efforts to survive the un-survivable. If it is love that we want to manifest in our lives, and deep within there is an abyss of toxic, fermented negative beliefs about love, we hold a fear that is more powerful than our longing. We cannot expect positive results from our strongest conscious efforts to manifest love in our lives if we don't believe in love. If our relationship with money is guilt and fear-based, we cannot expect our efforts to override our subconscious negative belief system.

Affirmation, prayer, meditation, and chanting help us to channel our wandering thoughts into a single stream of energetic intention. These positive thought-forms, summon our intentions into manifestation. A pure and focused thought-form can assist effectively in magnetizing our own electromagnetic force field to attract our conscious and subconscious desires by Divine Will. It is, therefore, a spiritual mandate that we are very sensitive in detecting and banishing negative thought-forms that may be projected from within, or from an external source. It is equally important to reinforce positive thought-forms that work in favor of manifesting our highest good.

The mind can be a powerful ally or a mean-spirited, fickle bully. Our own minds can be the most dangerous psychic attacker we will ever encounter. That is why there must be time set aside to silence it so that it can rest and heal, or it can cause damage to the entire body system. Sometimes the mind longs to be liberated from its vain, petty preoccupations so that it can return to its natural, peaceful state of surrender to the I AM, the Essential Self.

The Emotional Self

Studying Mystical Meditation impacts our emotional stability in a positive way by offering a sense of sovereign security in spiritual practice. We learn to take full responsibility for all aspects of our life. Some people really are better off being a part of a consistent support group or circle that offers a forum to vent, heal, and be understood by people who are, themselves, coping with the fears associated with spiritual warfare.

Some chose to be loners while coping with Psychic Self-Defense issues rather than associate with people who would unintentionally introduce triggers that would slow the remedial process. Though it is a fact of life that it fluctuates, there is an emotional balance that must be kept. When depleted, energetic balance can be restored by constantly cleansing our own emotions of the spiritual burden and heaviness of guilt, jealousy, envy, anger, and hatred. Forgiveness, whether it is deserved or not, is important to maintain our positive energy. The emotional must yield to the spiritual because unstable emotions can cause fear, panic, and grief attacks. These attacks are directly related to specific triggers.

The Physical Self

The part that the physical self plays in walking the path of the Natural Mystic is often ignored and considered unrelated. Our physical condition can either make us a fit or unfit vessel for the flow of creative, mystical forces. To facilitate the safe and effective performance of prayer and Mystical Meditation, we must give proper attention to certain aspects of our physical health.

Pharmaceuticals and over-the-counter medications must be used with caution. The side effects of certain drugs can cause energetic damage and create auric ruptures, opening portals into our consciousness that are not easy to close. A perfect storm of discordant elemental energies can leave us vulnerable to all manner of physical, mental, spiritual, and emotional trauma.

Tai Chi, certain systems of Yoga, Chi Gong, or sound disciplines of personally compatible forms of meditation and exercise are helpful in establishing the groundwork of mystical practice. Many mystical and spiritual disciplines promote the maintenance and well-being of the body's seven major energy centers, the Chakra System. This text offers exercises that are helpful in that effort. A holistic approach … mind, body, and spirit, can facilitate a healing that can cause a radical and positive shift in energy.

We must not underestimate the potential for protection and healing offered by practicing the energetic exercises recommended in this and many other spiritual texts. Our goal is to strengthen our energy centers, maintain a healthy aura of protective Light, and energetically close portals through which we may be invaded or occupied. Our well-rewarded sacrifices mark our concern about the care and maintenance of the health and well-being of our many "selves" as guardians of the Temple of our Creator.

The use of consciousness-altering chemical substances, legal or illegal, is generally not recommended in most common spiritual practices. It can leave us wide open to energies and forces we may not have the experience or strength to be able to manage. Even on spiritual paths that do use substances that will alter consciousness, it is generally practiced in a prescribed, supervised, and sacred manner. It is always advisable to consult both spiritual and medical experts to determine what best serves our individual needs.

There is an army, visible and invisible, of Divinely commissioned guardians to guide and protect us on our journey through this life with all of its light and shadows. There are accessible states of consciousness that exceed the capability of any drug or consciousness-altering substance known on this plane of existence. Access to these realms can be spontaneous or induced. I have personally experienced both on more than a few occasions. These experiences were so profound that I have no words to describe what happened. There are no set rules, only amazing rewards for our longing on our sacred quest for the Unattainable.

The Soul/The Ether/The True Self

The soul is the least dense of our being. It, like its Source, can only be expressed as Silence. This silence is not the silence of the absence of sound. It is a silent awareness, a spark of the Flame of the Ultimate Essential Being, That which created all.

The soul has no form or substance in the way that beings of other levels of the spirit world may have. Even though that is true, it is not beyond manifesting a form to be perceived for whatever time and reason. It cannot be identified by the same standard as an incarnate being with an endless list of archetypal and personal qualities. It cannot be bought or sold. If it finds itself feeling fractured or scattered by some traumatic event, it can be mystically gathered up and retrieved, becoming stronger in the broken places.

It is the drop of water that embraces the ocean and ultimately becomes it. That drop can feel either diminished or enhanced. It can feel as though it disappears in the vast sea of its own element. It is at home. It can claim a higher understanding, as the sea in all of its vastness. That is the choice we have. Do we cling to a multitude of self-defining identities in the face of the opportunity to become One with the Source of all existence? … Or do we engage an ego-fueled argument as a wave rising on the ocean, declaring sovereignty?

The soul is not something that I feel inclined to speculate on, as though I can define it. All is speculation because none of us can say that we really know. It is of the Realm of The Unknowable. A truth of it, I sense, is that it does not belong to us. We were manifested by way of it, individuating as us, emerged from the Source of all.

The Aura in Psychic Self-Defense and Sleep Paralysis

The Aura is a luminous Astral Plane substance that creates an energetic force field surrounding the human body, much like the glow around the flame of a candle. This force field can reflect the spiritual, mental, emotional, and physical state of an individual to those who are sensitive enough to see and read the human aura. It is the environment of these emanations that we often tap into to extract energy or tap into to cleanse the energy.

The energetic field of the aura creates a *charge*, or *current*, that can affect the practice of meditation and prayer. This energy can be transferred between people as well as objects. In certain forms of meditation, crystals, and other semi-precious stones, charged with positive energy, are used as a catalyst to boost the force and depth of the meditation. These stones are charged with astral material associated with the essence of the individual who charged it. Objects carry a vibration, and the meditator taps into the frequency, much like scanning the band of frequencies on a radio, to find a clear signal and a channel with music agreeable to our personal preference. Energy is gathered by relaxing into the clearest possible channel and listening to the subtle voices that we will learn to distinguish from those of our own thoughts.

In a similar way, that energy is channeled in such practices as the *charging* of Holy Water, anointing oil, candles, and other objects. Energy is transferred and shared in a common energy field. It can be a factor in the discomfort felt in the presence of some people and the pleasant feelings experienced in the company of others. It can even explain why certain people with a "green thumb" are better at growing strong, healthy plants than other people. The energies of some are more conducive to nurturing the Life Force of plants than others.

We have all seen examples of the aura, illustrated in the many renderings of historical characters of great spiritual significance, depicted as being surrounded by a white or golden Light or having a halo of Light around their heads. The rainbow colors of the aura can perform a fabulous light show, varying according to the spiritual, mental, emotional, and physical state of the individual it surrounds. Often the aura contains impressions of pictures or symbols that display relevant information about the person emanating it. This light display can provide accurate information that serves to be helpful in determining the cause and cure of problems a person may be experiencing that require knowledge of Psychic Self-Defense.

Certain colors tend to be associated with emotional states of mind. Often these colors demonstrate a correspondence to the colors of the chakra energy centers and their representative energies. However, there are no hard, fast rules about the interpretations of the colors of the aura. People have their own unique emotional reaction to and interpretation of these colors, which may differ from textbook correspondences. Which is right? Your intuition will give you the best information as to the meaning of the colors and impressions of viewing the aura of another person.

The aura can be charged or magnetized by the energy of our emotions to either attract or repel many of the experiences of our lives. Through proper physical and spiritual care, the aura can be magnetized to protect us from spiritual and physical damage. Before entering a meditation, and as part of a healthy spiritual practice, *visualize* your aura surrounding you as pure white Light, a brilliant illumination that continually grows more intense with the rhythm of your breath and heartbeat. Envision yourself comforted by the Pure, Radiant White Light of Divine Protection as a shield and barrier to any presence of harmful intent. Visualize yourself encapsulated in an egg-shaped body of Light, which extends several feet from the physical body. Nothing penetrates this powerful barrier except that which is Divinely Ordained to do so. Prayer and remembrance of The God as our Protector empowers these visualizations.

It is important to the effectiveness of spiritual work that the aura is well-maintained and not polluted by substances known to be toxic to both the physical and Light body. The aura is magnetic and very sensitive. It is important to avoid the damage that alcohol and drug abuse can cause the aura. There are certain vibrations, even lighting, such as fluorescent and strobe lights, that are very damaging to the aura and can affect our physical health.

The aura can be influenced by our thoughts and emotions, as well as the thoughts and emotions of others. Due to extreme emotions of injury or trauma, the aura can sustain damage and become dirty, ruptured, or lowered in vibration. Particularly damaging is our own unbridled anger and that of others who may direct it toward us. This energy can literally take on a life of its own as a *thought-form* that can attach itself as astral material to the aura, creating negativity that can ultimately lead to attracting misfortune and poor health on every level of our being. Many emotions, even love, though positive, can be damaging when the object of this attention does not welcome the perceived invasive energy. It is important to develop skill in the verbal expression of emotions and seek to communicate with an effort to resolve emotional conflict in a timely manner. We must seek spiritual guidance with regard to the virtue and mandate of forgiveness. We will exercise humility and compassion in the expression of our volatile spiritual and emotional energies.

Suppression of negative energy does not guarantee that it is under control. In fact, it can cause an escalation of the negative energy and create a critical mass scenario building to an explosion or implosion, equal in intensity to the degree of suppression. These energies can be seen in colors and images floating around an individual in his or her aura. This can occur when one is obsessing or brooding over a particular thought, either consciously or unconsciously. The energy spins and gains momentum. Intention directs this concentrated emotional energy around him or herself and the object of the attachment. Anger and resentment can show up in the aura as a dirty, red hue. This phenomenon can also occur when someone is engaged in ego-based power struggles, attempting to influence, bend, or break the will of others. Our spiritual, mental, emotional, and physical condition can change the colors of the aura surrounding us. These colorful illuminations can be seen or sensed by those who possess that spiritual gift. We all can be trained to see auras, and it can happen spontaneously.

It is a spiritual imperative to devote our energy to the study and implementation of methods of insulating ourselves from the negative or invasive energy of others. It is a common occurrence that strong emotions bypass energetic boundaries and attach themselves as attacking thought-forms. Those who can see auras can identify the tainted aura as cloudy and polluted by the litter of floating Astral Plane garbage. The energy of fear and guilt rank high on the list of what makes a person an attractive target and increases the effectiveness of the negative, attacking energies.

A damaged and unclean aura is a precursor to physical illness, as negative energy penetrates both the aura and the physical body. The human energy field, or matrix, is the seed from which the physical form has grown. The formless Self existed *before* the physical form. That fact explains the phenomenon of phantom limbs of amputees who continue to feel sensation in a limb that is no longer a part of their physical body. Those who possess the ability to see and read the energy field can see these limbs. Traditional Chinese Medicine (TCM) approaches healing at the origin of the disease rather than merely relieving the symptoms of it. Practitioners have been known to treat organs that have been surgically removed because they recognize that the organ is still there on an energetic level and can still be the source of illness.

In this great study we have chosen, our primary concern with the aura is to keep it free of the attachment of unwelcome thought-forms, the absorption of negative energy, and the leaking of positive energy. The symptoms of maladies that result from these conditions can range from an inability to concentrate all the way to going barking, stark raving mad. Thought-forms could attach themselves, but they are perceivable intuitively. If you are aware of them, they can be banished. If you are not aware of them, they can influence your decisions, concentration, and behavior. These negative thought-forms, entities, and energies feed upon the energies of fear, guilt, and anger, using them in much the same manner our physical bodies use food for nourishment. A sound clearing or cleansing ritual is an effective way to release these energies before they turn us into a magnet for unpleasantness in many forms. They can manifest as interference in our relationships with other people. They can manifest as interference in our relationship with our Self.

Those who seek to drain us of vital life-force energy can deposit spiritual parasites into our aura. I am sure that everyone has experienced the company of a person who is invigorated by spending time with us yet leaves us feeling physically and emotionally drained of energy … lifeless and empty. This is often the work of people who are completely unconscious of what they are doing. It is not always possible to avoid the company of people with such vampire-like energy. It becomes important to replenish our energy resources after having been depleted of energy. We must seek restoration from positive sources rather than any random source available. Reaching out indiscriminately trying to fill that type of energetic emptiness can lead to bad habits and substance abuse and cause further damage by leaking vital energy through ruptures in the aura. Incorporate methods of Psychic

Self-Defense suggested in this book and others, into your daily spiritual practice for protection from those who are either consciously or unconsciously corrupting our positive energy.

The archetypal personality of an energy vampire is referenced in my book FACELESS: THE SACRED RELATIONSHIP as the archetype, The Undead. I share it later in this book for a reason. FACELESS reviews the major archetypes of humanity and how our lives are healed by understanding them and then transcending them, choosing to live as the True Self … *every* time.

The Undead is particularly relevant to the study of the aura and the energetic body in general. If people who fit this character archetype engage in a conscious or unconscious meditation or fixation upon us, in or out of our presence, they can have a powerful influence upon our aura. These character types make their appearance in the lives of anyone who has a trace of positive energy and Light for them to feed on. They can be dangerous and treacherous, yet many of them are passive-aggressive and can appear harmless. We must study this dangerous archetype because the knowledge of them helps us defend ourselves against them. The best defense is identifying them before they attach themselves too securely to our lives. It is worth the effort to shield ourselves from them and banish their toxic energy. As we examine the energy of The Undead, we must examine our lives for their shadows, as well as our own.

Care must be taken in cleansing the residual debris from encounters with them. After they leave us drained, a salt bath or smudging with sage, along with life-affirming prayer, helps restore balance. Some people replenish low positive energy levels by hugging trees, gardening, swimming, or being submerged in the ocean if that option is available. Taking a nature hike, exercising, and horseback riding, even listening to certain types of music can have a cleansing and balancing effect. Ancient practices of Tai Chi, Qi Gong, and breath control meditations are helpful in rebuilding our energy levels.

Another method of revitalizing positive energy and recharging the Chi or life-force of the person, the home, and the work environment, is the study and practice of the ancient mystical science, Feng Shui, the art of placement. It extends from the ideal placement of furniture in the home or office to intricacies of the architecture of the building. The Chi energy of the home or office is enhanced by elemental, symbolic, and mystical cures to any energetic obstructions and interferences. The goal is to provide a healthier flow of Chi energy in the home and work areas while keeping our positive vibrations and overall well-being at optimum levels. This can be assisted through the use of aromatherapy, flowing water, lighting, colors, crystals, mirrors, flowers, and plants, among other remedies.

Wearing certain properly charged crystals can divert, absorb or diffuse energetic attack. Never lose touch with the most basic truth …
The power of prayer exceeds all else. When we feel uneasy, as discordant energies try to penetrate our energy field, one way to immediately protect ourselves from them is to cup our hands close to our mouth, catching the breath of intense prayer. Perform an ablution (cleansing) with the breath of the prayer affirming the nonexistence of anything but The One God. All else must concede. Nothing exists but The God.

Healthy Aura

Polluted Aura

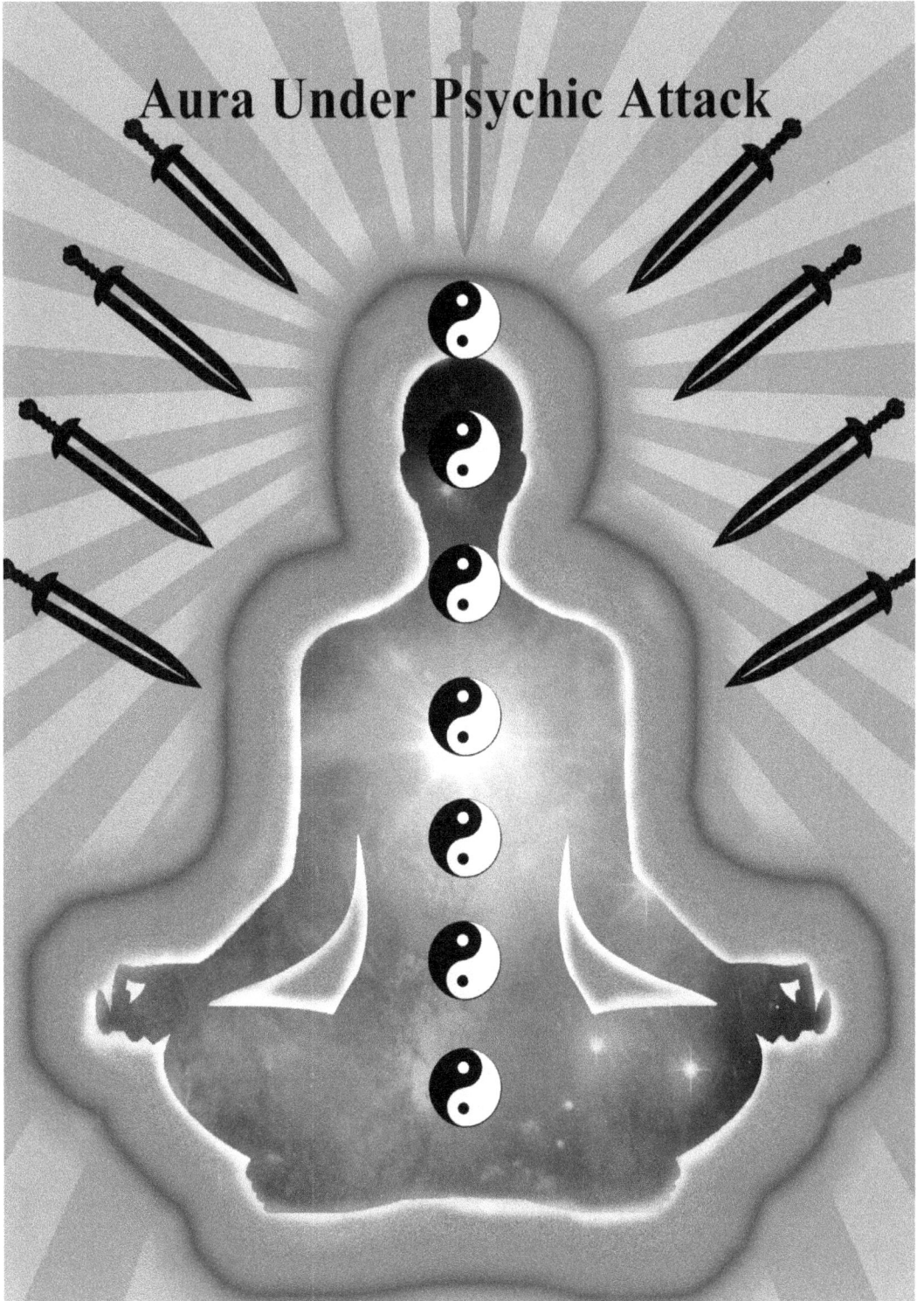

Aura Under Psychic Attack

Light Sphere of Protection

Refuge

The MERKABA is our Chariot, our Vehicle of Light

APPENDIX TWO

The I AM
and
Non-Physical Existence

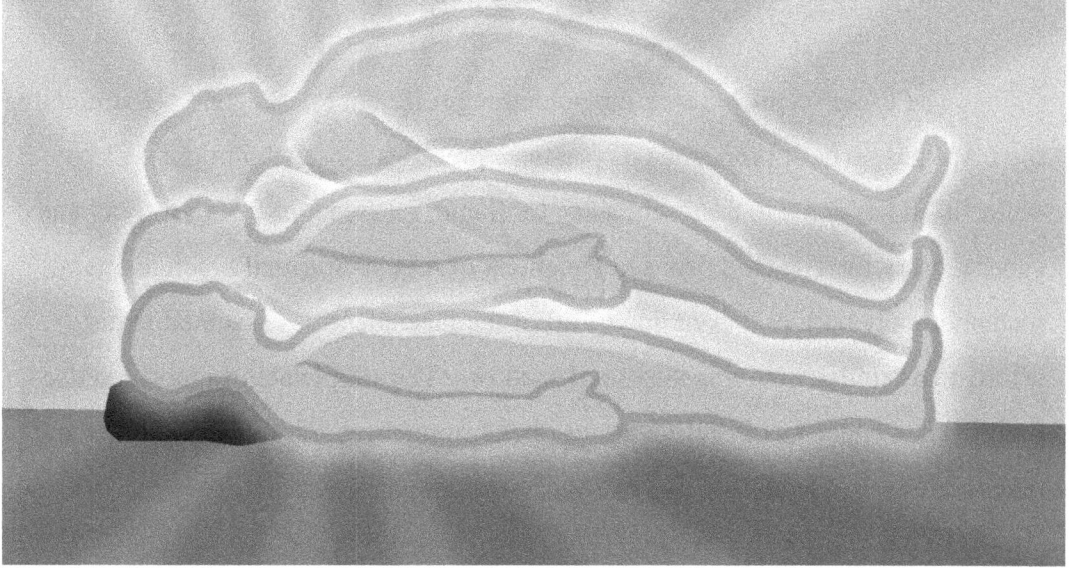

The Meaning of the I AM

The I AM defies definition. We are dreams born of the sacred realm of the I AM, delicately clothed in matter. Only the blind spots of our own vision would make us believe otherwise. There are many common names for the energy of this subtle and powerful field of conscious energy. There are many manifestations of the I AM. It is the object of our Self-Inquiry, that conversation between the ego self and the Higher Self. The energy of the formless, eternal, transcendent being of pure consciousness is the higher Self that we are. The I AM has deep significance in many mystical traditions and goes back into antiquity thousands of years, representing a pure, Timeless, formless Self that witnesses the physical expression of Itself as us. We manifest in form as the clay creatures we are, driven by That Sacred Breath, powered by That Light of Origin, sustained by the same. The heart must embrace this perspective to be released from the bondage of self-identification with transient forms covered with labels and become a truly Self-Realized being. This is not an event. It is a path through the mystical gates of Self-awareness into the eternal domain of the I AM that we are.

The I AM seems to represent something different to everyone. Historically, the I AM has no definition since its presence precedes those who might seek to define it. It has come to represent a cry for home, for freedom from captivity and slavery, a cry for The God. As a key element of regular spiritual practice, many metaphorically burn or "chant down" all of the false identities assumed in our efforts to assimilate into this theatre of shadows. The simple act of ignoring false precepts and concepts of Self facilitates the burning away of counterfeit inner and outer realities that lead us to our spiritual corruption and destruction.

The vibration associated with the I AM can be maintained through disciplined spiritual practice, faith, and reliance on the seen and unseen for guidance. It is represented in this text as a dimension of consciousness accessible to all of us, for WE are the temple that houses the energies of the Eternal I AM, the Creator of all we are and all we know. It is only a matter of exercising and flexing the muscle of remaining in the I AM, pulling ourselves back from every cage of bogus definition we assign to our true Self. Even though notions of Eternal existence are commonly associated with a past life, a future life, or an afterlife, it can be entered without experiencing what we call death. To view existence as the I AM or to remain within the myopic vision of a one-dimensional self-concept is a choice. When we have suffered sufficiently from this limiting and terrifying perspective, we expand our focus to explore the nature of who we really are.

Who we really are is not limited to that reflection we see in the mirror. Even the mirror has enough sense to know that our reflection is not who we are, so it does not cling to anything we show it. It accepts and releases. It does not look for yesterday or tomorrow. It does not record or identify with that image. It is our own minds that tend to do that. But we are not the mind. We are not the body. We are That … That which preceded the mirror and all false concepts of the "I." The real "I" is that formless, Timeless, storyless being expressing itself as the form it witnesses in the mirror. "That" is the I AM. From that perspective, we ask, "Who am I?" From this perspective, we affirm that there is no death, no time, no story, no form. Then, after the rush of freedom we feel from that realization, we must ask, "Can the seer be seen? Can the witness be witnessed? What witnesses the witness?" At this point, Self-Inquiry begins. The fire is kindled, and the process of awakening to freedom has begun. Time is escaped. The bullying of the flesh is checked and put in its place as a cooperative subordinate to the Higher Self and the Most High.

From a state of consciousness mimicking a coma, we awaken to the dawn of every new day, rejoicing that we are blessed with the opportunity to renew our commitment to the purification of our hearts. We commit ourselves to cleansing the controlling, manipulative energies of desire, attachment, and aversion. There are many roads to the spiritual mindset of the I AM. There are many names ascribed to the Ultimate Witness. Opinions, cultural conditioning, and choices only add to the diversity of the colorful mosaic of our collective journey. The fact that someone else is traveling a different path than our own does not mean that they are lost. There should be no unfavorable comparisons, nor should these paths and respective deities be set up in competition with one another for rightness. If we have images, qualities, or even the intonation of a name, that reference is still not of the Ultimate I AM, the Unknowable and most subtle in density.

In the Baha'i temple in Wilmette, Illinois, one of the most beautiful I have ever seen, there are nine doors, each representing a different faith. Each of the doors represents a path to the experience of what is characterized in this text as the realm of the I AM, the realm of the Sacred. There is nothing that must be done to earn one's place as the I AM, only to strive to gracefully master the balance of unconditional acceptance of the perfect balance inherent in creation. Everything has a balance that must be kept to progress from negative into positive existence. There is no such thing as all good or all bad. That type of terminology is subjective, relative, and can turn on a dime. Communicating this philosophy is the sacred symbol commonly referred to as the Yin Yang, illustrated in this text at the end of the following section.

The Yin Yang is a sacred symbol that represents all of life as a circle, rather than seeing it as linear. A horizontal timeline suggests that there is a distinct beginning and, at some point, an ending. A vertical timeline may suggest the same. But there is no end within the circle, especially this circle. It is divided into two parts, not in a straight line but in an "S" shape. One side is black, illustrating the void from which the Light emerged. The white side illustrates the Light. The two small circles of opposite polarity on each side mean that nothing is just one way. Duality is our nature and the nature of creation. It requires us to be more merciful and compassionate in our judgments of everything, including ourselves. Everything and everyone is a composite of two sides, each necessary to the other.

Whatever name you want to call it, and there are many, our souls are well familiar with the energies of I AM, naturally seeking its serenity for survival. The longing is the connection. If prayer were a government, its name would be I AM. Its flag and national anthem would be "the Eternal OM (AUM)." Its race is the *human race*. The President's name could only be expressed by silence. The I AM is our safe refuge from the evil influences and attacks of mischievous creation. The streets on this sacred journey are littered with broken hearts and vanity-based dreams. That Which Created us is sufficient to guide us through the challenging experience of material form and will be there waiting to welcome our grateful spirits home. Unconditional Love is the Soul of the I AM.

Protect the I AM

The Light essence of the I AM is sustained more easily when the body Temple has been cleansed of the toxic, negative energies that collect in the normal course of our daily lives. The nature of the I AM is a request for the respect and purification of our physical bodies as a vehicle of transportation assigned to our immortal soul by The Creator for this temporal experience. The essence of our immortal soul is one with That of The Creator I AM, the One that is the Witness of the seer of the experience of our form. Our physical form or container represents the temple of The Creator. Our indifference to the desecration of the temple of The God will cost us in all ways because we are not our own. In some ways, we take ourselves too seriously. In other ways, we do not take our real Self seriously enough. We are unique and peculiar in creation, and respect should be born of healthy spiritual self-esteem.

In the process of the cleansing of our temple, physical, mental, and emotional balance can be maintained by surrounding ourselves with the supportive energy of like-minded people. There is no need to become anti-social in relationship to people we determine to be unlike ourselves. Some fulfill this basic need in the environment of a church or spiritual organization of people. Others are fortunate enough to find it within their families and circle of interpersonal relationships. The Internet can even provide a safe and effective way of communicating with like-minded people. It is most important to know that the Temple of our Soul is within. Yet, a social journey can provide powerful revelations of The God and The God within ourselves and others, holding that delicate balance between Heaven and Earth, clay, and Ether. Even though the strongest spiritual connection is kept through focused prayer and meditation, the nature of the I AM can occur harmoniously as a chord rather than exclusively as one single note. Those who have chosen to submit to the Divine Will of The God can be a choir in celebration rather than a form of sacrificial, solitary confinement.

The body is as much affected by loneliness, grief, fear, anxiety, and stress as it is by toxins and chemicals that we ingest and are exposed to every day of our lives. Regular physical activity and a daily practice of some form of transcendental physical discipline, such as Yoga, Martial Arts, Chi Gong, or Tai Chi as a form of meditation, is highly recommended. This discipline will assist in the maintenance of a fit and worthy vessel to host the energy flow of the I AM. These activities can be done in a group to keep the spirit stimulated by new input and new acquaintances.

The path of the Natural Mystic on the road to the realization of the Self can lead us to peace with no borders. It can also lead us to bouts of loneliness and the isolation of spiritual solitude. A social circle that is either too small or too large is not healthy if it becomes a form of bondage. A well-chosen social environment, which respects the integrity of our immortal soul, is a taste of the "rapture" on this Physical Plane of existence. The journey takes on a synergy that multiplies and intensifies our individual energies by our association with the energy of an entire group with the same focus and tuned in on the same frequency. I quote a well-known Spanish saying, "Mejor solita que mal acompañada" … "Better alone than in bad company." Group Karma can be experienced because of the company we keep or groups we energetically align ourselves with.

The I AM can be associated with many of our considerations of Heaven and the afterlife. Heaven, like hell, can exist as a dimension or frequency. As with the abyss, once we have gazed into the Realm of the I AM, it has also gazed into us. We have to keep reminding ourselves that as the forces of good are realized in the I AM, so are the forces of evil well anchored in their I AM. Both frequencies can be tapped into at will or may choose to tap into us if we are open and available. For that reason, becoming well-versed in Psychic Self-Defense is very important as we pray for the virtue of spiritual discernment to continually grace our lives. There is no reason to live life fearfully. Fear is nourishment for negative energies and entities. They feed on it. That Which created us is sufficient to protect us from anything outside of Divine Will. Nothing outside of Divine Will exists. Consequently, protection is a lifestyle, not an occasional ritual. Anchored in the energy of our Higher Self, nothing can do us harm. The I AM is Pure Awareness and cannot be harmed.

I AM Consciousness Rising

The human condition requires that we observe the first Law of Nature, Self-preservation. Survival of the fittest has always extended beyond physical boundaries into the invisible realms. Knowledge is power. The belief that what you don't know can't hurt you can invite disaster as you've never imagined. You do not need to be involved in any type of mystical study or practice to require the knowledge of Psychic Self-Defense. We are energy, and there are energies all around us all of the time that can, and will, affect our lives on many levels. These energies rise from many physical and non-physical sources. They can rise to personally target us, or it can be a matter of being in the wrong place at the wrong time. We will examine many forms of attack that I am familiar with. They are not necessarily from a physical source. Many are fire elementals from the jinn kingdom, angels, discarnate beings, and their countless manifestations.

In this text, we approach the subject of spiritual warfare from apparently physical sources, asking, "Who is being attacked?" The answer is … A person who is presumed to lack the knowledge of who they are. Who defends? A person who does not know who they are. Who is the attacker? A person who does not know who they are. All of those questions and answers lead to the revelation that we have nothing to fear. If we know who we really are, and the power associated with living as our Higher Self, then we know we have nothing to fear. From that perspective, we accept that we are made of the same Eternal Essence of That Which created us. We are That. What should we fear? "Nothing!" … answers the I AM Consciousness Rising. It does not matter how many candles you have to light. It does not matter how many mantras you know to chant. It does not matter how much sage you burn. Nothing will save you more than knowing who you really are.

In Psychic Development classes I have taught, I spend a lot of time and energy dispelling the fears associated with mystical studies. Knowledge is the best cure for fear. This particular type of fear can be the result of negative programming and cultural propaganda. One factor in the propagation of such fear is the judgment and oppression imposed upon seekers, by some who claim to represent the *only* "Truth" of "God." Some organized religions, and spiritual paths tend to regard certain types of spiritual independence as threatening, dangerous, and even evil.

I could drop a defensive posture on the issue and say not all warnings about the dangers of certain prepackaged mystical practices are completely unfounded. I could take the offensive and condemn them according to their own Law, which leaves all Judgment to The God, not to someone who decides to play God. However, I now see both sides. I know that there are undeniable dangers, particularly to impressionable, naïve, or spiritually compromised people. I now know there are undeniable dangers to spiritually sound, strong, and stable people as well.

Certain mystical paths and studies can cause us to become magnets for phenomena that can be disturbing, at least. The more common victims of potentially dangerous spirituality tend to be those who profile themselves as outcasts and vulnerable loners estranged from family, friends, and social contacts that could provide balanced feedback. These people are often drawn to philosophies and groups offering the well-baited hook of "home" and "family." A diverse support system can provide a caring voice of reason that serves as a reality check from many perspectives.

Many of us have found out the hard way, through tragedy or trauma, that there are things in this life beyond our control or explanation. Feelings of helplessness can fully engage a desperate pursuit for the power to survive it. It can then take on the spirit of a power monger attracted to radical mystical paths to manipulate the events and circumstances of life. Some just want attention and embrace controversy as a means to achieve that end. Whatever it takes to drive us to these studies, know that approaching it with an ego-based agenda will not yield good results.

A major event may prompt a quest to control the things we can, no matter how inconsequential, often manifesting as OCD (Obsessive Compulsive Disorder) behaviors. Others just want what appears to be "something for nothing" or a quick fix instead of putting in the spiritual work required for healing. Real change requires adopting a sustainable, holistic lifestyle that supports a more evolved consciousness. This is not for cursory study or entertainment. I can relate to many of these psychological and character profiles and confess that control issues, namely the desire to control my own life, made me embrace and travel spiritual paths of study and practice that could have been dangerous to me. By Divine Grace, my soul's path ultimately led me full circle, back to my mother's favorite prayer as a child, the 23rd Psalm, The Bible (KJV), representing a cornerstone of faith and spiritual practice.

> *Though I walk through the valley*
> *of the shadow of death,*
> *I will fear no evil, for thou art with me*

It is no wonder that the study of the mysteries has come under intense scrutiny and criticism by spiritual conservatives. But we are the honest ones. We are the sovereign ones. Many practices may be "judged" by some to be unacceptable, yet they are powerful and spiritually correct. With *all* paths, there are positives and negatives, and even that determination is a judgment to some degree. On this sacred journey, the path is the destination. Most important in essence, is that the path is focused on the pursuit of a beautiful, loving relationship with Universal Law and That Which Created all. Any path can lead to detours and confusing crossroads. I don't believe that in all cases throwing the "baby out with the bathwater" is required. They all may have their merits. To choose to travel NO path defies the Laws of a Universe that is in perpetual motion, evolving, expressing, and unfolding in its revelation of who we essentially are.

Whether we are studying mysticism or just trying to carve out some sacred space in a whirlwind life, it is important to know how to protect ourselves, not so much in a defensive way, but more so in a preventative way. One of the most important recommendations is to exercise sound discretion and critical judgment in our choices of associates and friends. Friends are like clothes; they say a lot about us. Everyone has heard the horror stories of cultish organizations and irresponsible rogue spiritual groups. We must make sure we know, as best we can, the spiritual orientation of those from whom we seek spiritual classes, friendships, or advice.

Imagine what life could be like vibrating at a frequency where there was no way to hide wickedness behind cloaks of apparent good intention, where all is seen, all is known, and all is Divine Love. Imagine a world with no ambition to strive every day to subject beings to needless suffering.

We are people of many dimensions. On one side, our visions. On the other, their visible manifestation. We are free. We walk our path in knowledge, not fear, of ourselves or anyone else. We walk the path of the Natural Mystic with those who have traveled before us. We merge as energies with those receiving guidance through the relationship we maintain with The Creator. In every dimension of our Ultimate Reality, we are loved and protected by The Most High. Our greatest danger is our own ignorance.

Many of the mystical experiences people report make the concept of Spiritual Self-Defense as important as breath. Most of us have, at some point in our lives, had a spiritual experience; some good, some ecstatic, some scary, some threatening, some even dangerous. After such experiences, one cannot expect to ever be the same again. It can represent the first stirrings of the evolution of spirit, a quickening, a confirmation of our connection to the world of non-physical existence.

There are safety issues on this unpredictable spiritual path when mingling with energies, entities, and unseen forces. We address these issues as they arise with the wisdom of the ancients, as our problems represent a modern spin on old themes. There is nothing new under the Sun. Understanding this works to our advantage in matters of Psychic Self-Defense. It allows us to access the wisdom of the ages and appropriately apply this knowledge and improve the quality of our lives.

The first step toward spiritual protection is our wise and discerning choices regarding the company we keep and what we choose to share with other people. Being friendly with a person does not necessarily mean that person is our friend. Uncensored disclosure of personal mystical experiences can open the doors to ridicule or judgment and expose us to danger. That is why it is so important to pay attention to the company we are in before beginning a spiritual or any other type of self-expose. I believe these things to be private and have no place in common, casual conversation. It is unwise to feel too free to engage in random small talk about our spiritual experiences among people who have no foundation for understanding such issues. We must first look at the spiritual and cultural mindset of the people around us and ask ourselves if these are people we really want to disrobe our souls in the presence of. If not, we should respect boundaries regarding the depth and extent of our disclosures, depending on who we are talking to.

We must accept the fact that it is "normal" to have what some see as paranormal experiences. It is far more common than we may think. Some try to explain away mystical phenomena as evil or crazy. It is to our advantage to pursue and embrace an understanding of the spirit realm and its relationship to the rich world of mystical practices and study. It will make our lives make more sense as we expand our understanding of the many dimensions of our temporal life. We are complex mystical beings, challenged to discover that within the context of physical experience.

Life is a gift to be examined, cultivated, and preserved. The spirit of ourselves is who we really are, apart from our clever packaging. Many of us get emotionally attached to the packaging. Many never rise above a dirt level consciousness that anchors our spirit to the perishable, then breaks our spirit because it cannot conform to the concrete boundaries we set in place. We cannot endure our physical reality if we refuse to broaden our vision of Self to include the imperishable, immortal duality of our nature.

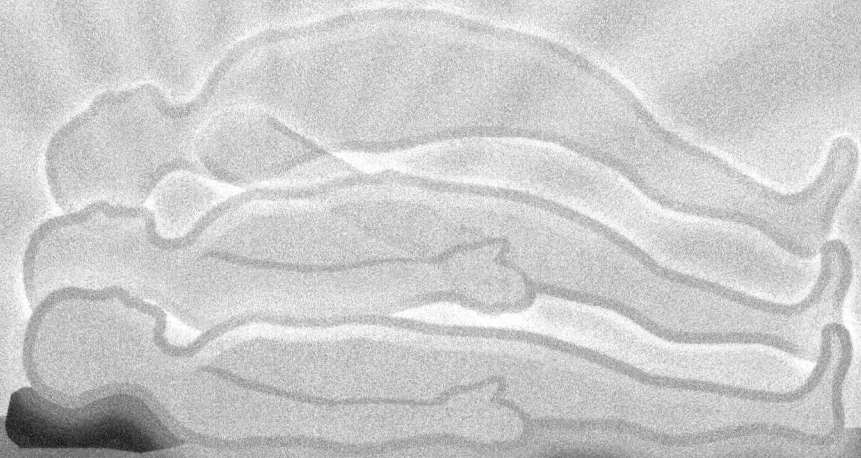

The 'self'
that fears
for its safety
is not real

WHO ARE YOU?
The one that the physical eye cannot see …
the witness, not the one that the witness observes.

The Ego Under Attack

That ego "I" image of us is so full of vanity-based energy, spinning in such powerfully distracting circles of illusion that it often cannot defend itself from the attacks of psychic bullies. That is the first thing any bully attacks, the ego of the intended victim. This malevolent spirit stalks, looking for weaknesses, tentatively sensing someplace for the attack to land, some open door of the psyche through which to direct the negative energy. As it is on the playgrounds of the schoolyards of the world, so it is, in the cosmos, on the physical and ethereal planes. That type of energy predates our collective history on this planet. However, if there is no fertile soil to root in, no hump to ride, there is nowhere for that plane to land. It has to keep on flying, generally on the flight plan of a boomerang. Journaling will show you how the surrendering of the false "I," ego-based identities, naturally coincides with the dismantling of psychic attacks and attackers.

If we feel some aspect of our life is under attack, we must ask the "I," Self, "WHO is the target of this attack?" Who is the "I" that experiences the phenomena associated with this attack? Is it the "I," me, my, mine, one-dimensional self-concept? Or is it the formless, nameless, identity-less "I" of the Eternal I AM that expresses itself as us … the shadowy forms we take far too seriously and at the same time, not seriously enough. Who is that "I" that is under attack?

The stereotypical attacker is generally targeting the "I" we see in the mirror. What defends the "I" is the "I" that can only be seen with the eye of the soul, The I AM. It is secure in its defense because the Ultimate "I" witnesses all and can and will intervene in our affairs. The psychology of the attacker is petty and shallow in its mental perceptions and projections. It is covetous. It is jealous. It is mean. It is cruel. It has a hunger that can only be satiated by the suffering of others. It preys upon the vulnerable at their weakest point and strikes below the belt to the heart of ego self identity. It literally chants down its victim until those voices become a shared mantra with the victim until the victim joins the attacker in the dismantling of his or her self-esteem. Often the target becomes depressed and takes on self-destructive behaviors, all symptoms rather than the cause. Rarely is the attack without motive, as senseless as it may be. More often than not, the attack is rooted in some form of competitive jealousy or some level of malignant envy. The attacker perceives the intended victim as having something that they feel was denied to them and that they are worthier of it. They may become overwhelmed by uncontrollable, self-serving compulsions that they feel are best satisfied by violating others, passively, aggressively, or both. Generally, these far-reaching tentacles extend out of empty desire, fueled by narcissistic ego self identity.

The attacker who wages war against the innocent does not approach from a position of strength, security, or confidence. They are blind to the knowledge of their own Higher Self and choose to operate from the shadow realm due to thought-forms of "not enough." Happy, secure people don't act that way. This sort of an attack can even be unintentional, a wicked thought-form riding on the wind of a full Moon, damaged pride, and low self-esteem.

Attackers count on a runway into our consciousness, welcoming any and everything that tries to land there. If we do not provide a landing strip, if we do not allow our own egos to leave our psychic doors open, many attacking energies will escape our awareness. To ignore the ocean, and respond to every wave of emotion and judgment, is to become the attacker of our own peace of mind and well-being. As an attacker of self, we are then robbed of our primary advantage as a spiritual warrior, our innocence.

An attack of any sort is a gamble riskier than feeling drunk and lucky in a Vegas casino on payday. When someone initiates an attack, they have no way of knowing what they are up against. After scrutinizing a person believed to be known, even intimately, by the attacker, there is still no possible way to truly predict how the target will respond to being attacked. It is not possible to know what type of spiritual security system the intended victim has in place around them. There is as much a credible danger to the attacker as there is for the intended victim.

Upon determining that it is the ego self "I" that is under attack, it is important to process raw emotions of anger and counter aggression, seeking a refined form of energetic expression. For example, imagine we find ourselves in a situation where someone is sending desperate, attacking energy, targeting us based on a perception that it is we who are triggering those feelings within him or her. That doubles their anger. First, they are disturbed by what they know or see that sparks their envy, jealousy, or hatred. Then enters the distorted perception that it is the fault of the perceived trigger, and that person is to blame for their suffering. There is never an acknowledgment of personal responsibility.

"Hater" is a word that started as slang but has found its way into mainstream vernacular. Everyone knows what a "hater" is, and everyone has a few, no matter what we do. All we can do about it is not to become one. All we can do about it is to keep our energy grounded in spiritual integrity and gratitude for the blessings we have and our faith in The God. An army of forces, energies, and entities are already set in place, sufficient to guide and protect. We are not required or advised to petition them directly. All we are required to do is surrender to Divine Will and respect the ongoing process of that sacred surrender.

The study, practice, and discipline of meditation will allow us to see life from a witness or observer's perspective, even a Timeless perspective, from which we are better able to understand time and the relationship between it and the events of our lives. We also view our journey from a time circle rather than a "timeline."

We are in uncharted territory. Meditation is a valuable tool for connecting the dots of the messages, signs, and visions we receive. The words "random" and "coincidence" have no place in our consciousness.

APPENDIX THREE

Planes of Existence

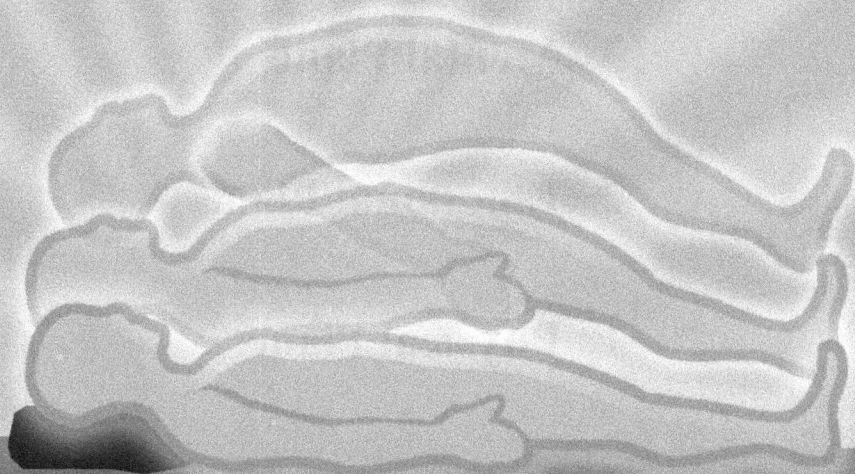

Planes of Existence

0. Unknowable

7. Realm of Divinity

6. Archetypal Realm

5. Etheric Realm

4. Astral Plane

3. Mental Plane

2. Emotional Plane

1. Physical Plane

I share excerpts of the section on Planes of Existence from my book, FEARLESS: PSYCHIC SELF-DEFENSE, Transcend the Fear of Spiritual Warfare, for their relevance to an examination of our fear-based relationship with multi-dimensional realities and related mystical experiences.

Planes of Existence

In both an individual and collective context, we are each a composite of all of the Planes of Existence. To view them separately does not imply specific or actual locations in our being or psyche. All of the Planes and their inhabitants coexist in an interdependent, interactive, symbiotic relationship. References to "Planes" and "Realms" are used interchangeably and conceptually. The Planes are distinguished primarily based on density, from the subtlest state to gross matter. These Planes, Dimensions, Worlds, and Realms of inter-penetrable consciousness, ranging from ethereal and invisible to physical and perceptible expression, are considered abstract and theoretical, based on religious, philosophical, and esoteric beliefs. This elaborate manifestation is believed to emanate from One Timeless, Unknowable Source that is beyond comprehension. One Supreme Being sent out this energetic force of unmanifested creation from the Realm of the Unknowable through sound vibration … the Cause that resulted in the Effect of all that we know as reality. Many meditation practices are based on the chanting of mantras, intonations, and repetition of sacred words associated with that Creative Force.

0 – The Unknowable

There are no words in this realm. This realm precedes thought and form. I have heard it referred to as the realm of "Self-Illuminating Triple Darkness," the Unknowable Realm of Unlimited Potential. I have heard it called "Dark Matter," not to be confused with anti-matter or black holes, "Invisible Matter," "Dark Energy," "Negative Existence," or "Zero Point Reality." There is more Dark Matter than there is matter, and it precedes the existence of all thoughts, words, concepts, or precepts. Focusing on this subject is futile because the scientists admit to knowing more about what it is not than what it is. It is generally understood to be:

- The Unmanifest;

- Self-Illuminating Triple Darkness;

- Beyond the concept of Negative Existence;

- Negative Existence is beyond definition;

- When it is distinctly defined, it ceases to be Negative Existence;

- The Negative Existence that does not pass into a static condition;

- Beyond the concept of limitless expansion;

- Beyond the limitations of the rational mind;

- Beyond the limitations of the intuitional mind;

- Beyond the limitations of concepts, constructs, time, body, and mind;

- Beyond the concept of transcendence;

- The experience of the Realm of the Unknowable as the release of all attachments to egoic desires;

- The experience of the Realm of the Unknowable releases one from all attachments to body-mind, time-space identification;

- Independent of human senses;

- Independent of human perception;

- Nameless and formless reality;

- Beyond existence;

- Beyond duality;

- Unobservable;

- Unimaginable;

- Omnipotent.

7 – The Realm of Divinity

A "Divine Realm" is not really suitable as an "address" for The God. Due to the Omnipotent nature of That Which cannot even be named … an "address" would, in a sense, express an expectation of confining The God to a place or a realm, which denies the very nature of The God. Attributes of the Realm of Divinity include:

- An Energy, a Frequency, The Realm of the Limitless One;

- The Realm of the Holy Spirit;

- The Angelic Realm;

- The Awaliya (Friends of The God);

- Angels that are known as the Messengers, Apostles, or pure beings of Light that were created to establish the many aspects of God;

- The Ascended Masters and spirit beings among us in diverse manifestations who assist others in the experience of enlightenment and ascension;

- The Realm of Indivisible Oneness;

- The Realm that demonic forces and entities cannot access;

- It is sanctified beyond human comprehension;

- It is beyond our scope of finite, intellectual knowledge of Creator/creation;

- The embrace of the understanding of Divinity as infinite;

- The embrace of the reality and nature of our intimate relationship with Divinity as infinite.

6 – Archetypal Realm

The Archetypal Realm is the prototype existence that manifests in the Physical Realm. It is the parallel world that generates the masks of identity that we wear, and believe them to be who we really are. In the context of our True Self, the Timeless, unborn, undying, Eternal beings that we are, we can live a shadow existence in a waking dream world. This occurs when we accept archetypal influences blindly, spinning in and out of delusional, binding, attachment and aversion scenarios. Our ancestors are among those who inhabit the Archetypal Realm. Cultural systems, customs, social structures, spiritual science, and all manner of archetypal wisdom of the ages are alive and well in that boldly interactive realm. That is a gift as long as we acknowledge the memetic nature of archetypes. They change from age to age, from generation to generation. They are supposed to, and we are supposed to embrace Annica, the Law of Impermanence. Instead, we often cling to our perceptions of static realities and dualities, fleeing from the truth that *nothing* is fixed or permanent. Everyone and everything we know is changeful and impermanent.

Attributes of the Archetypal Realm include, but are not limited to:

- *Archetype* is defined as the original model or prototype from which the attributes of people and the cultural realities of our world are copied, patterned, or emulated;
- Patterns of archetypal realities that manifest as symbols and imprints that permeate our psyches to the extent of having a hypnotic effect on our collective persona, behavior, and environment;

- The energies and entities of the Archetypal Realm can use subliminal influences to trigger aspects of collective memory to revive, destroy, or shift the reality, even the memory of our reasons for being, and the truth behind the illusory masks we accept as identity;

- There are forces in the domain of the archetypes that have the full potential to affect and create interpretations of observed phenomena through influences of nonphysical beings, thought-forms and energies, ancestors, deities, concepts, ideas, and alter realities;

- Archetypes can often convey messages through symbolic frequencies, subtle language, and thought-forms, that verbal and written information cannot;

- We can become aware of the subtle influences of individual and universal archetypes in meditation, dreamtime, remote viewing, or other out-of-body experiences. They also affect creative art forms, music, fashion, advertising, and design.

5 – Etheric Realm

The concept of Ether, the Fifth Element, refers to the subtler realms of consciousness that interpenetrate the physical realm as an animating force. The beings of various realms are ethereal in quality. The etheric body is the energetic or subtle body. Within this parallel realm to our own is the matrix from which our world, and many we are unaware of, have risen into conscious reality. Evanescent Ether is an immaterial, intangible substance, yet it is very real. Attributes of the Etheric Realm include:

- Everything that exists on the Physical Plane has a subtle etheric form and counterpart;

- The human Etheric Realm of consciousness is an interconnecting and intercommunicating network of energy from which our body matrix or blueprint is created;

- The Etheric Realm is the bridge between the Physical and Astral Planes. Nonphysical beings and entities are inhabitants of the subtler planes, and yet they exist within realities of the physical world. An etheric body double can pass through walls and other apparently solid objects and still be connected to its physical counterpart, as well as being able to visit places and interact in the physical world;

- Telepathy, remote viewing, and other psychic abilities are elements of the ethereal plane of consciousness;

- The energies of fear … the fear of living, as well as the fear of dying, can attract ethereal and astral entities that are able to invade and poison our reality on all levels of our being;

- The etheric and astral bodies are not two entirely separate bodies. They each have different characteristics and features of mutual importance, relative to their essential purpose;

- Our mastery of the levels of the subtle planes can influence the strength of our electromagnetic energy field and how we are able to effectively connect with the Realm of Divinity.

4 – The Astral Realm

The Astral Realm is the realm of Dreamtime, where we go when we sleep. Things have no specific structure and more fluidity, meaning nothing is solid, even if it seems to be momentary. Everything changes as frequently as our thoughts, and in the Astral Realm, they are made manifest. It has parallel aspects to this world but is more bright, colorful, and responsive to our emotions. Qualities of the Astral Realm include:

- The Astral Realm is a non-physical realm of existence parallel to our own;

- It is beyond space-time;

- It is the home of the astral/etheric body double and its perceived simultaneous reality;

- The Astral Realm or spirit world is inhabited by non-physical beings and entities. They can be perceived as good or evil and exist as realities of diverse manifestations;

- We perceive the spirit of our True Self in the context of an inner life. The Astral Plane is an external environment for non-physical realities, beings, and entities;

- The Astral Realm is a platform of expression for thought-forms, dream symbols, and Universal Archetypes;

- Non-physical aspects of beings can get trapped in the Astral Realm. These astral entities and energies can create possession scenarios and psychic interference drama. Although we may be unaware of their presence, our lives can be altered in extreme ways. We may find our energy depleted and feel drained of Life Force. Our sleep patterns may be interrupted or disturbed. Our health may become compromised as we develop chronic illnesses such as recurrent headaches and unexplained body aches and pains;

- The Astral Realm is the domain of dreams, altered states of consciousness, Sleep Paralysis events, astral projection, remote viewing, portal jumping, spirit journeying, Out of Body experiences, and Near-Death experiences;

- Accounts of 'Heaven,' 'hell,' 'abyss,' and 'purgatory' experiences in consciousness are an element of Astral Plane reality;

- The subtle/dream/astral body's ascent from the physical body into astral reality has been described as an ecstatic, blissful Out of Body experience. It is known to have sparked mystical, even prophetic revelations from the higher realms;

- The astral body is seen by some as a visible aura of swirling colors;

- Memories, thought-forms, spiritual beings, apparitions, and visionary landscapes may be witnessed as astral phenomena.

3 – Mental Realm

The Mental Realm is the Plane of Thought, as well as the moments of the "Great Silence" in between them. From the ocean of primordial stillness, the Macrocosm of Divine Mind radiates its intense Light into the realms of names and forms … of energies and entities … of vibration and frequency. The mental realm exists outside of Cosmic Law and beyond Time. Qualities of the Mental Realm include:

- The mental realm relates to the domain of the individual as well as the cosmos;

- It is the realm associated with knowledge, intellect, reasoning, understanding, and perceptions, even referring to concepts of intuition;

- The mental plane, which intermediates between all of the realms, is symbolic of the marriage of Heaven and Earth, spirit and matter;

- The mental plane is associated with a type of "seeing" (mind's eye, psychic eye, Third Eye, evil eye) … all generated from the realm of thought;

- It is an aspect of the realm of the Timeless Now for having the capacity to escape Time;

- It is the plane of consciousness, awareness, and the unmanifested energy of thought;

- It is the plane of Manifestation through the projection of thought-forms;

- Thoughts are things. From a "thought form" realities are created;

- Just like magick, as one thinks ... so it is! (by permission of Divine Will);

- Sharing in characteristics of the Archetypal Plane, it is the world of original prototypes of the physical world;

- Thoughts are not just the consequences of brain functioning;

- Thoughts can operate on their own sovereign agenda, independent of physical reality;

- Thoughts have been proven scientifically to affect physical reality.

2 – Emotional Realm

The Emotional Realm is a common source in the generation of psychic phenomena directly connected to the Mental Realm. The arena of unguarded, reckless, unbridled emotion is the breeding ground of manifestation of powerful thought-forms, both positive and negative. Emotion is linked to thought; Thought is linked to desire; Desire is linked to manifestation; Manifestation is linked to attachment; Attachment is linked to suffering. Qualities of the Emotional Realm include:

- The heart as the "bridge" between the upper and lower realms of consciousness;

- The heart is the home, the throne of Divinity;

- It is the Realm of Union between the Divine and human;

- It is the emotional connection between humanity and The God;

- It is the realm of thought-forms being generated through the mystical power of emotion that causes the spark that triggers manifestation;

- The primary target of a psychic attack is the heart;

- The primary emotional triggers of spiritual attack are the emotions of anger, hatred, envy, jealousy, desire, and attachment;

- It can be the realm of magnification into states of overwhelm due to extreme emotional states of depression, fear, grief, rage, anxiety, and jealousy;

- It is the realm of connection of beings through relationships.

1 – Physical Realm

All realms are here, now, and within. The Physical Realm is the visible reality of Space and Time, energy and matter, Cause and Effect, the densest of a series of planes of existence. It does not exist apart from the other subtler realms, worlds, or dimensions, which interpenetrate themselves and physical reality from the center, as they were sent out as sound vibration into various densities of manifestation. The Absolute is The Ultimate Reality, whose center is everywhere and whose circumference is nowhere … The Infinite. Qualities of the Physical Realm include:

- The Physical Plane is the realm of dense matter;

- It is the vehicle of consciousness and non-physical awareness;

- It is the personal manifestation of temporal, perishable form, identified as the human body and physical existence;

- It has the physical means to provide for and sustain physical beings;

- It is bound by the Three Marks of Existence; Anicca – The Law of Impermanence, Dukka – The Law of Suffering, and Annatta – The Law of Non-Self;

- It is subject to Space-Time, Cause-Effect, and Life-Death realities;

- It is inextricably connected to and affected by 'Something' beyond the Physical Realm, that created it and serves to sustain it;

- It is sacred, in the context that it is the vehicle which contains our Essence, and demonstrates the full potential for our transcendence;

- It is the bridge between the inner and transcendent planes of consciousness and being.

The enemy of our fear is our knowledge. If we understand that our formless Self is not threatened by Anicca, the Law of Impermanence, or death, our fears will dissolve, and a unique type of freedom will take their place. The practice of Mystical Meditation can induce journeying through realms of consciousness we commonly associate with the death process.

The death experience involves the many planes of existence. Meditation and prayer can take us on an excursion through the Astral Planes, opening gateways to dimensions beyond imagination, promoting healing on many levels. If we open our minds to the meaning of "as above, so below," we will discover the key to understanding what the practice of meditation really involves. The condensation of thought-forms seeking manifestation can cause precipitation of the best and the worst of energies upon our lives.

We are given meditation and prayer work as tools to catalyze our energy to transcend our own self-made temporal reality and venture beyond Space-Time, where the past, present, and future exist as one. We are able to access puzzle pieces of past events and things to come, to construct a portrait of life on any plane of existence. We are able to see ourselves as who we *really* are ... Timeless, Eternal beings. A nonlinear portrait extends beyond present realities and reveals the true significance of time and its relationship with the events of our lives. This vision may reach years into the future to provide glimpses of tomorrow based on the effects of the choices we are making in the present, or have made in the past.

Of all the fears of matters regarding both sides of the veil between worlds, it is the contemplation of the inevitability of death that challenges our courage the most. One of the most primal of all fears is our fear of not existing anymore, of just disappearing. Knowing that there are many planes and forms of existence THAT can serve to assure us of the fact that *we do not die.* It will give us comfort to contemplate and consider what death really is.

One simple way to demonstrate the way a relationship between planes operates is to make two fists, placing the left *above* and the right *below.* The left fist represents the bird's eye view of our world from the Astral Plane. Its position offers the advantage of viewing all events in what we distinguish as the past, present, and future. The right fist represents our world of matter. It moves in a continuous circular motion. We are moving with the right fist, trapped in the life-death, Space-Time continuum. We perceive the experience of a distinct past and future without the conscious ability to see an outcome until it has occurred within our linear framework of present time.

Planes of existence are not to be viewed as locations above, below, or beside one another. The Astral Plane and its inhabitants exist just beyond our fixed perceptions and parallel to the Earth plane, as demonstrated by the left fist. This perspective offers an objective overview of life, death, and time. The past, present, and future are clearly seen as fluid or occurring *simultaneously.* The perception of life and death is seen as a mere transition from one plane to the next, or death to one plane and birth into another, upon the release of the physical vessel.

There is in-depth literature readily available, offering a journey into the world of spirit. The inhabitants of the Astral Plane are much like those of the Earth plane. Some are good, and some are not. The subtle planes have been described as being similar in appearance and form to our denser plane of matter, but multidimensional and holographic in imagery, defying our marginal linear vision. In the Astral Dimension, sound vibrates at frequencies that sometimes create the hollow toned sound we may associate with echoes and whispers. Some colors appear as they would on the Earth Plane; other colors may appear exceptionally vivid and vibrant. The senses are enhanced by the depth and intensity of our experience of the Astral Planes, where our rules of weight, density, and limitations of the physical form do not apply. The fears of life and death no longer seize and control our positive energy. We are no longer slaves to our concepts of Time and Space. We have the power and freedom to manifest our conscious thoughts, creating the reality we choose to experience.

We have the power to free ourselves from the bondage of fear and attachment to the perishable. We have the wisdom to embrace Timeless reality. We cannot prove the existence of an afterlife or lateral existence, though many report having had such experiences. There is evidence sufficient to presume that we do not die. At the intersection of science and mysticism, we affirm, *we do not die*.

Manifestation: As Above, So Below

After meditating on the basic but profound reality of "as above, so below," we must acknowledge the fact that some energies, both above and below, are less than wonderful. There are people in this world that we would rather not communicate with, people we would not invite into our home, and people we would not want to meet by chance on a lonely street at night, unarmed. The same is true of the spirit world. I do not intend to evoke fear, but common sense is required when dealing with certain Astral Plane entities and energies. Not having a body is no indicator that an entity will be any more intelligent or good-natured than they were while traveling in one. There is a shadow side to the astral realm and its inhabitants, as there is in all of creation. For this reason, people are generally cautioned against using mysticism for entertainment purposes. It is foolish and dangerous to play with ancient spiritual science as though it were a game, and I don't recommend this type of study to those who seek only a cursory knowledge of what should constitute a lifetime of spiritual study and practice.

There are age-old techniques used to cleanse and banish undesirable, trespassing presences. Some techniques are as simple and as common as a prayer. It is not wise to enter a deep meditation without ritually dismissing unwelcome energies that may be present. Such practices present in some common traditions as simply as blessing the food before eating a meal.

Psychic doors must be locked to uninvited party-crashers by invoking the White Light of The God. We surrender our ego-based will to the Compelling Will of The Divine One with faith that the protection of The Creator envelops and secures our souls. Study the basic suggestions and precautions shared in this manual. It is beneficial to document experiences, insights, and visions on this beautiful adventure. It will contribute to spiritual safety and show respect for a sound check and balance system of accountability. We are seeking wisdom and knowledge of the highest vibration, not an unpleasant experience.

Some wonder, "Why, then, don't we just go directly to The God and leave the use of mystical studies and practices out of it?" My response is, "How can you say with authority, that it is not the wisdom of The God that we are tapping into directly through the use of Mystical Meditation? Some ask, "Do you believe that spiritual intercession can occur and intervene in our affairs?" I can answer on faith and experience that the Spirit of all Spirits, the Holy Spirit, is the bond that reinforces our relationship with The Divine One and Divine Guidance. I believe that angels watch over us continually and communicate with us in a multitude of ways. They are called by many names, awliya, loa, orisha, spirit guides, guardians, and ancestors. They can take whatever form they need to get our attention, even in shocking or dramatic manners and ways. It is absolute hypocrisy to profess a belief in angelic, seen, and unseen presences, and yet believe that it is evil or witchy to acknowledge the role these undeniable non-physical phenomena play in our lives. It is commanded that we seek refuge *only* in The One God. We can trust in the Wisdom of The Divine One with regard to who, from this army of guides and protectors, is best suited to be permitted to intervene in our lives. An element of Mystical Meditation is seeking the presence of and communion with The Absolute, The Ultimate, The Divine, The One Creator.

The highest and purest purpose of practicing Mystical Meditation is for our personal spiritual growth and development. A meditation may induce revelations, visions, and can even give us a *forecast* of possible future scenarios, since its perspective is beyond time, space, or form, as we know it. Our Free Will may be guided by the wisdom of either embracing a possible fate or avoiding it in the most beneficial way for all concerned. Meditation is a powerful conduit for the transmission of messages of the highest intentions. Any abuse of it speaks only of the intentions of the abuser, not of the practice. Mystical Meditation is a form of becoming the prayer we pray and should be approached with that same level of respect for the sacred.

Angels mingle among us in many forms bringing messages of comfort, healing, and assistance. In the process, it is not possible to avoid messages from The Source of all, from that Timeless place where there is no difference between what we label as the past, present, and future. All things occur in the "now" or present tense. Anchoring our energies in the "NOW" causes a 'perspective' shift of Time and Space. The past and the future have been and will always be the now. Within this state of meditative 'now-ness,' all that is Divinely Permitted to be seen and known is seen and known. That which is not Divinely Permitted to be seen will not be revealed, regardless of what methods are used.

Meditation inspires a transcendent perspective. When we meditate, we are placing ourselves in a position of consciousness to receive visions of what we have named past and future physical and non-physical realities. Meditation can trigger spontaneous 'visionary seeing' beyond what we believe to be the capacity of our horizontal senses. In this regard, there are oracular properties associated with Mystical Meditation, as well as possible encounters with hyperdimensional entities and energies, which require the unwavering observance of spiritual responsibility and protocol.

The nature of the messages we receive will reveal whether the source is of the shadow worlds or Divine Light. The highest principles of any spiritual technology can be corrupted. The star or cross can be turned upside down. Verses of Holy Scriptures can be recited backward or used out of context, as weapons, even as a sick justification for cold-blooded murder. The use of inverted interpretations of sacred symbols and scriptures, reflect the negative orientation of those who choose this corruption, not of the symbols and scriptures themselves.

Mystical practices such as meditation can open doors to receiving communications from ascending and descending angels. Such phenomena commonly occur in Mystical Meditation. Messages of guidance and protection, comfort, healing, and Light are exchanged on these spiritual bridges. This also explains the apparitions and non-physical presences that occur in a waking dream state of Sleep Paralysis.

If the messages received are positive, there is no cause for concern. If not, it is best to withdraw from the meditation and retreat into prayer. After discovering the cause of, and cure for it, we are safe to resume our meditation practice. Prayer, intuition, and the gift of spiritual discernment are the most reliable and trustworthy guides. It is understood that any communication that has the potential to cause harm to anyone, including ourselves, is a voice to be silenced. If our highest moral values are threatened, compromised, or violated by a communication, it is a sign of a Spiritual Emergency.

Often a negative communication may be Divinely permitted as a test to determine if the suggestions of whispering demons have a place to land, that we may not even be consciously aware of. We pray that we keep our spirits cleansed through prayer, fasting, and meditation, and to have the spiritual discernment to know the difference between good and evil in all its many expressions.

The objective of Mystical Meditation can create, launch, and then anchor an ethereal thought form from this plane with prayer, meditation, sound, Light, symbols, and words of power. Prescribed protocol intensifies it. More than any of the paraphernalia you may gather to place upon your altar, *emotion* is the single most important catalyst to launch a stated intention into ultimate manifestation. Lukewarm emotional flatlining produces results directly proportionate to the energy brought to the spiritual work.

Depending upon the nature of your spiritual practice, certain lunar and planetary aspects are not recommended to work under because they are not conducive to a clean, positive outcome. However, it is not wise to be singularly dependent upon these aspects to practice because we were here before the Moon and its phases. We were here before the planets. It is preferable to "abide" in Divine Presence.

Many mystical paths will teach of Universal energies and how they work with us to achieve goals that can enhance, heal, and improve the quality of our lives. Some will experience a level of sensitivity wherein we will feel these energies call upon us to respond immediately and appropriately, then instruct precisely how to do what needs to be done to accomplish our spiritual goals.

I will never suggest that there is any ritual, meditation, petition, affirmation, or visualization that would enter the arena of the intensity of a single, sincere prayer. No sincere prayer goes unanswered. Prayer is our most powerful way of communicating with The Divine One and represents the most direct path to the experience of Oneness. The most basic level of respect for The God advises that we perform certain practices that are common to any communications with anyone, for example, cleaning ourselves, providing a clean environment, and providing an atmosphere conducive to the purpose of the communication. For example, we would not conduct a business meeting in a loud nightclub. Nor would we attend a business meeting dressed for and behaving as though we were attending a party.

Propriety and respect are key considerations; however, there is nothing that should be used as an excuse or reason not to pray. Even though we are instructed to wash the hands, face, and feet in some reverent prayer traditions, it is also taught that if provisions for this "ablution" are not available, the cleansing may be done with the literal breath of one's own prayer, or even with dirt. Common sense is the wisest instruction when engaging in any spiritual work. Never forgetting the objective is the wisest mindset. The objective is to "talk" with The Divine Presence until the two Voices and Intentions become One. The objective is to live in thanks and gratitude for the blessings of The God. The objective is to live in praise of The God. The higher our level of respect for humility and service, the stronger the bond of Love between the "I in I." That is the connection we seek, the sacred bond of the "I in I," causing a mutual Will for the manifestation of the highest good of all.

What Causes Sleep Paralysis?

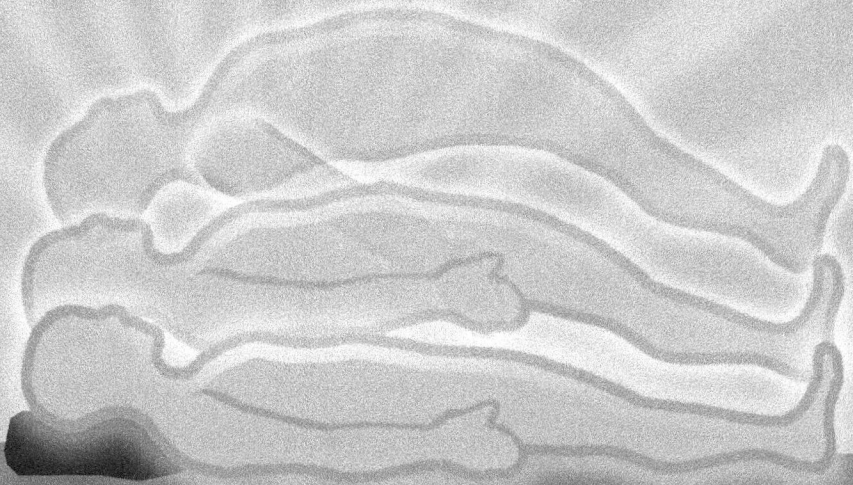

Signs of Natural Psychic Abilities

Some people are more psychically sensitive than others. These people are sometimes forced into the study of Psychic Self-Defense just to manage energies that are a normal part of their everyday lives. They are not strangers to sometimes disturbing mystical and paranormal experiences. They are magnets for it. This is not an exposé about horror stories of rampant wickedness and how to fear it. It is a holistic collection of suggestions from many paths, beliefs, and experiences. Only what resonates with the energy of your Higher Self should be considered. On any path of mystical study, many have experiences that are difficult to explain. These experiences are a natural part of our multidimensional existence, both perishable and imperishable, as they demonstrate our dual and transcendent nature.

The subject of Spiritual Emergency and the phenomenon of Sleep Paralysis is essential to the study of Psychic Self-Defense. I think it warrants being studied in greater depth than other phenomena because I have observed that elements of a Sleep Paralysis event are precursors to manifestations occurring in common spiritual/psychic practices, and may not really qualify as a Spiritual Emergency. Sleep Paralysis can manifest as one of the many natural sensations associated with an intentional, voluntary mystical experience.

The nature of Sleep Paralysis suggests that the onset of these experiences/attacks could well be the unveiling of the fact that we may *be* the portal, not necessarily, the victim. As disturbing as it is, the experience of Sleep Paralysis is a precursor to mystical experiences people are trying for intentionally. (Lucid dreaming, Out of Body Experience, Near Death Experience, Remote Viewing, Astral Travel, Portal and Dimension Jumping, Time Travel, Merkaba Activation, Mystical Meditation - Journeying). What presents as a surreal nightmare could be an initiatory Rite of Passage, designed to get our attention. At the very least, it may simply be a sign of possessing a mystical gift.

Some unsettling experiences may include, but are not limited to:

- The sensation of being pulled out of body by an unseen force, feeling paralyzed, and unable to "get back into" the physical body. This may occur just before falling asleep or being lulled into a deep sleep. It can begin as a Lucid Dream, nightmare, or Sleep Paralysis.

- Dreamlike visions or apparitions.

- Dreams that come true, either literally or symbolically.

- Dreaming in color and experiencing Lucid Dreams with an unusual, surreal feeling.

- Strong feelings toward certain people, either positive or negative, that turns out to be a sign or warning.

- Having thoughts about someone and they call or visit soon after.

- Having seen an illumination of varied colors or aura surrounding the body of a person.

- Having mysterious knowledge of unknown events with no apparent reasonable explanation.

- Recognizing and having knowledge or memories of places never visited before.

- Having the feeling of recognizing a person unknown on a conscious level.

- Dreaming about someone unknown and later meeting them and recognizing them from the dream.

- Having recurrent dreams or visions of another time period wherein there was a feeling of having been present.

- Sensing an unseen presence.

- Having heard a voice that had no possible physical source.

- Having seen someone, or something, a light or shadow, in the peripheral vision, then turning to look and finding nothing.

- Identifying a scent with no possible physical source.

- Having canceled or altered plans for trips or appointments without having a conscious reason, only to discover later that something happened that you would have chosen to avoid.

- Having had memories of life before the age of three.

- Having known what other people were going to say before they say it.

- Having felt the sensation of freezing cold pass through the entire body, with no apparent physical cause or source.

- Having become extremely angry with someone and they have experienced an unfortunate and unusual turn of luck soon afterward.

- Having dreamed certain details of another part of the world and subsequently traveled to that place and recognized those details to be accurate.

- Having seen things move with there being no physical cause.

- Having traveled to places without physically being there or astral travel.

- Having experienced physical death and being revived, mental faculties intact, with the experience of having traveled to the "other side."

- Having had the experience of being transported to another place, either in or Out of Body, and communing with what appeared to be aliens, spirit beings, or deities.

- Having felt that prayers or touch was a factor in the healing of someone suffering from an illness.

- Being born with a "veil" (a sheath of skin) over the face.

- Having had premonitions of events to come and they actually occurred.

- Having dreamed or had visions of information that have caused a win in a game of chance.

- Being regularly singled out of a crowd and asked for advice.

- Having had dreams of flying and experiencing a shocking feeling of sinking or falling when awakened.

- Having experienced intuitive feelings knowing that it is logical to override worldly explanation.

- Having had physical symptoms (headaches, nausea, itching, burning, panic attacks, shortness of breath, dizziness, diarrhea, unusual bleeding, insomnia, choking, or heavy pressure on the chest) seeming to correspond with some unexpected event.

- Having some unusual identifying mark on the physical body, believed to be spiritually significant.

- Having had many compliments on beautiful or unusual eyes.

- Having had an emotional reaction to being in a certain place, around a certain person, or coming in contact with certain objects (uncontrollable crying, fear, laughing, panic, sadness, grief, loneliness, peace, comfort, or relief).

- Having looked in the mirror and seeing images of people or places on the other side of the mirror.

- Having looked into a glass or body of water and seen images of people or places in the water.

- Having written unfamiliar things and not having any conscious recollection or control of the writing.

- Having always been curious and attracted to the mystical.

- Having a strong belief of having lived before.

- Having felt that energy directed by mind or emotion has affected the operation of electronic or mechanical equipment (blowing out light bulbs, stopping clocks and watches, draining batteries, altering the functions of televisions, radios, cars, etc.)

- Having appeared to cause animals to behave strangely.

- Having moved objects with the mind.

- Having seen or had communication with an apparition of someone known to be dead.

- Having had a spiritual or religious experience and given a communication directly from The God or angels.

- **Having been instructed by voices with no physical source, to do something that was completely against moral belief, and following, or not following their instruction. This is particularly true of messages suggesting self-harm or harming others.**

- **Having experienced the sensation of an energy, entity, or spirit entering and controlling the physical body with or without consent.**

You would be surprised to know how common all of these experiences are. It's not something that people are anxious to communicate to one another for fear of being called insane. It would be most unusual if we did *not* experience these types of phenomena. The more of them we have experienced, the easier and more rewarding the study of Psychic Self-Defense will be. It offers spiritual independence and freedom from our fears.

Some of these experiences may be quite frightening or even devastating. However, I believe that by the time you have finished reading this book, you will at least have a better understanding and frame of reference. Acceptance of the diverse manifestations of non-physical reality is much easier if there is a sound knowledge of just how common it is. It is fascinating to study how to control it, banish it, or even embrace it.

There are two exceptions to embracing it. If you have experienced any of the **bolded** phenomena from the basic checklist above:

- **Having been instructed by voices with no physical source, to do something that was completely against moral belief, and following, or not following their instruction. This is particularly true of messages suggesting self-harm or harming others.**
- **Having experienced the sensation of an energy, entity, or spirit entering and controlling the physical body with or without consent.**

Please know that if these experiences occur, it is cause for great concern. You must consult physical, mental, and spiritual professionals for help. *Consider any variation of these particular experiences an issue of great urgency, and seek help immediately.* It would *not* be a good idea to engage or continue any type of mystical study without consulting physical, mental, and spiritual professionals to determine the cause and treatment of your Spiritual Emergency. Your highest priority should be the study of how to get your life and your soul back.

If you have experienced any of those above, consider yourself among those for whom the veil between the worlds of spirit and matter is very thin. You are not necessarily crazy. You are not necessarily evil. You are not necessarily weird. These abilities, however, can be very disruptive and counterproductive to leading a "normal" life. Choose to see these experiences as a gift and a blessing even during times it may feel like a curse. Embrace these Timeless, priceless adventures and use them to benefit the highest good for yourself as well as others. Wisdom would also choose to be cautious with whom these experiences are shared. There are some who are not spiritually open-minded enough to accept or even discuss unfamiliar spiritual reality without judgment and fear.

Spiritual gifts are not to be abused. There is a thin line between "use" and "abuse" and a very large, tedious gray area in the interpretation of "use." One rule of thumb is to determine whether or not you are using your gift to harm, take advantage of, or manipulate anyone against his or her Free Will. If you feel you have done or intended to do this, approach the issue in prayer and ask for guidance and forgiveness. It is not worth the consequences of crossing the line.

Don't risk turning a gift into a curse. Many do not understand the serious consequences of choosing to be a negative energy that causes others to require Psychic Self-Defense to protect themselves from your attacks. Energy is neither good nor evil. It just is. It is the intention and the outcome that makes the difference. Any energy directed into the lives of others to cause harm will effectively turn into a boomerang that returns to the sender. The only one we curse in the end is ourselves.

Any energy that seeks to force issues and manipulate Divine destiny will be fruitless. There is nothing that we should desire outside of Divine Will. However, the reality of creation is there is nothing we *can* do other than what is permitted by the Will of The God. None of our mystical practices can transcend or change the Permission of That Which Created all. The consequences of the *desire* to impose our personal will upon ourselves or others will return three times into our lives. If the intention was to cause harm or manipulate the Free Will of someone consciously, Cause and Effect and Karma would return it to us three times three. It is not worth anything we could think to gain, knowing that we are bargaining and playing dangerous games with all we truly are, our souls, and our connection to The Source. Imagine a world full of gifted people who choose to direct their powerful spiritual energies to bring love, healing, and peace to creation. Imagine a world full of gifted people who choose to act just out of love for and connection with The Creator, The Source of all gifts. Imagine!!

Spiritual Warfare

We are energy. Our electromagnetic energy field can be affected by other energies. Many mystical practices cause energetic shifts that affect us on every level of our being. Energy is neutral. It is neither positive nor negative, good nor evil. What differentiates positive mysticism from negative mysticism is *intention* and *outcome*. Some call it black magic and white magic. On some paths of Western mysticism, some change the spelling of the word *"magic"* to *"magick"* to distinguish magical tricks from mystical practice. There is a thin line between the mystical and the magickal, but drawing that line is not the purpose of this text. I choose to call it either positive or negative mysticism. Any thought or act intentionally committed to creating a negative outcome is referenced here as "negative mysticism." Any thought or act intentionally committed to creating a positive outcome will be referred to as "positive mysticism." If the *intention* is negative, regardless of the outcome, it is considered negative mysticism. At the same time, if the outcome is negative, regardless of positive intention, it is still negative mysticism.

A judgmental, jealous, envious, or hateful thought about another can be a projection of negative energy associated with the practice of negative mysticism. This projection of condensed negative energy can take on a life of its own as a 'thought-form.' It can be used as a weapon as damaging as a bullet fired from a gun. It feeds upon the energy resources of its target. Thought-forms can and do create havoc, discord, and illness. They can even present life-threatening issues by way of subtle frequencies and powerful energy currents influencing the electromagnetic energy field of the intended victim. Some know this as a psychic attack. It qualifies as the practice of negative mysticism because a projected intention has caused harm to someone. Some of us even psychically attack ourselves by entertaining our own negative thoughts!

Some of the most flagrant practitioners of negative mysticism are many of the very same people who are its' most judgmental critics. Even the most sacred of practices, such as prayer, chanting, and meditation, can be used in such a way as to cause harm. That is why to only have a cursory interest and knowledge of certain spiritual paths can be dangerous.

The reason I direct attention to the irresponsible throwing around of projected energy is the fact that every spiritual practice, including meditation and prayer, each in its own powerful way, are the elements that make any mystical practice work. We are the magic that we seek. Many of the rules of Western magick trace their roots to ancient mysticism and can operate within the same framework, except that with mysticism, there is no frame. There is only our intention, cooperative with Divine Intention.

We determine what type of mysticism we are practicing. Any time the mind becomes focused on anything or anyone, the object of that attention has somehow been affected or changed. If it is anger, hatred, envy, or jealousy that is focused or meditated upon, then projected at the object of this negative emotion, it is as evil as a wicked magical spell. These attacks can occur subconsciously if the practitioner is in a state of denial. The subconscious attack can be more dangerous than the deliberate attack. What is not consciously known cannot be easily controlled. It must first be identified to exercise the power to control it. If the same projection of energy is positive, sending loving, healing, and protective energy, it would be one of the strongest forms of prayer.

Many of us frequently practice positive mysticism without realizing it and may call it by a different name. The most powerful form of positive mysticism is prayer. It has been said that Jesus was known as one of the most brilliant positive mystics that ever lived. It is said that he performed healings. He had the gift of prophecy. He walked on water. He communicated with the spirit world. He resurrected the dead. He even rose from the dead. Certainly, these phenomenal feats qualify as positive mysticism, at the very least. Jesus taught that we, too, could perform such feats and miracles with sufficient faith and trust in The Divine One, with faith the size of a mustard seed and the heart of a child. The prophets and messengers from most spiritual paths have been ascribed to have possessed mystical powers.

We must keep in mind that The One God protects us all and is everywhere present in our lives as we consider the dangers of spiritual practices as innocent as meditation. Prayer is essential to our protection from the unpleasantness of the spirit world and the physical world. Every one of us has had unpleasant encounters with the phenomena of negative mysticism, whether we know it or not, even if we have never practiced mysticism of any kind. The veil between the worlds is quite thin. I do not intend to evoke fear, only to inspire awareness and commitment to study. We will discover that in the process of our spiritual evolution, we will become increasingly sensitive to the subtlest of energies, their patterns, and their many manifestations. The energies that we are uncomfortable with can be avoided and banished. There are spiritual cleansing practices that are recommended in most traditions. Hopefully, this text will cover many that will keep this spiritual journey cleansed of both Astral and Earth Plane garbage. Refer to the section on "Prayer" for a mosaic of protection prayers from many traditions. The Light Meditation audio recording is provided with this text to perform before daily prayer and meditation rituals.

Signs of Positive Mysticism

Positive mysticism, in any of its many forms, either intentional or unintentional, can emerge from the following common human tendencies:

1) There is an overwhelming desire to connect with The God and submit to Divine Will and the Divine Plan for our lives. This is not about religion. It is about a glorious sense of confidence in the connection between the I AM that we are, and the Creator of That, of Its Own Essence.

2) The commitment to improve the quality of life of self and others is a resounding sign of positive mysticism.

3) There is a desire to be a conduit of healing and an instrument for transmissions of sacred wisdom. The expression of this longing manifests in many creative forms.

4) There is a commitment to the study and research of our connection with the Earth and nature. There is a strong interest in the study of the ancient mysteries.

5) There is an evolved understanding of the forces of nature we are at the effect of.

6) There is a desire to commit random acts of kindness and compassion.

7) There is a desire to be a part of solutions rather than the voice of problems.

8) There is a desire to be a co-creator of miracles.

9) There is a desire to create peace in the face of discord.

10) There is an innate consciousness of the Natural Mystic that dwells within.

11) There is a belief in The Creator and the rejection of all that is not That.

12) There is an overwhelming desire to connect with The God and submit to Divine Will and the Divine Plan for our lives. This is not about religion. It is

about a glorious sense of confidence in the connection between the I AM that we are, and the Creator of That, of Its Own Essence.

13) The commitment to improving the quality of life of self and others is a resounding sign of positive mysticism.

14) There is a desire to be a conduit of healing and an instrument for transmissions of sacred wisdom. The expression of this longing manifests in many creative forms.

15) There is a commitment to the study and research of our connection with the Earth and nature. There is a strong interest in the study of the ancient mysteries.

16) There is an evolved understanding of the forces of nature we are at the effect of.

17) There is an empathic connection with the energies of others. There is an innate desire to alleviate needless suffering and extend kindness and compassion.

18) There is a desire to be a part of solutions rather than the voice of problems.

19) There is a desire to be a co-creator of miracles.

20) There is a desire to create peace in the face of discord.

21) There is an innate consciousness of the Natural Mystic that dwells within.

22) There is a belief in The Creator and the rejection of all that is not That.

23) A strong sense of Kismet, Synchronicity, Fortune, Fate, and Inner Guidance.

24) There are excursions in consciousness that become commonplace.

25) Visitations of angels, ancestors, loved ones on the 'other side,' and prophetic revelations are common in Lucid Dream events.

26) Reiki and forms of Energetic and Remote Healing.

27) Mystical Meditation (Meditations that inspire mystical phenomenon).

Signs of Negative Mysticism

Negative mysticism, in any of its many forms, either intentional or unintentional, can result from the following common human tendencies:

1) There is a tendency to shoot a fly with an elephant gun, and swat elephants with fly swatters, based on transient erratic emotional states. Such compulsions can be an indicator of a conscious or subconscious psychic attacker. We must have a committed prayer and meditation practice in place to give us strength in these days of unprecedented spiritual warfare. We must approach petitions for protection as basic as a prayer with impeccable discernment to avoid creating an unpredictable outcome or an attack against innocent people.

   One must have 20/20 Third Eye vision, see all perspectives, and choose to act with sound judgment, which, by definition, means someone can get it twisted and try to play god. The Karmic debt incurred is not worth the fleeting satisfaction of revenge. Vengeful, unforgiving, grudge-holding people must elevate their frequency through prayer and meditation to avoid attracting negative energy and providing a place for it to land. Allowing unresolved conflict to cause psychic energy to spin out of control harms both the sender and the target. A wise mystic controls their energy and avoids either over or under-reacting to the challenges of life. Seek fair and equitable conflict resolution in a timely manner. Practice forgiveness.

2) There is a tendency to seek to avoid destiny by attempting to alter it, whether it be at their altar or in the spinning thought-forms of their obsessions. We can manipulate fate, but it is an exercise in futility to attempt to manipulate destiny. To fulfill our destiny, whatever it may be, is among the most profound of human goals and achievements. Nothing but Divine Grace can alter destiny. Nothing good can come from efforts to stand our personal willfulness up in opposition to destiny. It is a waste of energy. At the same

time, know that you need to keep an open mind with regards to determining what your True Destiny is. The process of awakening is a natural one and cannot be conformed to the rules we often play by.

3) There is a desire to manipulate or control the fate and will of others, regardless of how noble we perceive our intentions to be.

4) There is a tendency to suppress or deny deep subconscious feelings to the extent that when we approach our mystical practice for intervention, we may meditate on a wave and create a tsunami of pent-up emotions.

5) There is a tendency to avoid responsibility. If a failure is experienced, there is an inclination to blame external forces, blame the process, but never blame ourselves for having created the cause. Journaling is a very important tool to help us review our documentation objectively, connect the dots, and understand the circular nature of time and the relationship between events. Journaling makes it easier to observe the Law of Cause and Effect at work. If we feel our spiritual practice is not as effective as we would like it to be, it is because we were a cause, or at least an influential contributing factor, that resulted in the compromised outcome.

    If a lamp is plugged into a fully functioning power source and it doesn't work, we check the lamp for the defect because we are sure that the source works. If we ask for something in prayer and don't get it, don't assume the prayer was not heard. All prayers are heard. Perhaps the answer is simply, "No!" The Source is all-powerful and knows all things, including how and when to say no. Let your journaling be the cause of new good habits forming after observing consistent Karmic patterns.

6) There is a tendency to want to be a "member of the club" without paying dues. Spiritual endeavors require a tremendous commitment and investment of energy, study, and practical experience. Shortcuts and quick fixes disrespect the process and can ultimately lead to disaster.

7) There is a tendency to deny the Natural Mystic of the "I in I," the unfathomable power of the Higher Self. If we do not see ourselves as *being* the magic we seek to create in our mystical practice, our most energetic efforts are futile and will render negative results. When we cannot see the spark of the flame of The God ... the "I in I" that we are ... we are limited in our efforts to love ourselves unconditionally. To love the Self can be complicated if we insist on seeing ourselves as the "s"elf, in its changeful revolving door of identities we find in the mirrors of our minds. The knowledge of Self gives us the unlimited ability to emit a higher frequency of love for all beings and becomes an example of what beautifully mystical beings we all are.

8) There is a strong tendency to see Universal Order as a phenomenon that occurs outside of the self. There is a Self-observing-self phenomenon that would better serve us. We are the keepers of the Universal Order that we are. Our choices dictate our relationship with Universal Order. Choose for the Eternal being that we are, not the perishable form that rises in like a wave on an infinite sea. We are a phenomenon, seen and unseen. When the manifestations we seek to create are aligned with our destiny, the Universe will align itself behind the strength of our commitment to fulfilling that destiny.

9) There is a tendency to give permanent reality to temporary conditions and situations. Toward an effort of avoiding personal responsibility for our lives, we can trivialize the major issues we need to address while maximizing the importance of trivia. The mystical process of prayer and meditation ritual is sacred and should not be treated profanely with spiritually empty, vanity-based transient pursuits. We approach all ritual as the I AM with love for all beings, affirming that the Self cannot be harmed.

Like all beings, we would prefer an attack free life, yet attack cannot become our central point of focus. These situations come and go. They may create annoying and even disturbing phenomena, but the worst thing we can do is give too much attention to the phenomena. We must maintain focus like a laser beam on how to detect and dismiss negative energies. Our center of attention must be focused on being that field of energy that is our Higher Self. We are learning here how to defend ourselves above the storm and under the radar against any form of attack.

10) There is a tendency to deify physical manifestations and give too much energy and significance to distracting phenomena. The ultimate of all phenomena is the knowledge and understanding of the multi-dimensional, phenomenal beings that we are. We don't have to chase phenomenal experiences to convince ourselves or anyone else of anything. If we can embrace our real Self, the I AM, as the observer of the self of our conditioned perception, our energy field is fortified against attackers.

Extend to observing "What" observes the observer and the real inquiry has begun. What can attack consciousness engaged in that elegant dance and win? The battleground and the common ground of our lives begin in the formless realm. It is amazing how some create a beautiful altar and then begin to worship the forms and objects they place upon it. It is like worshiping a telephone as a friend rather than seeing it as an instrument that facilitates communication between friends.

11) There is a tendency to conform phenomena to substantiate our beliefs rather than proceeding with the strength of faith and trust in Divine Providence. The application of *any* given force affects the object at which it is directed. It is up to us to determine the nature of the force that would best suit our intention, trusting that the application of it will create change by The Will of The Most High. The Universe has nothing to prove to us. If we paid as much attention

to what we can contribute to the Universe as what we demand of it, our names might outlive our self-imposed boundaries. It has no spiritual integrity to practice Psychic Self-Defense only when there is a fear of attack. One's lifestyle must reflect respect for the wisdom traditions that teach us how to manage the energies that affect our lives.

12) As an old saying goes, there is a tendency to try to "plant corn and get wheat." We cannot attract anything other than what we are. If we seek to refine what we are, that which we attract to ourselves will be of higher refinement. We are that which we seek. We cannot be a spiritual warmonger and think that we get to live in peace. The most powerful form of Psychic Self-Defense is ... Do good!

13) There is a tendency to see the nature of a "should be" as being real enough to divert our attention from the truth of what is. Often in the face of what appears to be chaos and suffering, our greatest spiritual growth is underway. We are not to seek to use mystical practice as a "quick fix" to escape from the work involved in facing the challenges of life. Consider that the way it is, is the way it is meant to be, right now, for a reason. Challenging that can result in transforming mysticism as a positive energy, into a negative force. Be careful what you wish for. Be even more careful about what you demand.

14) There is a tendency to be controlled by anger, jealousy, desire, greed, obsession, and fantasy or illusory romanticism. These are very strong emotions that create strong force fields of hungry, predatory, toxic energy. It is a powerful discipline to master resisting being controlled by our emotions.

15) There is a tendency to have a complete disregard for consequences. There is a wide range of manifestations, from a dysfunctional personality to mental issues that venture into psychosis, sociopathic narcissism, or even spiritual possession.

16) There is an instinctive knowledge of magic and mystical sciences often triggered by expressions of negative emotions. The transmission of mystical knowledge can occur in many ways. We may receive messages in Dreamtime, in meditation, from past life and genetic memories. I don't spend a lot of energy reflecting on past or future lives. I choose to keep my awareness firmly in the now.

It is common that past life memories sometimes bleed through into present life experiences. With that can come uncanny mystical knowledge that can't be explained away. That remembered knowledge is accompanied by accountability for our actions, and the causes and effects we create. We are mystical beings. We all have natural mystical powers. We must use them to heal and never to harm. If we are being harmed, we seek refuge in the I AM and the Observer of the I AM. If we find ourselves tempted in any way to allow our willfulness or anger to energetically harm ourselves and others, we seek refuge in The God from our own transgression.

17) In the practice of "magic" or "magick," as it refers to the mystical sciences, we participate as co-creators in the manifestation of some desire in our hearts. Before you are faced with a pressing matter that inspires you to go beyond common prayerfulness and take a work to task at your altar, ask yourself a few questions. What is the nature of this manifestation? What is the nature of this heart which seeks this manifestation? What is the motivation behind this work? Why is a formal ceremonial approach believed to be required to accomplish it? Against what odds do you strive to manifest this work? Are you sure it is in cooperation with the Divine Plan, or is it an attempted manipulation of it? What are the known and unforeseen consequences of this work, as manifested within the time frame of the worker?

We must be careful when we arbitrarily decide that we know what is best for the highest good of everyone concerned in an attempt to manifest a new reality. If we find ourselves working outside of the framework of Universal and Divine intention, we are treading on dangerous ground. It is not like there is a possibility that our ambition alone would lead us to our imagined success. Nothing can be manifested unless it is permitted by Universal Law and Divine Plan, regardless of the worker's skill or best intentions.

When our personal ego willfully flies out of control, and we feel we know beyond the Knowing of the Knower of all things because of an emotion, an opinion, a judgment, a fleeting desire. It is just not worth the consequences for a momentary rush of a power trip that promises to do a U-turn, derail, crash, and burn.

At the risk of sounding preachy, it is just not worth the dangers involved when the Karmic turnaround presents. The energy will boomerang in mind-boggling, ironic ways. If it goes beyond a prayer of surrender, consider it a red flag. These subtle energies are sacred. When that sacredness is violated, the entire Universe and the very Essence of The God that created it will rise up against you. Do not *practice* magic. Become it.

Spiritual Emergencies

There are many manifestations of what is classified as a "Spiritual Emergency." I have attempted to cover as wide a range of possibilities and probabilities as my own experience and studies can confirm. What constitutes a Spiritual Emergency is the disturbing occurrence of phenomena that are impossible even to attempt to explain or describe to *anyone* outside of the direct experience of it. It can mean becoming so overwhelmed with such life-altering, crippling fear and panic that one may feel cast into some sci-fi realm of the unknown while knowing for a fact that it is all quite real. It more than likely means that you can't confide in family, friends, acquaintances, or colleagues without the risk of compromising relationships and being called insane. It means that seeking help from the average therapist can get you diagnosed, labeled, and drugged, if not locked up. It can mean that you can't even get help from most sources of spiritual counsel without being victim-blamed and exorcised of some perceived demon that you are judged for having somehow invited in. Sometimes helpful and knowledgeable sources of spiritual support are practitioners of secret arts beyond your comprehension. You may not be ready to step into a shared energetic field with some of them, or the entities and energies they wrestle with constantly, as a part of their own practice.

Spiritual Emergencies Induced by Spiritual Practice

There are precautionary warnings on every spiritual path regarding protocol associated with mystical experiences and practices. I am not demonizing or casting shadows upon the traditional spiritual practices I mention or inferring that they are dangerous. Some are no more triggering of nonphysical phenomena than an afternoon nap. Others require that you become knowledgeable of possible or probable risk factors. Some that come to mind are Yoga; Meditation; Vision Quests; Soul Retrievals; Ceremonial Sweat Lodge; the use of any consciousness-altering substance in mystical/ceremonial practice; hypnotism; past-life regression;

future-life progression; trance channeling; clairvoyance; clairsentience; clairaudience; psychokinesis; oracle reading; Ouija boards; music with backward masking; visits to certain sacred sites or spiritually charged places with residual haunting energies; profound grief because of a loss of some sort; visitations with energetic or disembodied, nonphysical beings or entities; giving or receiving energetic healings; out of body experiences; lucid dreaming; astral projection and travel; remote viewing; non-observance of basic spiritual and Feng Shui protocol. All of these mystical gifts and practices can trigger what appear to be random phenomenal events in the home or in the person. *Anything* that would cause a trance/altered state of consciousness, whether or not it is substance-induced, intentional, or spontaneous, can serve as a powerful trigger. Being the target of an energetic attack or even on the receiving end of some random projection or influence can leave even unintended targets vulnerable to the experience of a Spiritual Emergency.

There are signs to watch for in a necessary practice of Self-witnessing. Many of the red flags and indicators of possible spiritual emergencies are depression; feeling haunted; feelings or signs of being possessed; changes in eating or sleeping patterns, having visions or hearing voices that make disturbing suggestions and communications; anti-social behavior, and feelings of alienation, isolation, shutting out family, friends, and peers; relinquishing personal power to the control of someone or something outside of Self.

Group Karma

Group Karma can be experienced when a mystical interest becomes aligned with groups of others on the path. It is wise to be cautious with regards to mystical groups that are exclusionary, dogmatic, and cult-like, seeking to micromanage the lives of members. Beware when initiatory degrees or rites of passage are introduced which engage in any manner of violent hazing. Overt or covert manipulations and influences are often accomplished using methodical mind-control techniques and reward/punishment scenarios. The lure of fraternity and belonging to a like-minded "family" is attractive to people who feel displaced. Approval and acceptance seeking begins with the destruction of past self-concepts while cultivating and nurturing the evolution of a new self. When social isolation/exclusion, breaking bonds and ties with family, friends, and peers, and distancing members from any manner of support group outside of the "family" becomes a factor, it is a cause for concern. It is of particular concern when kept in place with the connective cords of fear, guilt, humiliation, peer pressure, and loss of identity. At the breaking point, letting go of the former "self" may take on the form of confessional self-hatred and self-judgment in exchange for an illusory promise of a "new self" to become. Some of the conforming methods used are sleep deprivation, food deprivation, control of attire, and control over sexual expression. Often initiatory rites of passage or rebirth involving oaths, agreements, and renunciations serve to commemorate the slaying of the former self.

Doctrines that employ certain elements of brainwashing are used to maintain the state of mind that has been set in place, for example, Memorization, Repetition, Re-languaging (using language only known and understood by the group), Isolation, and Resocialization. All social reference points are redefined. Powerful control is taken over even the most strong-minded individuals using threats of shaming, harsh discipline, ostracizing, or excommunicating the victim. These threats are usually made with references of Divine approval. If the victim seeks understanding or guidance with regard to feeling misaligned, often cruel and degrading techniques like "gaslighting" and "stonewalling" are used in a manner that discredits questions and the questioner.

Highly disciplined and restrictive lifestyle choices may well be conduct associated with a Hermetic Order to anchor a cleansing, spiritual practice. A path of renunciation does not necessarily constitute a cult. However, if it is represented as the *only* path to spiritual enlightenment, to the exclusion of all others, or if harm is done to anyone, that is indeed an obvious red flag.

Spontaneous Kundalini Awakening

Kundalini is a Sanskrit term for the primal energy that sleeps, coiled like a snake at the base of the spine, in the area of the Root Chakra. It is the source of latent concentrated power, grounded strength, and profound will. The uncoiling of the Kundalini is the manifestation and realization of optimum potential as a complex being. As this powerful energy rises, it revitalizes and transforms all of the chakras in a manner that can spark a spiritual paradigm shift that reconstructs the experience of everything.

The Root Chakra (the first of the column of seven energy centers of the body) has a shadow side when it is out of balance. Care is to be exercised in meditations that concentrate on the clearing or activation of this area. A spontaneous Kundalini Awakening event is an experience that some have not survived intact. I experienced this phenomenon after a spiritual breakthrough in my studies. I retired from a night of intense study and was awakened by what felt like a bolt of lightning, violently surging up from the base of my spinal column and out through the top of my head. I shook for over twenty minutes as if gripped by a seizure of some sort. After medical professionals failed to explain what had happened to me and ruled out any physical cause, I consulted a trusted spiritual professional and established the connection between that experience and an overwhelming spiritual epiphany that occurred prior to it.

In certain cases, a spontaneous Kundalini Awakening, such as the one I experienced, can be considered a Spiritual Emergency and can have extreme and unpredictable manifestations and consequences. The process of raising the Kundalini force up through the Chakra System should be a gradual one. It can however, be much more complex.

My cursory research using basic classes and internet sources, primarily Wikipedia, yielded so many energetic elements of so many spiritual and traditional paths that they all began to collide. Each path had different languages, traditions, and cultural twists and turns, but at the bottom line, they are more alike than they are different. Terminology associated with *Yogic and Tantric traditions (Indian)* is becoming more mainstream every day in Western cultures. The *Tan Dien* and the *Dantien* are referring to the same thing (some English spellings are phonetic). *Nadis* and *Channels* are the same thing. These terms were not unfamiliar to me because of years of mixed Martial Arts training growing up. My Martial Arts practice was also my first exposure to mystical healing paths of meditation.

- *Dantien* literally means "elixir field," but a better translation might be "energy center." It is located in the area of the lower abdomen. It is a natural reservoir for storage of the body's vital energy. These are important focal points for meditation, t'ai chi ch'uan, qigong, and other Martial Arts and energy healing techniques in Traditional Chinese Medicine (TCM);

- *The Lower Dantien* is about three finger widths below and two finger widths behind the navel. It is called "the golden stove," where the process of developing the elixir by refining and purifying essence (jing) into vitality (qi, chi) begins;

- *The Middle Dantien* is at the level of the heart, which is called "the crimson palace," associated with storing spirit (shen) and with respiration and health of the internal organs, particularly the thymus gland. This cauldron is where vitality (qi, chi) is refined into shen (spirit);

- *The Upper Dantien* is on the forehead, in the area between the eyebrows, known as the Third Eye. It is associated with the pineal gland. This energy field is where spirit (shen) is refined into Wu Wei (emptiness);

- *The Hara* is in the area of the stomach. In the Japanese medical tradition and in Japanese Martial Arts traditions, the word Hara is used as a technical term for a specific area (physical/anatomical) or energy field (physiological/energetic) of the body. The hara is a core power-source that resides beneath the auric field of the human body. It is housed inside the tan tien, existing on the level of intentionality. The hara is also known as the core star connection;

- *The Nadis/Channels* transport Life Force energies, the cosmic, vital, seminal, mental energies, (collectively described as *prana*). In the physical body, the nadis are channels carrying air, water, nutrients, blood, and other bodily fluids. They are similar to the arteries, veins, capillaries, bronchioles, nerves, lymph canals, etc.;
- *Nadis – Sushumna, Ida, and Pingala*, pull from reservoirs of the latent, potent energy of animation of the Three Tan Dien, to distribute throughout the body.

The Sushumna Nadi – connects the *Muladhara* Chakra to the *Sahasrara* Chakra, and is the path for the ascent of *Kundalini* energy up the base of the spine into the Sahasrara. It is considered the central channel for the flow of prana throughout the body and unites all other chakras in the body.

On either side of the Sushumna Nadi are two other Nadis that partner together and cross over the spine, meeting in the center of the Sushumna Nadi:

Ida Nadi – located to the left of the spine and carries feminine lunar energy. Starts in the Muladhara Chakra and ends in the left nostril;

Pingala Nadi – located to the right of the spine and carries masculine solar energy. Starts in the Muladhara Chakra and ends in the right nostril.

When done in the prescribed manner, as a highly evolved Sadhana (committed spiritual practice), it can be a transformational, healing meditation experience. However, in the case of a sudden involuntary awakening of the Kundalini energy, it can occur as a traumatic event that can feel like an implosion and look like a seizure. After experiencing such an awakening, I approached the line of study that I believe sparked the event with more caution. A sound meditation practice begins with studying under a knowledgeable and experienced teacher and guide … someone you feel you can trust.

Use this information more as a glossary than a course of study on this specific subject because it is cursory and contains just enough information to accomplish nothing at all. This is hardly more than a casual mention, considering the profound depth of all of these sacred, ancient traditions that will never cease to fascinate me. Use these terms for your own research and join me in the effort to be a student for life. An entire book could be written about each topic. Our survival depends on incorporating the transcendent wisdom of these powerful paths into our daily lives.

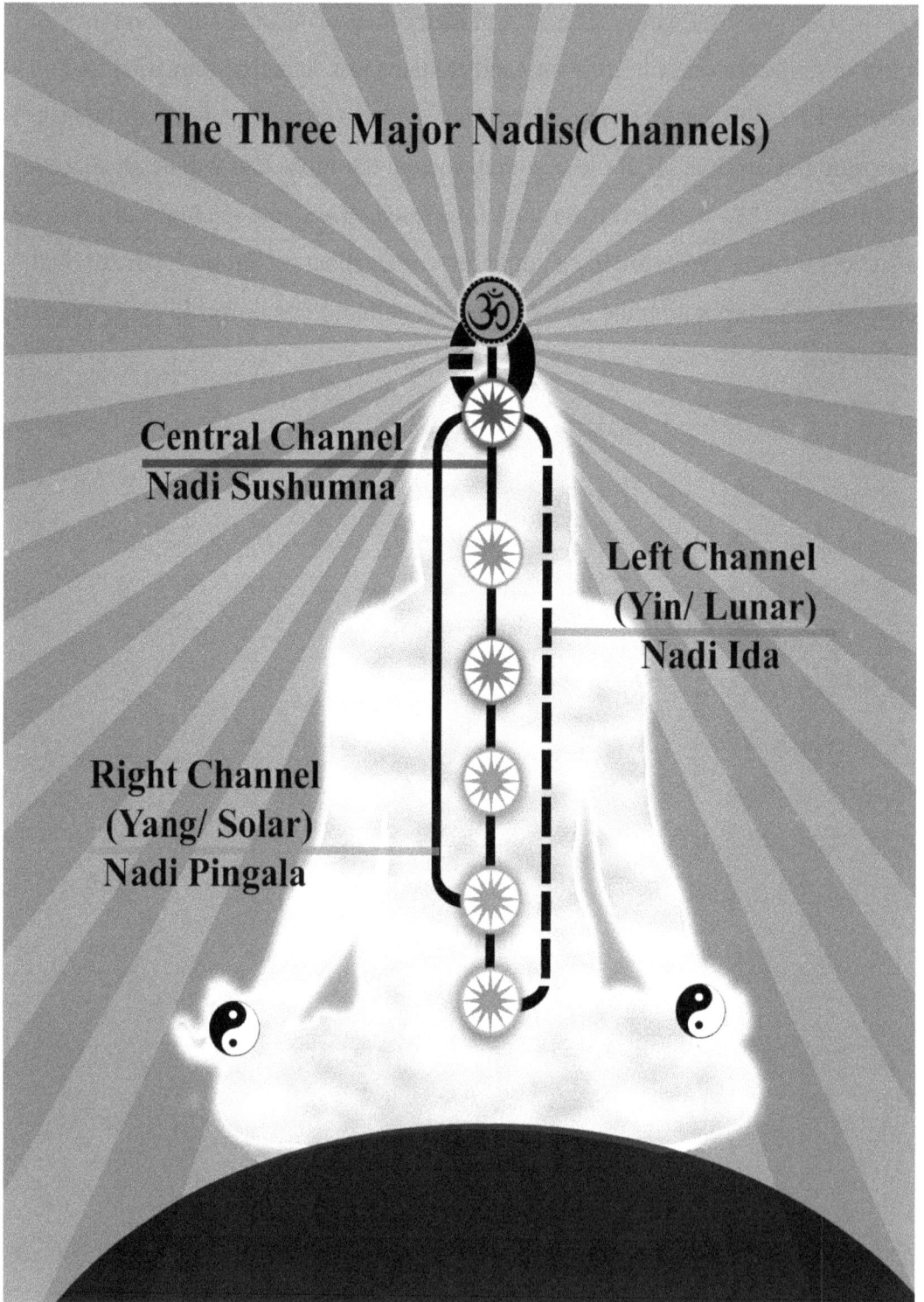

The Three Major Nadis(Channels)

Central Channel
Nadi Sushumna

Left Channel
(Yin/ Lunar)
Nadi Ida

Right Channel
(Yang/ Solar)
Nadi Pingala

The Three Energy Chakras

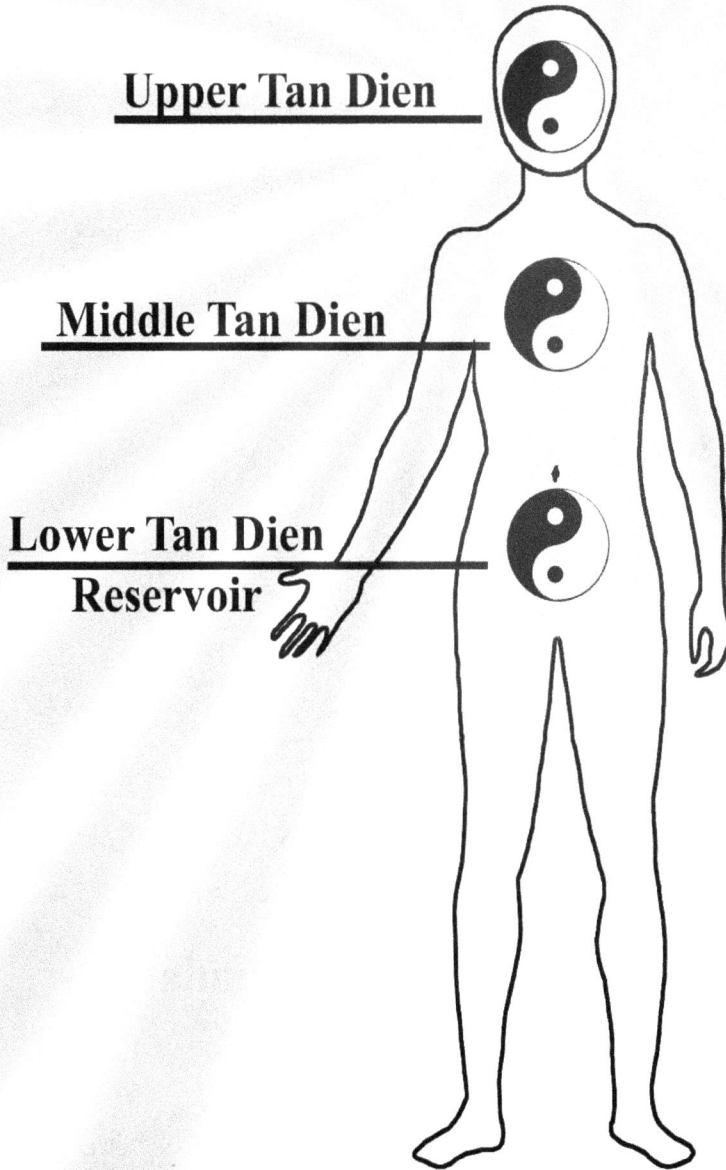

Upper Tan Dien

Middle Tan Dien

Lower Tan Dien
Reservoir

Subtle Energy Bodies (The Three Nadis)

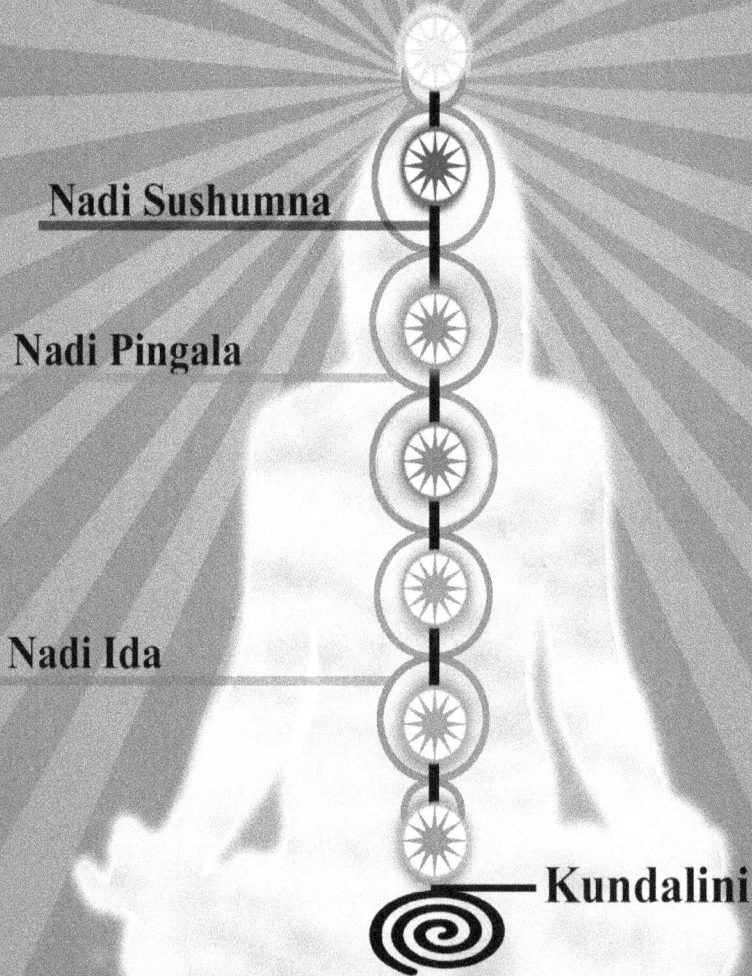

Nadi Sushumna

Nadi Pingala

Nadi Ida

Kundalini

Mystical practice is often blamed for spiritual emergencies. A Spiritual Emergency can also be triggered by prayers of every tradition I can think of … even to the extreme of experiencing what is known as a complete *awakening*, which can only be viewed as a blessing. That is why journaling is so important. In the event of any type of Spiritual Emergency, regular reviews become helpful in connecting the dots to identify triggers. If you note that a certain activity or practice stirs up phenomena that you are uncomfortable with, you will need to investigate whether or not you are practicing correctly or even if that particular practice is right for you.

Yoga Samadhi and Sleep Paralysis

Could altered states, labeled as Samadhi, actually parallel the experience of Sleep Paralysis? When compared with Sleep Paralysis, there are many similarities between Yoga Samadhi experiences, which include:

- Paralysis of the physical body, unable to speak or move;

- Altered or heightened awareness;

- Hearing voices and sounds with no apparent source;

- Seeing shapes, visions, apparitions;

- Sensing of a nonphysical presence;

- Disabled physical senses;

- Labored, restricted, constrained breathing;

- Panic, unusual speaking, or movement;

- Feelings of terror or euphoria;

- The sensation of floating, falling, or levitating;

- Hovering outside of, or "above" the physical body.

Some have experienced symptoms consistent with the experience of Sleep Paralysis during Yoga and/or certain types of meditation practice. Some have reported that a sense of terror or panic has ensued after a feeling of no longer being "in control" of breathing, body movements, or speech, accompanied by feelings of losing voluntary command over the body and/or floating outside of the body. Some may even associate that feeling with "bliss" or transcendence while remaining aware that they were no longer in control of their physical body.

The Danger of Cultural Appropriation

A solid warning: When we believe in (and practice) things that we don't understand, we invite a level of suffering that we may never recover from. There is longstanding traditional and spiritual protocol in place, so exacting that for you to attempt to practice it without fully understanding and respecting certain specifics could worsen the situation you are seeking protection from.

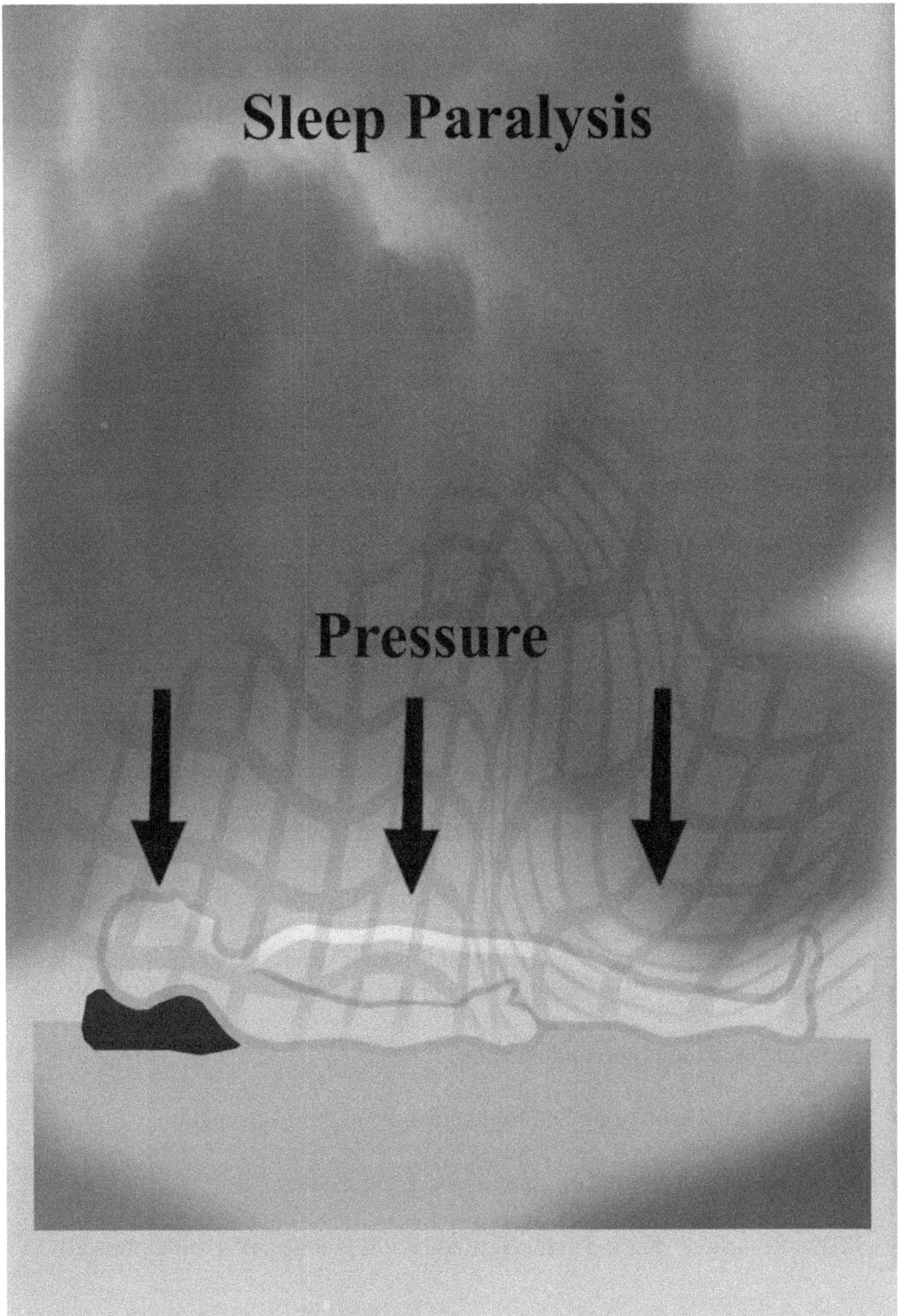

Regions of the World and Names for Sleep Paralysis and Associated Entities

Among a wide cross-section of the world population, the victims of Sleep Paralysis all seem to be reporting the same bizarre, supernatural activity ... with traditions, cultures, primarily religions, creating the narrative to explain it and cure it.

- China, "bei gui ya" (held by a ghost)

- Indonesia, "digeunton" (pressed on)

- Fiji, "Kana Tevora" (being eaten or possessed by a demon)

- Turkey, "Karabasan" (The dark presser/Assailer, nightmare)

- Thailand, "Phi Am" (a spirit that sits on a person's chest during the night)

- China, "Pinyin: Gui Ya Shen; Pinyin; Gui Ya Chuang; Pinyin: Meng Yan" (ghost pressure)

- Japan, "Kanashibari" (bound up with metal)

- Korea, "Gawi Nulim" (being pressed down by something scary in a dream)

- Mongolia, "Khar Darakh, Kara Darahu, Kharin Buu" (to be pressed by the dark)

- Tibet, "Dip-Non (Kham) or Dip-Phok (Ladakh)" (oppressed/struck by shadow)

- Cambodia/Laos, "Phii Am and Khmout Sukkhot" (that one or more ghostly figures are nearby or even holding him or her down)

- Hmong, "Dab Tsog" (pressure demon)

- Vietnam, "Ma De or Bong De" (held down by a ghost or shadow)

- Philippines, "Bangungot" (nightmare, or dying in sleep)

- Malay Peninsula, "Kena Tindih (Ketindihan In Indonesia)" (being pressed)

- Kashmir, "Pasikdhar or A Sayaa" (invisible creature who attacks residents of houses where God is not worshipped)

- Pakistan, "Shaitan, Bakhtak" (the sleep demon who has taken over one's body)

- Pashtun, "Khapasa" (nightmare or night hag)

- Zanzibar, "Popobawa" (evil spirit or shetani)

- Bangladesh, "Boba" (speechless)

- Tamil Nadu and Sri Lanka, "Amuku Be or Amuku Pei" (the ghost that forces one down)

- Nepal/Newari Culture, "Khyaak" (a ghost-like figure believed to reside in the darkness under the staircases of a house)

- Arabia, "Ja-Thoom, jinn" (a spirit capable of assuming human or animal form and exercising supernatural influence over people)

- Persia, "Bakhtak" (The sleep demon)

- Kurdistan, "Motakka" (demon that attacks people in their sleep)

- Egyptian, "jinn" (a terrifying jinn attack)

- Zimbabwe Shona, "Madzikirrira" (demon pressing one down)

- Ethiopia, "Dukak" (an evil spirit that possesses people during their sleep)

- Africa (Nigeria), "Ogun Oru" (demonic possession of the body and psyche)

- Southeast Africa (Swahili Speaking tribes), "Jinamizi," "Strangled by jinn" (creature sitting on one's chest making it difficult for him/her to breathe)

- Morocco, "Bou Rattat" (a demon that presses and covers the sleeper's body so they cannot move or speak)

- Finland, "Unihalvaus (Dream Paralysis) Painajainen" (pusher or presser)

- Hungary, "Lidercnyomas" (witches' pressure)

- Iceland, "Mara, Goblin, Succubus (Generally Female)" (*martröð* or mare ride)

- Malta, "Haddiela, Wife of the Hares" (haunts the individual in ways similar to a poltergeist)

- Greece/Cyprus, "Mora, Vrahnas or Varypnas" (Spirit who tries to steal the victim's speech or sits on the victim's chest causing asphyxiation)

- Catalonia, "Pesanta" (an enormous dog (or sometimes a cat) that goes into people's houses in the night and puts itself on their chests, making it difficult for them to breathe and causing them the most horrible nightmares)

- Sardinia (Italy), "Ammuttadori" (a ghoulish creature that sits on the chest of the sleeping victim, suffocating him and, sometimes, ripping the skin with his nails)

- Latvia, "Lietuvens" (the soul of a killed (strangled, drowned or hanged) person which attacks both people and domestic animals)

- Mexico, "Subirse El Muerto" (dead person on you)

- Brazil, Pisadeira ("She who steps")

- Northern Indigenous Canada, Greenland, and Alaska (Inuit) – uqumanqirniq, aqtuqsinniq

- Hawaii, "Press Down Ghost" (Stories About the Press Down Thing)

- Newfoundland, "AG ROG" (hag-ridden), "Old Hag" (set of eyes in the dark, bringing with her a sense of pure evil)

- Netherlands, "nachtmerrie" (night-mare)

- Germany or Old Norse, "MAHR or MARA" (supernatural being who lays on people's chests, suffocating them)

- America, "Witch Riding, Old Hag, alien abduction, possible drug abuse, plant medicine, prescription drug side-effects, physical problems, sleep disorder, possible mental issues or emotional problems" (Associated with portents of tragedy or accidents).

Experiences/Symptoms in Common
Reported by Victims of Sleep Paralysis Worldwide

- The sensation of being "eaten," consumed, absorbed, smothered by an ethereal demon;

- Visitations by the spirits of recently deceased relatives with accompanying physical symptoms of Sleep Paralysis;

- Seeing spirits with an agenda, mission, unfinished business, or bringing news;

- The victim would be perceived by an onlooker to be making interdimensional communications with invisible astral beings;

- Able on occasion to converse with spirits, therefore able to experience clairvoyant visions and receive direct transmissions with those in the spirit world;

- An astral being known as a jinn holds down the victim, restricting any type of movement, beginning with the sensation of strangulation;

- Witnessing a jinn depicted as a tall, shadowy male figure with a wide-brimmed hat. This apparition projects an ethereal cording with a binding grip that is difficult to break;

- "Kane" (metal) bound or fastened in metal, and "shibaru" (to bind, to tie, to fasten), ghost pressing on the body, or ghost pressing on the bed;

- "Being pressed down by something scary in a dream." Associated with belief in a ghost or spirit lying on top or pressing down on the sufferer;

- Even a person lying in bed next to someone experiencing an attack may be unaware that the attack is happening;

- Shadow, referring to a kind of spiritual pollution;

- Attacks from these entities have been known to leave bruises and show signs of physical contact with the victim;

- Boba, Speechless;

- Held down by a ghost. Held down by a shadow;

- Surreal nightmare in which one or more ghostly figures (intruders) are nearby;

- The sufferer is in a state of full-body paralysis, unable to call out for help;

- Being "pressed down" … incidents are commonly considered the work of an evil presence, occurring in what is explained as "blind spots" in the field of peripheral vision, described as demonic figures;

- Shaitan (Satan), evil jinns, or demons who have taken over one's body;

- Assumed to be caused by black magic, performed by enemies and jealous people;

- It is a demon that attacks the victim while the person is sleeping, pressing on their chest and stealing their breath;

- Some homes and places are also believed to be haunted by evil ghosts, satanic or supernatural beings, and they disturb people living there, especially during the night;

- Involves an acute night-time disturbance that is culturally attributed to demonic infiltration of the body and psyche during dreaming;

- Creature sitting on the chest of the victim, causing difficulty in breathing;

- Attributed the experiences to the work of shamanistic forces, often a hex placed on the victim by a shaman who practices negative magic;

- Visitations by owls, various animal totems, discarnate entities, skinwalkers, wetiko, interdimensional beings;

- Ghost-like creature or demon tries to steal the victim's speech or sits on the victim's chest, causing asphyxiation;

- An enormous dog or cat that visits in the night and sits on the chests of victims struggling to breathe. Victims are said to experience horrific nightmares;

- A ghoulish creature that sits on the chest of the victim, suffocating him and sometimes ripping the skin with his nails;

- "Torture" of being strangled. The soul of a murdered, strangled, drowned, or hanged person and attacks both people and domestic animals;

- The spirit of a dead person. It lies down upon the body of the sleeper rendering him unable to move;

- Supernatural assaults by shadow people. Victims report four different entities, a man with a hat, the old hag noted above, a haint riding, and a hooded figure;

- Sensations, memories, and hallucinations consistent with alien abduction;

- Tall, skinny, elderly woman, with long dirty nails and dry toes, white tangled hair, a long nose, staring red eyes, greenish teeth, and an evil laugh, who steps on the chest of those who sleep with a full stomach;

- During the Salem witch trials, several people reported night-time attacks by various accused witches that may have been caused by Sleep Paralysis. In many parts of the Southern United States, the entity is known as a *hag*, and the event is said to portend an approaching tragedy or accident;

- A harbinger of misfortune, such as poverty and unemployment, ill health, and chaos;

- Beings are associated with smoke. For example, the shadowy figure, the "Hat Man" entity, has been witnessed with smoke surrounding it. It appears with smoke rising off of the shadow.

Sleep Paralysis is common, in some form, to all cultures, and it is almost always associated with nocturnal evil. Cultural and religious overtones addressing the phenomenon of Sleep Paralysis are a fascinating study. Ethno-cultural traditions of diverse demographics have approached this phenomenon using various labels from different languages and perspectives.

The fact that folklore tracks "origins" of reports of Sleep Paralysis events linked to mysterious entities, commonly known in the Middle East and Africa as jinn (djinn), is a good place to begin studying the nature of this phenomenon. When the effects of this phenomenon have reached the point in someone's life that remedies and treatments are required, research shows that many of the cures seem to have roots in religious/mystical beliefs. From an Islamic perspective, it is believed that holding and/or reciting from the Quran aids in dispelling evil creatures; from a Christian perspective, a Bible, and recitation from it, aids in discouraging demons; some belief systems may require types of sacrifices or offerings to ward off evil spirits. These cures vary from one cultural tradition to another.

The book, *Sleep Paralysis: Night-Mares, Nocebos, and the Mind-Body Connection*, by Shelley Adler, a professor at the University of California, San Francisco, documented a study of the Hmong ethnic group of Laotians who immigrated from Southeast Asia to America in the early 1980s. Within months of their arrival, one by one, 116 of the 117 died in their sleep. They were all young men, with a median age of 33 years old. The men were all healthy, except one. There were no obvious abnormalities found in their autopsies. But whatever was happening to the Hmongs in their sleep killed them.

The general consensus among the Hmong was that they were being attacked in their sleep by a nonphysical entity they called Tsog Tsuam (a pressure demon), sitting on their chests, constricting their breath, paralyzing their bodies, and sometimes attempting to strangle them. It is a case used to reveal the connection between a belief system and the victim's response to these attacks. The fact that strong belief systems, coupled with intense fear, can open one up to attack, increase the intensity of the attack, and even result in injury or death is a factor to consider and study.

Adler spent years researching traditional belief narratives and what she called "nocturnal pressing spirit attacks," dab tsog *(pronounced 'da cho'),* also called Tsog Tsuam. The attacks were believed to be linked to what scientific literature refers to as sleep palsy or Sleep Paralysis. In-depth studies led to an unsettling argument that the power of the "nocebo" (the flip side of the placebo effect), contributed to their sudden physical deaths (SUNDS – Sudden Unexpected Nocturnal Death Syndrome). What is known as "the placebo effect" can demonstrate healing benefits based on the patient's belief in that treatment. "Nocebo" refers to a patient's belief in the power of something being able to harm or kill them, creating such extreme levels of stress and fear that it could even result in their death.

These attacks are real. There are too many parallels between the experiences of a sufficient global cross-section of diverse people NOT to consider that these beings could be among different species of a certain classification of "entity." They all seem to have one thing in common ... somehow, being able to induce the experience of Sleep Paralysis.

The Hmong group were displaced and lacking access to many elements of their native cultural practices because of a U.S.-backed guerrilla war against the government of Laos during the Vietnam War. They lived in scattered communities across the U.S., so they were not able to procure by familiar means (both preventative and remedial) what was required to address spiritual emergencies. A shaman would have been consulted to attend to such matters, according to their sacred beliefs and practices. They were not able to worship properly, according to their customary ways. Considerations on their list of disrupted realities their displacement caused included:

- The traditional Hmong spiritual belief system was based on the idea that all things material in creation have an element of individual consciousness or spirit – Panpsychism;

- They believed that to have moved away from their homeland cut them off from the protection of their ancestral spirits;

- They believed that because they could no longer extend traditional conciliatory sacrifices to the evil spirits at least once a year, they had become more vulnerable to their attacks;

- They believed that because they could no longer feed the spirits of their ancestors regularly, they were no longer under their protection against the evil spirits;

- Their belief that they had consequently been made more susceptible to attack because their traditional practices stopped when they moved to America, and left them wide open to an extreme, potentially life-threatening fear response in the face of these nocturnal assaults.

This bizarre case attracted substantial media attention, as well as the concern of the CDC, and ended up becoming the inspiration behind the highly acclaimed horror film Wes Craven's Nightmare on Elm Street.

It is interesting to consider that they may have been killed, not only by their fear or their beliefs but the fact that their fear was inspired by the belief that their salvation relied solely on location dependent sources and forces *outside* of themselves. They felt powerless for their inability to perform their spiritual duty to appease the spirits. They felt abandoned and forsaken by those sources in times of their greatest need. They felt, therefore, undeserving or without expectation of the protection and refuge of their ancestors. They felt that way *knowing* that ancestor protection is not location dependent … *knowing* the realm of the ancestors is beyond the Life-Death, Space-Time continuum. They felt powerless before the very entities they sought protection from, for their own inability to perform their traditional obligation to appease them, based on their change of circumstances due to their displacement. I wonder if there was a belief system in place that would have had them seek refuge in an intimate connection and Oneness with a Higher Power … One whose ability to protect them was not dependent upon their location and offerings.

My approach to this has consistently been a sense of absorption into the Realm of Divinity, in complete surrender to the Mercy of The Divine One as my sole Source of protection and guidance. By "absorption," I mean the total dissolution of every trace of ego attachment to, personification, or individuation of deities or forces or associations that create a distraction from the singular focal point. This realization was not an event. It is an ongoing process of surrender; the sacrifice is the offering of my prayers, my sacrifices, my life, and my death to All that sustains, protects, and provides for every aspect of my being. It is not just a guardianship. It is a relationship and not a relationship of diverse energies. Our shared Light is our connection. My longing for Oneness with it is my connection.

Whispered prayers into Holy Water
drown magic spells of
hypnotic seduction
words of power
incantations

laced with poison offerings
toxic promises
of date-stamped love
conditional hope
illusions of salvation
fleeting comfort
They beckon
They hiss
through pursed lips
blowing on knots
bait affixed to hooks
planted seeds
that grew
into trees
that would never bear fruit
or offer shade
outside of Self
(True Self)
There is no refuge
I am dissolved in the Essence of
That
The Only One
The Beloved

No matter how hushed the secret, the tentacles of Sleep Paralysis reach across the seen and unseen world … global, in its range of experience and scope of concern. The nature of believing you are possessed or attacked by demons, regularly abducted by aliens, or have "the red-eyed hag" sitting on you at night whenever she wants to, or the "hat man" lurking in the shadowy corner of the room has caused people all over the world to just keep it quiet and internalize the fear. The stigma and judgment attached to the mysterious condition called Sleep Paralysis keep it crouching in the shadows of obscurity, preventing many people from seeking or receiving much-needed help. The more we study, the more we can understand the nature of multidimensional existence and how it can affect our life experience, dispelling levels of fear that can literally scare us to death.

Cultures with shamanic traditions know how to deal with interdimensional interference and have beliefs, customs, and healing practices in place that support handling the types of problems that can arise. We are generally advised not to interact in a sovereign way with these entities but to study how to delegate these matters to the Highest of Spiritual Authority. Some species of these beings have the strength of seven to nine young, fit men. Their strength is not limited to our basic body/mind strength. They are not necessarily more intelligent or "smarter" than we are in terms of reasoning, but the levels of their potential for malignant mischief, even violence, are beyond what we can imagine.

We are warned to not interact or engage and resort to prescribed methods of defense, primarily specific systems of prayer that employ techniques involving the use of prayer, words of power, frequencies, and tones that discourage and repel them. We must examine what it is about us that is attracting them and opening the doors and portals in the first place. We must structure our lifestyle to vibrate at higher frequencies that are not resonant with these entities. We must affirm our gift of access into a dimension they have no access to, the Realm of Divinity. They are the textbook monsters of our worst nightmares. Their brain is reptilian. They are wired differently and lack empathy and remorse. They are not our toys. They are not a sport. They are not a video game to play!!!!

Hat Man

Reported Causes or Triggers of Sleep Paralysis

Diverse perspectives and accounts of known triggers reported by experiencers of Sleep Paralysis:

- Jinn attack (Nonphysical beings/energies);

- Toxic prayer projection;

- Medical diagnosis of physical disorders;

- Disrupted sleeping routines and habits;

- Substance abuse;

- Psychic (energetic) attack from others;

- Elemental/entity attack from others;

- Practitioner of sihr (black magic, witchcraft, sorcery);

- Psychic attack of the self, Spiritual Emergency, crisis of faith, guilt, self-hatred;

- Extreme occult studies, interests, practices, and preoccupations;

- Random (wrong place, wrong time, wrong people);

- Manipulations of family;

- Religious/Mystical beliefs and experiences;

- Jealousy;

- Location;

- Pain;

- PTSD (Post Traumatic Stress Disorder);

- Extreme emotional shock;

- Physical/Emotional trauma;

- Sudden loss;

- Grief;

- Extreme depression;

- Recent death of family or loved ones;

- Yoga practice;

- Meditation practice;

- Hypnosis;

- Mystical or magickal practice;

- Dirty, cluttered, disorderly house;

- House energetically unclean due to unholy activities occurring in the house;

- Spells, incantations, and curses could result in ghouls haunting a person;

- Sufferer's Earthly encounters with "spiritual" spouse;

- Bewitchment through eating while dreaming.

How Non-Physical Beings Shape-Shift and Appear to Us

The jinn kingdom is said to live between the 3rd and 4th dimensions, the same realms as some spirits, but they are not the same. They are not discarnate Earthly beings who once had a body and died. They are memetic beings without stable form and are not of the Earth element. They are plasma beings of the (smokeless) fire element. They can appear in a variety of densities. They are able to see us, but most of us cannot see them. Their fluctuating frequency gives them the ability to shapeshift and appear as any being they want to, known and unknown to the subject.

They may appear as:

- Smokeless fire;

- Clouds of smoke;

- Shadow people;

- Having four digits on each hand, cannot use thumbs, reptilian;

- Hat Man;

- Spiders and other insects;

- Some species are mistakenly identified as aliens;

- Many manifestations of interdimensional beings common in fairy tales;

- Piranha fish;

- Satan, Iblis;

- Figure made of smoke with a trail of smoke behind it;

- Hooded Figure, Angel of Death;

- Flashes of light and shadows in the peripheral vision;

- An energy with tentacles.

THE ARCHETYPE OF THE UNDEAD
FACELESS: The Sacred Relationship

APPENDIX FOUR

The Archetype of the Undead

This section is an excerpt from my book FACELESS: THE SACRED RELATIONSHIP, a mystical journey behind the masks of the many faces of our associations. The Undead is shared here as an in-depth overview and character analysis. It is a dangerous archetypal personality, with respect to its powerful influence and relevance to Psychic Self-Defense. An archetype is a model or prototype personality/character that filters down through the ages, as personalities that manifest across time, into our lives, and into our own being, without invitation. They will shapeshift through sociocultural, psychological, and even spiritual conditioning, and resurrect from being buried so deep into our collective subconscious; we believe we are the authors of who we are being and with whom we share our lives. As we study the effects of vampiric and parasitic energies that drain our Life Force and leave us flat-lining on the floor of a solitary confinement cell we once called our life, gasping for air, this character simply cannot be underestimated, considering the potential for irreparable damage. This influence of the Undead can result in toxic and disturbing physical manifestations that disrupt our lives and the lives of those around us. Particularly susceptible to these subtleties are children and animals. Often people experience phenomena that appear to be bad luck or poor health, only to find out that their misfortune was a construct of some Judas-spirited sorcerer, once believed to be loyal family and friend. It is important to identify, expel, and banish these causative, negative energies quickly and thoroughly.

The archetype of the Undead introduces itself to you as a council and a warning. It is a shadowy energy, murky, incredibly dangerous, and void of authentic social skills, with the modus operandi of a malignant narcissist or sociopath. This energetic 'type' is a closeted, low vibrational force with the predatory energy of a low-frequency, compassionless, shapeshifting monster. Void of both empathy and remorse for the damage left in the wake of their primary, two-faced objective is to leave behind them in their paths, broken spirits, hearts, and trust. Though it looks like malignant hatred, behind the mask, who they really hate the most is waiting for them in every mirror. Who needs to focus on invisible enemies when their memetic nature allows them to shift into the relationships and mirrors of our lives, looking out of familiar eyes for new mischief to make and new souls to take. This phenomenon qualifies as a Spiritual Emergency.

Zero
0
The Undead

Planetary Association - Mars/Pluto

Ruled by the Fifth Element - Ether

I speak for myself. Look into my steely eyes. I am the fixed, rigid gaze and cold icy touch of the departed ones from the physical plane though I am a sovereign and ancient being. I am that demon behind the eyes, behind the vertical pupils of the spirit possessed. I am the screams and fearful tears of the innocent ... the wonder that casts shadows over the pure of heart in their amazement at just how far and how low I will go to exercise my evil intentions. I cannot help myself. This abysmal energy has become my nature. When I awaken to a new day, it is overcast by utter darkness, for the Light is my destruction, and darkness is my abode. When I close my eyes, my devilish mind knows no rest, nor does it sleep, never ceasing its relentless pursuit of souls to capture and spirits to break. When a light shines and comes up on my radar, I cast my net and gather energy for my next attack. It is not personal. It is my nature.

I dare not look into the mirror because, as a vampire, I cast no reflection. My soullessness and emptiness make me unbearable to gaze upon. I have died, and there was no funeral, no burial, no mourning, no obituary, no grave, nothing. There was no evidence of my passing away, only the vacancy in my eyes and the emptiness and hunger of a soul that cannot be satisfied by positive energy ... only by the destruction of it. I am relentlessly driven by an appetite that cannot be sated by anything but the living death that I represent.

I stalk the living from my one-dimensional world. After I feed upon their energy and Life Force, I leave my victims feeling spiritually, emotionally, physically, and mentally violated and drained to the point of exhaustion. Overwhelmed by a perpetual state of fatigue, I suck the very life from their souls, and as they become weaker, I become stronger. I will leave you battling forces you have become too weak to defend yourselves against. I will leave you in ill and deteriorating health. I will leave you feeling broken and confused, for I have an investment in making you question your own judgment or making you behave in ways that other people would witness and write you off. I influence you to make the "mistake" of perceiving me as a figment of your imagination. If you go into denial of me and become unconscious of my presence, the damage I do to your life leaves you spiritually empty, without the desire or energy to even seek help.

I stalk your inner and outer world to determine your vulnerabilities, which are usually found in what you believe you desire or need. All I want to know is, "What do you desire?" I am well skilled at extending a well-baited hook to draw you into the realm of my attack by the manipulation of your own desires.

I am not happy, as I exist between worlds, held in bondage by my own welcome ignorance. I hate myself for my primal evil and insatiable appetite for destruction and take joy in the fallout. I am a critical faultfinder with such low self-esteem that I seek to bring down the positive levels of self-worth of everyone around me. I wear masks ... the perfect masks that create invitations and opportunities for myself among the undiscerning, the trusting, the innocent, the desperate, the needy, the gullible.

Even the mirror refuses to gaze upon my face. Perhaps, if I could see the ugliness of myself, I would gross myself out and be open to change. That is the cruelest of my realities. I cannot see myself except by the Light of day, which would burn me to ash. That is why it appears I have no conscience, cannot be shamed, will not change. I entertain myself with energies associated with unprecedented tragedy and grief.

I attack, not even realizing I am harming the people closest to me. All you can do is kill me in your mind. I am worse than a devil. What is your victory over my brand of evil? Your only victory over me is The God. If you seek to destroy me by my methods of destruction, you will have become me. I am not stupid, not troubled ... both are elements of the mental and emotional planes. I am a contagious spiritual disease ... a virus.

Recognition of the archetypal Undead represents a necessary stage in the evolution of the soul and spirit toward the Judgment of self. The energy of these Undead beings of many species will slither around undetected, below the radar, among the living, as a virulent, ethereal toxin. These are individuals whose consciousness and belief system are overruled by an *exclusive* attachment to the Physical Plane and material existence. In some cases, a higher awareness is in place, but stronger is their refusal to accept responsibility for the negative manifestations they intuitively know their energy is causing. If they were to acknowledge and observe the toxicity of their energy, they *might* not find it so easy to penetrate and poison the lives of other people for the shame that it should make them feel. Within a linear context, their refusal to submit to the Command of The Most High constitutes a spiritual death. These beings walk among us, appearing to be alive, yet they are dead. They represent a danger to themselves and others as they sniff around in the stench of their various stages of decomposition, looking for fresh innocent meat to devour. Closure, with regards to the death of the spirit or soul, is not ritualized in the same way as a death on the Physical Planes of existence.

This unconscious, living, yet, dead person is wired differently and rarely finds a proper resting place in the conscious world. The Undead are sentenced to directionless wandering as a shadow until he or she is awakened to the reality of his or her own true spiritual nature. At every twist and turn toward their awakening, in the resurrection of this dead person, they become accountable for the damage caused by their condition. They must willingly accept responsibility for the effect they are having on their own lives and the lives of others. They must seek atonement for the shadows they have cast.

This deadly archetype expresses the most impenetrable shadow side of human character, capable of gross, intentional, and unspeakable mischief. So often, the incredible Light or disparaging shadow aspect of the Undead is cast over the lives it touches, manifesting a full spectrum of composite characters. The Undead, in a reading/Inquiry, can appear as a voice of counsel, an enabler of fear-based behavior. They can run interference in the quality and depth of a spiritual relationship with the Higher Self, rendering the victim broken by feelings of helplessness and co-dependence.

As a rule, we are not vulnerable to these predators because we are open, compassionate, loving, trusting, and loyal. Somewhere in our consciousness, we have provided a place for attacks of all types to land. We become vulnerable when we operate on the lower, ego-based frequencies of fear, guilt, and absence of accountability. Fear is the opposite of love. Fear sends out powerful, manipulative messages, becoming the puppeteer that pulls the strings of our dance with fate. The guilt consciousness magnifies our faults and anchors the thought-form that "we are not good enough," rendering us emotionally needy and insecure.

The Undead represents advanced stages of spiritual corruption and destruction, born mature into spiritual ignorance. This energy is an airborne "free floater" in the realms of both the Astral and Material Planes. One must always be on the lookout for this wicked force and its attempts to creep into and bring ruin to every life it crosses at the intersection of any major change.

The Undead appear in the vapor of our every aspiration or inspiration, at will. We will all experience the energy of every one of the many archetypes of humanity at some point in our lives. The Undead will always be the storm cloud that threatens to rain on the positive experiences of everyone within his or her force field. The Undead will always be a precursor to negative change and seeks to pull out of the shadows the secrets we keep, even from ourselves.

The Undead is a warning, not an indictment. It either warns us to stop or proceed with a heightened sense of caution. It always means not just to pray but to remain in a state of perpetual prayer. A state of perpetual prayer takes on different forms in different traditions. Most spiritual traditions use prayer, chanting, or repetition of a positive mantra, sufficient to provide a spiritual shield of protection. We must be mindful as we examine our lives to determine if we are the target of malevolent attacks or influences. The most dangerous thing we can do is respond to this warning with fear. Fear is their nourishment. They feed upon it. Prayer is the neutralizer and healer.

The nature of the Undead is much like that of what we have seen ascribed to the classic mythical "vampire." They can be victims. Many are left soulless for having somehow been robbed of it. Though they may have been a victim, at some point, they are transformed into predators, perpetrators, murderers, and thieves of souls. They are attackers and destroyers of the spirits of other people whose souls and consciousness have sustenance enough to be a source of energy that feeds their insatiable appetite. Their targets, however, may have reasons for willingly opening the door and inviting them in. There may be feelings of neediness, instability, insecurity, or the perception of themselves to be weak in character, which inspires their feelings of guilt and worthlessness.

To have suffered the experience of trauma may have destabilized their spiritual resolve, or some unfortunate events or circumstances caused the Undead to fall into such a perilous situation that they are left open and vulnerable, fruit from a poisonous tree, ripe for the picking. The most effective defense against them is to never let them into your energy field in the first place. Avoid involving them in your affairs to the extent they can get close enough to do great damage. Feed them with a long-handled spoon. Better yet, don't feed them at all. We must examine ourselves and find the shadows of our *own* spirit that attracted them and then heal that condition. These are birds of prey. They feed on dead things. Determine what it is they identified as dead within you. Make your life depend on healing that spiritual void and becoming someone new, maybe even new to you ... your True Self.

The Undead are possessive, jealous, controlling, arrogant, selfish, empty shells. Often, they are hostile under the passive-aggressive guise of wolves in sheep's clothing. Fear is a weapon and tool for the taming of the intended victim. They want to know what a potential victim wants and fears. They function at the emotional level of a spoiled, self-centered toddler. Their behavior tends to be childlike, mischievous, and unbecoming of an adult. Consequently, they are abysmally lonely because these are not attractive qualities and will eventually cost them everything and everyone they believe they care about or covet. Loneliness is a powerful energy that keeps them fueled on their deadly prowl. They are bored and frustrated to the point of implosion. They hate themselves. Soon they find they have driven every positive energy and force out of their lives, as all things positive are sent running for their souls. After such loss, bloodthirsty and alone, they are right back on the hunt for new victims.

The Undead often use tools of isolation, repetition, sensual deprivation, spiritual starvation, and (re)languaging, or (re)culturing to mesmerize and disable their intended prey. They have nothing of substance to offer and seek to destroy or cut off any source of spiritual sustenance to their victim. They seek to take control of the lives of their victims, assuring that they have a convenient and constant source of nourishment for themselves as they go on with their lives, leaving their prey without one.

They show up among our families, in our relationships, in the workplace. They hide behind the forced smiles of counterfeit friendships and can be hidden beneath a shallow embrace of love. They are everywhere. And as we draw toward the end of a major time cycle, their efforts and energies are stronger than ever because they need more of that Life Force they seek to deplete … and closer proximity to that Light they seek to extinguish. Their attacks constitute the making of more undead as they spread their contagion. We will ultimately find many of their characteristics becoming a part of our own as we have fallen under their spell.

They are plagued by fantasy-oriented sexual issues, which they perceive to be completely beyond their control, in behavioral patterns of addiction. They are comfortable with harsh judgments of others, while they have enough skeletons in their closets to fill a large cemetery, with the most haunting being the ones they keep in their minds. Sex, among other drugs, can become an addiction, obsession, or compulsion that only instant gratification (with the option of discarding the victim) would satisfy. These appetites are insatiable. In the face of accountability, they shrink from responsibility for the consequences of their actions following their frequent voracious feeding frenzies.

Being the victim of this narcissistic hatred is a confusing experience because when confronted with their behavior, observe:

- They are masters of the "blame game." It will always be your fault;

- They convince you they celebrate your success when what they actually want, and will construct, is your failure;

- They will sabotage and ruin every special occasion. They dampen the experience of whatever gives you pleasure or makes you happy;

- They do not encourage activities that will contribute to your skillset, health, or your future prosperity;

- They will never teach you anything that serves your higher good;

- When they feel they are losing control over you, or find their mask is slipping, they will, in subtle ways, conduct a smear campaign against you to separate and isolate you from anyone that could help you;

- They play the "victim" and seek to make the target of their attack responsible for their own suffering;

- Their reprehensible behavior can manifest as arrogance, cruelty, and a lacking of empathy and compassion;

- They condescend and demean their victim as being weak and deserving of their suffering;

- They see themselves as superior to others;

- They exaggerate and inflate their accomplishments and achievements and exalt themselves over others, seeing themselves as examples or models to be emulated;

- They are spiritually empty though they may claim to profess some kind of spiritual belief.

Once they are discovered, and attempts are made to exorcise them from our lives, they become more vicious than ever, determined to control and disable the victim on all levels. This is the point at which survival depends on spiritual fortitude. We must affirm that nothing happens outside of the Will and Permission of the Almighty, Creator of everything. If we harbor strong feelings of malice against them, even though they have earned it, we open ourselves up to physical and spiritual disease, issued through the portals of our anger and hatred of them. We observe, in bewilderment, the ruins they have left our lives in and the evil-spirited joy of victory they have taken from our suffering. They have no sense of fairness or mercy, so our cries and appeals fall upon blind eyes and deaf ears.

Would-be victims have a weapon the Undead did not bargain for … Belief, faith, and respect for Divine providence and protection. If they were able to transcend the core nature of their mischievous inclinations, they would not have to act the way they do to sustain their bleak lives. But isn't that like saying, "Spiders would not weave webs if they only had belief, faith, and respect for Divinity?" Spiders could meditate and pray for victory over web weaving, after which the spiders would ultimately perish for seeking to operate outside of their nature. We human beings are not spiders, do not have the nature of spiders, and do not get such a pass. We have a choice. There is something about us that is Essentially Divine. With that knowledge comes great responsibility.

A victim of the Undead is often defenseless within the margins of their own emotions. Emotions such as hatred, greed, jealousy, envy, anger, depression, rejection, and grief weaken our immune system and leave us vulnerable to attack. Spiritual discipline and learning to be in command of our frequencies is our only protection from them. If we find our standards slipping, STOP, and immediately, fully engage in a spiritual practice that will help to manifest balance and equilibrium through complete submission to the Will and Love of The God. A sound spiritual practice serves as a shield of Light that becomes our armor of protection against such spiritual attacks. It mystically closes portals of entry through which energetic harm may be issued in by forces such as the energies of the Undead.

The personalities of the Undead are inauthentic and fraudulent. Sometimes feigned kindness or generosity masks their angry, domineering, and hateful spirit. They are flamboyant with their comfortable acceptance of the deadly sins as a welcome part of their lifestyle; pride vs. humility, envy vs. love, wrath and anger vs. kindness, sloth vs. zeal, greed vs. generosity, gluttony vs. faith and temperance, lust vs. self-control, and vengeance vs. forgiveness.

The archetypal Undead can manifest as malefic spirits trapped in bodies, and therefore, these people are very much in touch with the spirit world. They hide under many disguises. They have a certain charisma, but just beneath the surface of that, they tend to be mean-spirited, brutal, cruel, inhumane, sadistic, vengeful, spiteful, and vindictive. Our efforts against them often end in disaster, especially if we do not understand the nature of what we are dealing with.

As we observe a person known to us as possessing behaviors that suddenly change from a kind, gentle, and humble person into an arrogant, mean, and violent person, it can be a sign that this person is either an attacker or under the influence of an attack. *Prayer* is the wooden stake that must be driven through the heart of the Undead. The Love of The God is the only defense against them. They fear the Sun and are burned to ash by it. Exposing them to the Sun in the form of the Light of The God is both their destruction and redemption. To destroy them is to redeem them. The only way to destroy them is to cause them to examine their own nature and seek the Light that will not only burn but purify their hearts. They must seek to annihilate the "self" that they are in order to become the "Self" they have the potential to be, after surrender to the intense Light and unfathomable depths of the Mercy of The God. To submit their ego self to becoming "slain in the Spirit of The God" could result in their surrendering and redirecting of their negative, self-destructive path.

They are not to be mistaken for those who have fallen into the Abyss. To fall into the Abyss is often the result of spiritual consciousness reaching critical mass and crashing. This type of crash or meltdown can often precede or follow a profound spiritual epiphany. The aftermath can manifest as anything from fluctuating, roller-coaster personality disorders to a complete shift of energy and disruption of the psyche. Some people survive. Some do not. When someone is trapped within the framework of such a spiritual crisis, they can display the symptoms of the Undead. This is sometimes the only way, in the natural process of spiritual rebirth, that a person can restore balance, cleanse, and heal vital energies. They save themselves only by surrendering their will to the Will of The Most High, The God. The Undead have seen the Light and chosen to succumb to the shadows.

The quickest way to identify the Undead is to observe their unyielding, relentless desire to manipulate their victims into giving up control of their own lives, to free up more of their Life Force to be drained. They desire to exalt themselves over other people to support the illusion that they are still alive and well. They are naturally jealous and competitive and cannot stand to see other people experience the happiness that they are incapable of feeling. There is an ugliness about them, no matter how physically handsome or beautiful they may be. They are soul-satisfied by enslaving the spirit of others and occupying their lives. They have no lives of their own and entertain their boredom with mischief that can leave a strong soul in mortal danger.

They have a strong investment in making their victims see themselves differently than who they really are, until the victim becomes transformed into the negative image of their projections. The Undead want to become the mirrors that show the reflections of their victims. The victim begins to see their own reflection through empty eyes and identify as the image conjured by the eyes of their beholders. They want their victims to judge and define themselves by their standards, which leaves the victim feeling like "nothing," sitting like a pet dog waiting for a bone of self-esteem to gnaw on.

At this point, if we find ourselves the victim, and I think we have all had this experience at some point, we must pray and run for our lives. Pray as though our very souls are approaching the gates of hell, and we see a detour. Many suicidal thoughts and behaviors, mental conditions, chronic physical ailments, depression, and even deaths, are the result of the vicious spiritual attacks of the Undead. On the subject of suicide, I recommend reading the section "Is it Even Possible to Kill One's Self" from my book, THE TIMELESS NOW: Healing from Grief and Loss. These walking dead people are dangerous and must be approached from a position of spiritual strength, not fear. That is often difficult after they have skillfully depleted our spirits of the positive energy necessary to defend ourselves against them. When we have approached the awareness of forgetting who we really are, we are in the most danger of succumbing to their attack.

If we choose to look at it from another perspective, we can emerge from these attacks stronger than ever. We must release our attachment to shallow, vanity-based judgments and acknowledge that we are not defeated, that we actually *are* "nothing." Our *only* existence is in the Light that we are and The God that we have within. We then seek refuge in our inner Temple and Sanctuary where That Which Created us abides, waiting there to administer a healing. Often, our own pride, arrogance, or ignorance increases the damage of the attack, as we hold ourselves in false esteem by the standards of the physical world.

A person operating from such a demonic force field must be examined for the cause of it, as far back as their early childhood. Something happened that caused them to become such dangerous hypocrites and parasites. Even in the committing of some of the most abhorrent acts of depravity and violence, they can be made to see some reflection of themselves and become disgusted, yet their uncontrollable impulses cannot easily be cured of these behaviors. "Do they have a soul?" would be a good question to ask. The difference between them and the physically dead is that it is possible to resurrect them from the grave of mental and spiritual bondage. As a mercy and gift of The God, they may be made to see themselves and how they are behaving. They may seek to resurrect themselves from the grave of their own ignorant choices.

The Undead must have a soul within because if we say they do not, it is a contradiction of the Laws and terms of the Divinity of humanity. The question is, "What type of soul is this?" People don't commonly hang around cemeteries trying to resurrect the dead unless they have some Jesus/Lazarus complex. That is why, without intervention, we can be defenseless against them. It is almost impossible for our souls to understand them. What we cannot understand, we cannot effectively defend ourselves against. It is especially difficult to identify them as they can look so normal, as long as you do not look into their eyes or their hearts. Many do not act out of hatred. They do it for the enjoyment. They do it because it is the nature they have assumed, and it fulfills them.

Exposing them to the Light of The God and sincere prayer is the best weapon we have with which to defend ourselves, and that is all that we can do. It is also the *worst* and most effective thing we can do to them, without jeopardizing our own soul by becoming them. It is like shining sunlight upon a vampire. We must close our doors, lock, and guard them. We must keep the Light on as we call upon the Great Light for guidance and salvation and withdraw from them for the sake of our spiritual lives. We are not to withdraw as in a cowardly act but withdraw and seek refuge in the Loving Embrace of The Divine One. If we are running from them and they are in pursuit, we are running them into the arms of their own destruction. If there is a bully harassing you, and you have a friend on your side who is powerful enough to destroy the bully, the attacker is forced to concede. To choose the energy of the Divine Embrace for protection and refuge directs them toward their own obliteration in their relentless pursuit.

Encounters with shadows such as these are usually designed to push our spiritual strength to a new level. It is a rite of passage or an initiatory experience. We may be the ones that were chosen to coax them to open their eyes, look within, and ask if they are comfortable with the life they are living. They must see themselves or be touched by The God in some way. They are wired differently, and the shame/guilt factor will not change them. They can even feel guilt, but it won't stop them, not until they look in the mirror and be repulsed by what they see. At that point, it is not just about bad behavior. It is about self-definition. The question becomes, "Who do you choose to be?

Our transcendence of their influences is a way of running them into the light where they must either choose that light or perish. As they pursue us, we seek refuge in that same Light that will destroy them. This retreat from their presence will serve to neutralize and transmute their energetic wickedness into Light, along with their entire being, if they resist. We may have to leave loved ones behind, trapped in the intricate web of the matrix. We would be required to sever our attachments and never look back at our tears, turning into a trail of salt. It may be our responsibility to help them free themselves by placing them in front of a mirror. This mirror is not the mirror of our judgment but a mirror of Divine Reflection and Revelation.

We must strive to avoid an evil versus evil scenario by casting judgment and damnation upon them. There are manners in which we can seek their destruction and cause our own. The Undead can do damage that extends beyond the world of the perishable, and inflict wounds that transcend the physical form, leaving scars upon every soul they touch. If they can tempt us into lowering our vibration to the level of theirs, they have accomplished their objective. Their conscious or subconscious objective is to crush and rob our spirit of its positive Life Force. Remain aware. Remain in prayer. We must never forget who we are.

Gaining Control
Over Sleep Paralysis Events

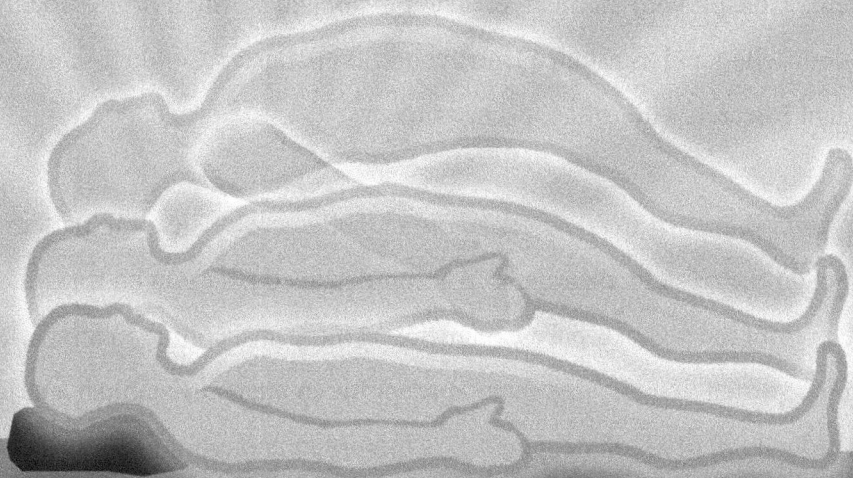

Gaining Control Over Sleep Paralysis Events

All information in this section is relevant to the experience of Sleep Paralysis. It is imperative to incorporate the knowledge of these common traditional practices into your daily lifestyle. The following are some that are *specifically* important.

Sever ties with the attacker. If you feel confirmed in the identity of the attacker, the first step toward ending the attack is to cut all conscious or subconscious links with the attacker. A change in environment may be necessary. Gifts that were exchanged should be disposed of, as well as all shared items. This may include gifts, clothing, furniture, or jewelry (especially anything made of silver). As challenging as it may be under the circumstances, we must cleanse our own energy field of anger, judgment, and hatred.

Document every detail of each occurrence of Sleep Paralysis. Your documentation will reveal what your triggers are. As these triggers are identified, avoid them. Consult with medical, psychological, and spiritual professionals to provide counseling and assistance if the condition persists. Conduct your own independent research with diligent discernment.

Train yourself to sleep regular hours. Rollercoaster sleeping patterns can cause any number of sleep disorders. A sleep-deprived person who transitions into REM sleep from the point of pure exhaustion is more susceptible to attack. Napping is reported to make one more susceptible to attack. Establish a strict regimen around the ritual of sleeping. It is important enough for our overall well-being to be the focal point of our attention when considering holistic health.

Embrace a prayer and meditation practice that is aligned with your highest spiritual intentions. Practice relaxation techniques and consciousness-expanding guided meditation for spiritual protection.

Do protection prayers before meditation and before sleeping. Never go into deep meditation or go to sleep without offering a prayer aligned with the tradition of your choice.

Sleep on your side. Do not sleep on your back (supine position). It is important to train yourself to sleep on your side. It is suggested that a pocket large enough to accommodate a tennis ball may be sewn onto the back of your sleeping garment to discourage sleeping in the supine position. This becomes important to know if Sleep Paralysis is a recurrent problem.

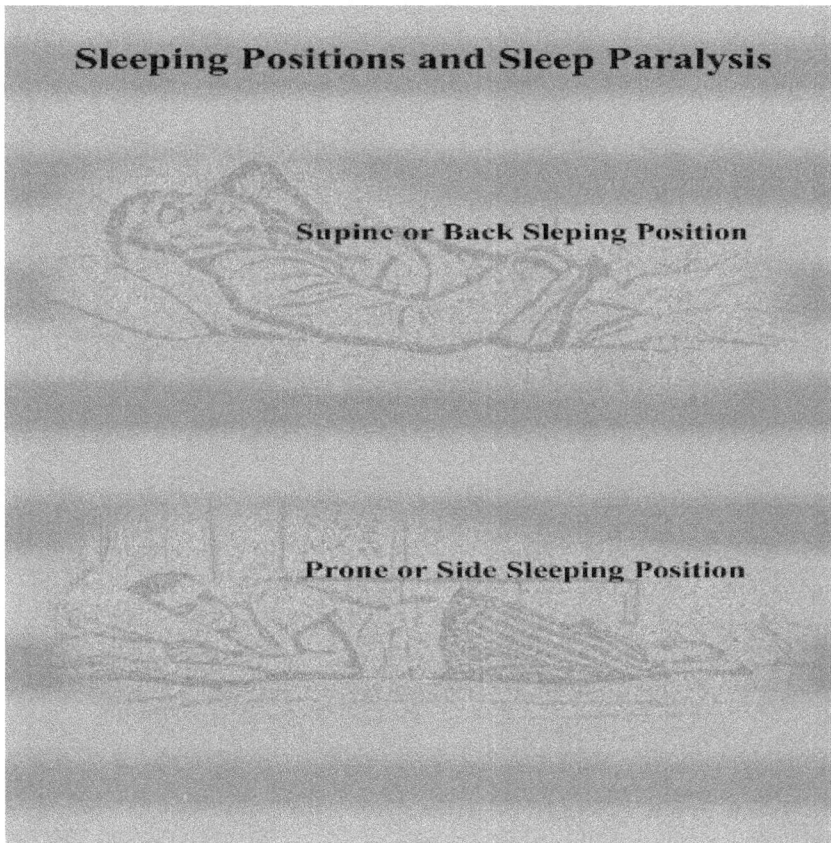

Sleeping Positions and Sleep Paralysis

Supine or Back Sleping Position

Prone or Side Sleeping Position

A pocket large enough to accommodate a tennis ball may be sewn onto the back of your sleeping garment to discourage sleeping in the supine position.

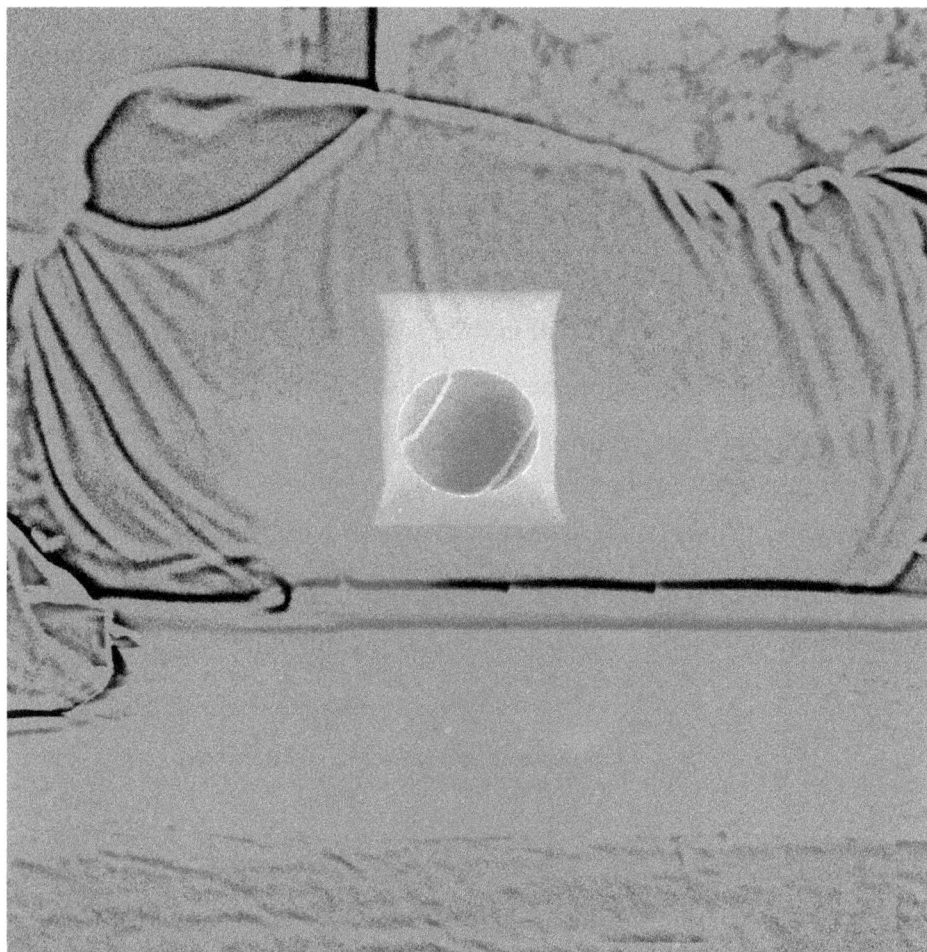

Perform a cleansing bath before prayer and meditation. Prepare a bath of warm water mixed with energy cleansing herbs and sea salt. Stir in with your right hand, infusing the water with the positive energy of sincere prayer, according to your own spiritual beliefs. Hold a focal point of intention as meditation. Air dry your body after the bath is complete. I have used sage, sea salt, baking soda, lavender, lemon, lime, rosemary, peppermint (Yerba Buena), thyme, pine, copal, Florida water, and eucalyptus. These and many other herbs, oils, and scents are available in metaphysical supply shops, Botanicas, and over the internet.

Praying, meditating, or chanting under a stream of flowing water, such as a shower, can augment the energy of your communicated intention. Before and after a cleansing bath or shower, *always* cleanse the bathing area with a mixture of water and ammonia, paying particular attention to mirrors and reflective surfaces. It is advisable to use a spray bottle for spraying other areas of the home and workplace, around entrances, windows, corners, and drains to dispel or discourage negative energies. Keep all drains covered when not in use.

Sleep in a clean and orderly environment. We must keep our sleeping area free of clutter and anything that would distract us from sleeping well. Before going to bed, take a spiritual cleansing bath to purify the aura. Information on how this is done can be easily found on the Internet. There are so many traditions that generously make profound wisdom available on spiritual protection, healing, and cleansing. Choose one that resonates with your energy. Make time to meditate and pray. Burn sage, basil, sweet grass, Palo Santo, frankincense, and myrrh. Be mindful of the type of art you display, avoiding images of people, animals, and statues. Cover all reflective surfaces, especially mirrors.

Study and practice Feng Shui. It is an Eastern philosophy and system that can bring harmony to our lives through the art of placement. It operates based on the management of the flow of Qi or Chi energy in our environment to enhance the overall experiences of our lives. It can represent the difference between traveling upstream against the current and going with the flow. Sometimes a remedy for energetic dreamtime drama is as simple as changing the position of the bed (always with the head in the East), or the colors, fabrics, and scents we choose. The sleeping area must be held to an energetic standard parallel to that of a prayer room. The most sacred space in our home is where we sleep.

It is worth committing to a lifetime of this fascinating study of energy and its management. A cursory approach to this knowledge is unwise. We cheat ourselves if we use this knowledge only to stomp out spiritual or energetic brush fires. Incorporate positive habits into your lifestyle to maintain energetic balance. Exercise impeccable discernment in choosing life paths and teachers. Stay centered in the knowledge and acceptance of who you really are. See everything through the filter of That.

Censor media exposure: Avoid horror movies, violent shows, video games, and literature with disturbing content. Do not allow political and social mayhem to lower your vibration into the realm of extreme anger, violence, and hatred. This is particularly true at bedtime and mealtime. After a dramatic shift of cultural norms, one of the worst continuing horror stories is the news, with its constant graphic coverage of horrific events. News has been turned into a twenty-four-hour media circus. All they break for is one million commercials. Technology is such that raw footage of every graphic detail of every tragedy and vulgarity on the planet is available in an instant and in real time, twenty-four hours a day, often delivering the experience of first responders to a layperson. To be caught in the loop of this type of repetitive, overwhelming, sensationalized, desensitizing, and conditioning hypnosis has a draining effect on our energy. It is not healthy to allow it to go on and on in our homes, cars, and workplace like white noise, just because they are broadcasting, and there is a screen to show it on. It is vital to stay abreast of what is going on in the world around us, especially in these volatile times. However, we must be intentional about keeping a healthy balance of positive energy flowing as we affirm that "Life is good … even now."

Avoid falling asleep with the television on. Our subconscious minds are aware on some level of television programming heard while sleeping. We can actually excel at learning a foreign language by listening to recordings of that language being spoken or taught while we are asleep. This amazing ability of ours can be used in our favor. It can work against our peace of mind as well. We do not want to be submerged in a sea of subliminal commercial messages and manipulative programming as we sleep. It is generally not recommended to have a television in your sleeping area unless it is enclosed in a cabinet or somehow covered.

Be mindful regarding your choice of music. Hypnotic rhythms and music can induce trance states. Certain music contains binaural beats that can be a trigger for an Out of Body Experience.

Place an uncovered glass of water by the bedside near the head of the bed before sleeping. The subject comes up again and again in conversations regarding Psychic Self-Defense. There are spirit, elemental, and energetic entities that can become mesmerized by the water, seduced into it, and trapped there. Do not drink the water. Flush the water down the toilet with a banishing prayer immediately upon awakening.

Study the significance and function of a dreamcatcher and hang one from the ceiling over your bed. The placement of a dreamcatcher suspended above the bed is a tradition of some Indigenous First Nation tribes, prescribed for managing nightmares and sleep disturbances. The webbing inside of the circular wooden frame filters out bad dreams and negative energies, trapping them in the netting until dawn breaks and sweeps them away. The hole in the middle opens to positive, healing thoughts and energies. The "Eye" in the center must be ritually opened and blessed. It, like any spiritual tool, is activated by being blessed and charged with prayerful intention. Otherwise, it is just decoration.

Place a "dream pillow" under your pillow filled with sea salt, fresh fragrant herbs, and sacred items. The alchemical properties can serve as a deterrent to negative energy while improving your sleep experience. It must be activated by being blessed and charged with prayerful intention.

Herbs and other items for your dream pillow: sage, garlic, rosemary, dried basil, nettle, mandrake root, black pepper, mint, eucalyptus, cloves, dill, anis, aloe, lavender, cedar, palo santo, salt, sweet grass, black tourmaline/obsidian, bay leaves, parchment paper, red marker to inscribe protection symbols, sacred scriptures, and prayers. The contents of a dream pillow vary according to tradition, tribe, and personal preference.

Grid your home: Refer to the section, *Methods of Spiritual Protection*, regarding "blessing" your home." Blessing your home is a wise undertaking whether or not you are experiencing Sleep Paralysis or any other type of spiritual phenomena. There are effective energy cures that can be set in place around your work, home, and sleeping area. If you are committed to a disciplined protocol regarding the cleansing and care of crystals, "gridding" your home is a powerful tool in Psychic Self-Defense. You do not have to be involved in any mystical practice to benefit from crystal gridding in your home, especially in areas where you meditate, pray, and sleep. "Gridding" is an involved process of creating an energetic network or grid of crystals and semi-precious stones positioned in strategic locations and configurations in and around the gridded area. They are situated in such a way that they are energetically connected and in communication with one another for one common purpose, providing a force field of protection. Gridding serves to transmute lower vibrations and frequencies and amplify positive energy. Gridding is an element of Feng Shui, energetically influencing balance and harmony in the home and workplace.

Gridding cannot be taught in a cursory way. It is worth the time and effort to pursue this valuable wisdom. I have heard of using mothballs, camphor tablets, sea salt wrapped in tea leaves, ammonia, or turpentine in the corners of rooms to enhance and cleanse the energy field of the home and workplace, warding off negative energies. Whatever symbols or elements of protection you put in place in the gridding of your home, make sure they are kept out of the way of children and pets. There are many traditions around the world to pull valuable information from regarding protective gridding. Study and practice those that resonate most with your own energy.

Keep your bedroom décor basic: Avoid placing statues, masks, and images of any living beings in the bedroom or house in general. Remove reflective surfaces. Avoid photographs, mirrors, televisions, and computer monitors in the bedroom. They can operate like an inter-dimensional portal.

Keep your home well lit: Use light sensor nightlights throughout your home to discourage shadows, particularly in the corners of rooms, entrances, and hallways.

Exercise regularly. Martial Arts, Tai Chi, Chi Gong, and Yoga are a few of the most helpful disciplines for maintaining the body's defense against assaults in both the physical and non-physical worlds. These practices promote a strong and healthy electromagnetic energy field, cleansed of unwholesome energies.

Eat Healthy. Avoid eating things that will disturb your nutritional balance and affect sound sleep. Avoid consumption of stimulants, toxins, alcohol, intoxicants, consciousness-altering substances, sugar, caffeine, and animals. Avoid eating too close to bedtime.

Exercise extreme caution using pharmaceutical and over-the-counter drugs: Research the side effects of any pharmaceutical drugs you may have to take. Avoid anything that can be replaced by natural supplements or lifestyle changes that are equally effective. Consult with your physician and discuss holistic solutions. Many prescriptions and over-the-counter drugs are known to scramble our frequencies enough to leave us with our psychic guard down and unable to defend ourselves. At the very least, our judgment can become impaired, and reasoning may be rendered faulty and confused. The worst-case scenario would be short-circuiting the fragile connection between our physical body and our body of consciousness, triggering chemically-induced Out of Body experiences. It is not rocket science to recognize the danger of losing or compromising that connection. It is vital to know that if it should ever happen, the same thing that connected us to this body, on this plane of existence, is sufficient to protect us and guide us back to safety.

Manage stress levels. Consider it a priority in life to manage stress and anger in ways you find relaxing and enjoyable. Get out into nature more. Pray more. Play more. Listen to music. Dance more. Avoid situations and people that trigger stress and anger. At the onset of a Sleep Paralysis Event, the most important thing to remember is that you are not left alone to defend yourself. That which created us is sufficient to protect us.

Call out the Name of The God three times. It is important to acknowledge the spiritual tradition that resonates with your soul's frequency and The God of your highest understanding. Say, "I command you, in the Name of (your manner of addressing The Most High) to be gone." I choose to refrain from using names specific to only one particular language, tradition, religion, or culture. If I am speaking English, or depending on my spiritual path, I may say in a banishing, "On the blood of Jesus or Yeshua, Yahweh, or Jah, I command you to be gone!" A person standing next to me may speak Spanish, and that person might say, "Por la sangre de Jesus Cristo, te mando que vayas de aqui!" The God and prophets of The God are called by different names in many different languages, according to many diverse traditions, but all respond to the unspoken language of Spirit.

Banish with authority any spiritual intrusion with the same energy you would if it were embodied and trespassed into your space. We stand up with courage and confidence, knowing that we are Divinely protected. We pray. We chant. We read selected passages from sacred scriptures. We will never have to wonder when a spiritual problem requires our attention. We will know. Dedicated spiritual discipline and practice is the only way to avoid the annoying task of stomping out the many brushfires of spiritual warfare.

Incorporate suggested methods of Psychic Self-Defense into a well-balanced, enjoyable lifestyle. Now, more than ever, these topics have gone mainstream, and help is easy to find. A support group of like-minded people is easy to find. Information over the Internet is easy to find. Classes and services are easy to find. Exercise the utmost of spiritual discernment in your choices of teachers, studies, and associates. Be mindful to resist falling into worship of the *process* as a crutch for understandable fear. Rebuke fear and maintain a high vibration.

Most people are attached to the idea of being in total control of the body and experience a spontaneous Out of Body Experience" (OBE) as an assault, an attack, or a violation, regardless of its cause. Most disturbing is the fact that episodes of Sleep Paralysis may be associated with spirit activity of low-frequency beings or entities called by many names from diverse cultures and traditions. Some of the entities I am most familiar with are called jinn, duppies, haints, press down ghosts, and dream stalkers, depending on the perspective of the culture, language, and belief system that describes them. This phenomenon is referred to by some as being "ridden by a witch or hag." Elemental beings (fire, water, air, earth, ether) from the outer and inner planes often appear as unusual physical manifestations involving the elements they represent. These entities are often associated with the practice of many forms of occultism but can, just as easily, arise from the practice of mainstream religion and spirituality, occurring consciously or subconsciously through the projection of highly emotional energy. Some are even conjured from the scriptures of sacred books.

We all have the innate ability to exit the body vehicle, in consciousness, and return to it intact. We do that every night in sleep. We disengage. We travel. We "dream" of experiences that may even have some relevance in our lives after we return. Follow the silver cord that connects us to that warm body of our temporary dwelling. We are also able to achieve the Dreamtime experience in deep states of certain types of meditation.

Sleep Paralysis involves the disengaging of the non-physical body from the physical body, much like what occurs in an Out of Body Experience (OBE). Sensations at the onset of a complete separation of the astral body from the physical body depend on the state of mind of the experiencer. Each unique episode carries a revelation of its own significance.

Protection Practices to Study and Incorporate into your Spiritual Discipline

I do not practice or support one spiritual tradition over another. This text offers experiential pointers and is not meant to "teach" you, only share research that will suggest how to find the help and support you need. Use the utmost of discernment in choosing a trusted spiritual professional, a Raqi (healer), according to your preferred tradition of practice and belief.

Some protection practices include but are not limited to;

- Discussing that you are experiencing Sleep Paralysis Events with your doctor might help you to receive help preventing future episodes. There are physical problems that have symptoms similar to spiritual problems. You should always consult with a medical professional when your sleep disruption and deprivation has begun to affect your life;

- Prayers recited out loud or in the mind from your most resonant spiritual tradition;

- Ruqya – (Recital of a prescribed, very specific form and system of healing prayer);

- Zikr – (remembrance), A system of repetition of mantra;

- Repetition of AUM, OM Mantra, silent or from a vibratory focal point inside of head; (See chapter on Repetitive Prayer)

- Repetition and contemplation of the HU Mantra (See Chapter on Repetitive Prayer);

- Zikr from a silent vibratory focal point inside of the head;

- Repetition of commanding words of spiritual power;

- Meditation beads (mala) to count repetitions of mantras;

- Repetition of Al-Falaq and Al-Nas from the Quran;

- Repetition of Ayat Al-Kursi - the Throne Verse is believed to grant spiritual or physical protection. It is often recited before setting out on a journey and before going to sleep;

- Repetition of The Lord's Prayer, 23rd Psalms, Psalms 91;

- Limpia (Spiritual Cleansing) of person, home, office, car;

- Seek help from TRUSTED and VETTED spiritual professionals Shaman (Curandera, Healer), Raqi (Exorcist), Priest, Lightworker;

- Avoid locations that are believed to be haunted by evil spirits, satanic or supernatural beings;

- Bless or Consecrate homes, buildings, and grounds prior to occupancy;

- Avoid consciousness-altering substances;

- The best shield of protection … DO GOOD. Forgive and repent from wrongdoing;

- Be mindful of shifts in the energies of your life. Many cases of illness, misfortune, imprisonment, school and professional failure, family breakups, and mental and personality disturbances are due to sorcery (sihr), at the hands of a person who practices witchcraft (sahir);

- Ruqya (exorcism), associated with reparation of damage caused by jinn attack and/or possession, black magick (sihr), or the evil eye (ayn hasad);

- Guard your associations. The most malefic type of evil eye is the one made by a group with a common intention;

- Whether or not the intention is malevolent, when people talk about or project energy upon someone, about their success, their beauty, their strength, or anything that could be envied or coveted, the subject's energy can be broken. They may suffer reversals of fortune, physical illness, and emotional slaughter.

- Cupping (Al-Hijama) is an ancient therapy used by many traditions to treat and cure many physical and spiritual problems. Some believe that if your problem is just physical, cupping can improve general health. Some say it is like a vacuum cleaner that eats negative energies. Consult with a medical professional to determine whether or not this practice is right for you;

- Avoid sleeping in total darkness;

- Do not wear outdoor shoes inside the home;

- Wash your feet before entering your home, or at least before you go to bed;

- Study the Yogic practice of conscious sleep and Samadhi - subconscious state, for a deeper understanding of methods of rest and balance of body, mind, and spirit;

- Some have declared order using a technique of disassociating themselves from their physical body during an attack and shifting from a body/mind perspective to a spontaneous transition into the essential, non-physical I AM perspective. The disassociated non-physical form, a sovereign entity, is a third-party objective "witness" that can have the clarity of mind to trigger the physical body to be receptive to merge consciousness with form and shake off the paralysis state. Consciously disassociating from form reveals the power of the True Self to be able to ground and merge, effectively causing the physical body to return to a fully conscious state;

- They cannot enter into the Realm of Divinity, which we have access to in absolute surrender to Divine Will, through prayer, meditation, dedicated spiritual practice, and Permission;

- Do not seek entry into the Realm of Divinity *only* in a fear-based attack/defense scenario. If you are under attack, seek refuge. If you are not under attack, seek refuge. If your spiritual discipline is committed and consistent, you will not be as much of a target.

- Do not fall into worship of the "cures," e.g., amulets, charms, incantations, talismans, taweez (Urdu word meaning amulet or charm), statues, or images. There is only one cure … That Which Created all.

- Shirk (širk) is idolatry, i.e., deification or worship of, association, or establishing "partners" with anyone or anything besides the One God.

Nothing to Prove

We must not drain our positive energy by arguing with, trying to convince, or defending ourselves against people who do not share our spiritual belief system. The fact that you are reading this book is evidence that you recognize the value of understanding the practice of Psychic Self-Defense with regard to the experience of Sleep Paralysis. Whatever the reason for this study, it is personal. Seek medical, spiritual, and psychological advice from a well-vetted professional. These are typically not conversations over coffee with a casual spa buddy, coworker, or classmate ... not even family, in most cases. Unfortunately, the dominance of one-dimensional logic, blind reason, and fear have suppressed many of our most basic mediums for the transmission of sacred knowledge. It is a waste of time to try to break through the stone walls of fear and judgment of others. There is an old saying, "A man convinced against his will, is of the same opinion still."

We do not owe anyone an explanation of the deeper levels of our spirituality or of our mystical or paranormal experiences. Mystical experiences are a natural element of our awakening. We must not leak vital energy giving too much attention to the occurrence of naturally rising phenomena. It is to be expected. These phenomena rise up and pass away into forgetfulness. It is the "I" that remains. It is the "I" (the essential, unborn, undying, Eternal Self), within the little I of our linear perceptions, that observes these phenomena, unchanging. It is worth the effort to rise above the need to lose ourselves in seeking the validation and approval of others.

It is generally unwise to feel too free to share personal spiritual experiences with others, even people we think we can trust. These soul-bearing revelations may create gaping chasms in the energy of our relationships, and may even threaten employment and reputation. Inappropriate openness can give "frenemies" potentially deadly ammunition to use against you and can taint the experience of the emergence of our new Light body Self, the "I in I," the I AM. For this reason, certain mystical studies have traditionally been held as well-guarded secrets, confined to discussion within the boundaries of the mystery schools and secret societies, shared only among fellow initiates. A wise person guards their tongue as they guard their life. In other words, unless we are speaking with a professional of considerable expertise in such matters, toward solutions, it's a good idea to keep our personal business to ourselves. Our spiritual experiences are as sacred as a prayer. Honor the privacy of that sacredness.

If you reveal your secrets to the wind,
you should not blame the wind
for revealing them to the trees.

~ Khalil Gibran ~

There will be experiences we will have that will be so sacred to us that we may not be able to explain nor describe, not to mention prove! The absence of proof is not proof of absence!

For people who trust your experience,
no evidence is required.
For people who doubt what you have actually experienced,
no amount of evidence will convince them.

We must pray for the strength to learn how to just let it go as we learn to pick our fights. The biggest mistake we can make is to allow our ego to become involved. The subject matter within the realm of spirit defies superficial science and mundane reason if one chooses to see it that way. Everyone evolves in his or her own time. We are not to rush or force issues regarding the spiritual evolution of another person, violating their God-given right to Free Will.

There will always be those who will seek to ridicule others for their differences. There will always be people who will frown upon the spiritual beliefs and experiences of other people in attempts to make them feel crazy, foolish, insane, wicked, and/or deluded, no matter the path or the pathless. Allow for the subtleties of the Universe to whisper into the consciousness of the soul of every individual as it sees fit. Everything happens in The God's time. It is not cosmically correct to laugh, tease, or gloat when whispers turn to screams and shouts, startling people out of their denial or lack of knowledge. *I told you so*" behavior displays spiritual ignorance and disrespect on the part of whoever engages in that type of immature conduct. Our own spirituality is enough of a responsibility, without seeking to stand in self-righteous judgment of someone else's.

There is no good reason to place our lives on the altar of public scrutiny. It will naturally occur that a strong support group will emerge and become a sacred inner circle. There are online groups and information available now, more so than ever before. Our world is expanding, not contracting.

Methods of Spiritual Protection

Spiritual discernment and trust in our intuition are critical to recognize the signs of spiritual problems that require our attention. There is a difference between paranoid superstition and having the wisdom to recognize the signs that we may have become the target of a spiritual attack. It is dangerous to be too attached to a tendency to write too many things off as coincidence.

There are many indications of spiritual warfare or unwanted energies that require a spiritual clearing or cleansing. Among them, you may experience;

- a stuffy or claustrophobic feeling in certain rooms, if not all of your home;

- a condensation of energy in your home;

- children or animals behaving strangely, reacting to something unseen;

- unpleasant odors with no physical source;

- things going "bump in the night," unexplainable noises from no apparent source;

- chronic or lingering illnesses which don't seem to be linked to a physical cause;

- cold areas or currents in the house or around your person for which there is no physical explanation;

- unusually frequent accidents or mishaps;

- an unusual occurrence of insect infestation;

- dramatic changes at home in the personalities of family, occupants, and visitors;

- unusual bouts with what appears to be a murky cloud of "bad luck;"

- strange pockets of energy in closets, storage areas, under beds, and in any dark or shadowed areas;

- an unusual increase in arguments and general conflict among household occupants;

- flashes of light or shadows in your peripheral vision, light bulbs malfunctioning;

- bizarre electrical problems, technical difficulties, malfunction of electronics;

- insomnia and nightmares of a graphic and visceral nature;

- chronic or sudden acute bouts of depression;

- suicidal thoughts and feelings of worthlessness and self-doubt;

- homicidal thoughts and a strong desire to harm self and/or others;

- pain or discomfort at the back of the neck and/or Solar Plexus area;

- chronic headaches and excessive fatigue;

- an unusual purging, diarrhea, vomiting, foaming, and especially bleeding;

- plants or pets dying from no apparent physical cause;

- apparitions, voices, and movement of inanimate objects;

- illnesses that involve blood. Blood conditions are the most severe and are referred to by some spiritual practitioners as 'the touch of Satan.' Waste no time in getting both physical and spiritual help. These cases are the most difficult to resolve. We must immediately look deeply into our lives for enemies who may have a motive for seeking our demise. These enemies may be hidden and under deep cover, even to their conscious selves.

We must humbly seek refuge in The God, heart, and soul to petition that the perpetrator is revealed and that the source of the energy is dealt with by Divine Will. We must also examine our own lives to unearth any deeply rooted, subconscious feelings of guilt for regrettable life choices. These life lessons may have resulted in the creation of a self-fulfilling prophecy of Karma that manifests in an energetic magnetism to misfortune. This can be cleansed and released through prayer, chanting of a mantra, and becoming very conscious of the people with whom we associate. We must observe with mindfulness the signs and guidance from the subtle realms. Pray for the strength to forgive and release those same energies we banish that also reside in ourselves.

There are symptoms far more extreme than those mentioned herein. If any of the troubling Psychic Self-Defense concerns discussed in this book become an issue in your life, it may be difficult to rely on a positive support system. It is unfortunate but true that such talk among average people will result in being perceived as crazy just for expressing your description and diagnosis of the problem. Understand that many symptoms of acute psychosis produce much of the same type of drama as listed above. The gift of spiritual discernment is often all that can differentiate one from the other. We may find ourselves on our own, isolated, with no trusted person to confide in, which only worsens the problem. If the indications of danger are severe enough, and we have ruled out the possibility of being psychotic, it is time to seek spiritual help from a trusted source.

Many people do not believe in the existence of certain psychic phenomena until they have come face to face with it. Even then, they may attempt to find logic-based explanations that suit their own limited, close-minded, unstudied, judgmental belief systems. If, however, we are fortunate enough to have a positive support group of people who are aware on the higher and subtler levels of mystical knowledge, there is no shame in asking for help. If not, then we must go within and know that we are not alone. We pray faith into our hearts, knowing that our needs are known and attended to in the subtle realms. Help is all around, whether we can see it or not. We will be guided through our complete submission to That Which Created All, which certainly has the ability to sustain and protect us. It does not sleep or tire. Satan stumbles.

I have gathered helpful tips from many traditions that can balance and fortify our electromagnetic field to attract our highest good. These age-old remedies are preventative measures, not just in times of apparent necessity, but as a lifestyle of mindfulness. When faced with a spiritual problem, these remedies are important to know, though it is just the tip of the iceberg. It is well worth the effort to conduct independent studies on this subject. We have enough spiritual maturity and discernment to separate alchemy from superstition.

Remedies to curb hyperdimensional interference:

Bless your home (Limpia/Cleansing): Traditional Shamanic methods of "house blessing" include smudging (fanning) the home and person with the smoke of sage, cedar, Palo Santo, or copal. Incense suited for spiritual cleansing is recommended, such as lavender, frankincense, and myrrh. Salt is believed to possess properties that serve to drive away negative entities and energetic attachments. Note that negative energies are not fond of bright lights and loud noise, especially certain types of music at high volumes. Some use gospel. I prefer what would be considered sacred music from many traditions, conscious reggae, and repetitive prayer. They are certainly not fond of prayer and commandments in the name of The Creator of all things. When performing the cleansing, use prayer and chanting to charge the smoke with the power of your intention, petition for spiritual protection, and the banishing of the invading energy or entity.

In cleansing a home of unwelcome energies or entities, it is important to consider that they may not be unwelcome. What if they are the spirits of our ancestors, spirit guardians, and protectors, or some 'familiar' that may not even realize they are in spirit. What if they were just passing through … just checking in on us. Generally, it is for a reason. In whatever way they make themselves manifest to you, ask yourself, "What is the message they are here to deliver." Some would be asked to stay for tea if they had a body. That is not advisable, and it would be weird. It is important to acknowledge the ancestral roots and energies that link you ancestrally to spiritual cultures and traditions that are a part of your inheritance. Some may be attempting to spark the flame of desire for connection.

It is not wise to seek to randomly interact with them directly, except through prayer, connecting through the Most High as Source. It can be a comforting and compassionate gesture, a healing for everyone concerned to light a candle and say a prayer to bless their journey. Some may simply need to be advised of their discarnate state and comforted by being directed into the Light. Some may be stopping by on a mission to let you know that they are "alright and not to worry" about them. Seek, on our highest level of discernment, the sign they serve as or the message they seek to deliver.

Spray a solution of water and salt, rosemary, or ammonia: Pay attention to the corners near the floors and ceiling, the interior of cabinets, drawers, closets, and drain pipes when you spray.

Place packets of Hawaiian salt charged with prayer, wrapped in tea leaves in the four corners of your home: Place them at entrances and exits, under and around areas where you sleep, as well as any other areas that you are guided to protect. You may want to wear this packet on your person as a talisman if it feels appropriate.

Frankincense and Myrrh: This combination of incense lifts and dispels negative energy. The smoke, charged with prayer, blesses and spiritually cleanses people, places, and objects. Myrrh is believed to be born from the mythical goddess Myrrh's tears. Myrrh has been used in religious rites as many as 2000 years before the birth of Christ.

Lavender: This word is a Latin derivative meaning "to wash." It offers an excellent spiritual cleansing when used with prayer and sacred words of power. It should be used for bathing, as incense, oil, or mixed with water to spray around your home.

Lemon or Lime: When mixed with water and charged with your positive intention, it can be used for blessings and purification.

Crystals: Commonly used as talismans or amulets, crystals are believed to protect the wearer when used in a spiritually correct manner. Fully understand that the crystal has no power other than that which you assign it. Consider it a container for prayers and praise for The Most High. Never look to a stone for protection. Look to The God. Wear or use them with responsibility. They must be stored correctly and kept clean and free from outside energies because they absorb them. Wrap them in silk and store them in a wooden box.

White candle: Charge and anoint a white candle in prayer and meditate upon its flame, requesting Divine protection. There are anointing oils available that will enhance the focus of prayer and meditation rituals. Olive oil is one good choice, and it is easy to find. A seven-day candle is best, observing standard fire safety precautions. There are color-coded candle rituals; however, I find them to be a distraction from my singular focus on The Divine.

Glass of water: Placing a full glass of water on a nightstand near the head of your bed before going to sleep is commonly recommended as a regular Spiritual Self-Defense practice. It is believed to attract and absorb directed negative energies and entities that may cause troubled sleep or worse. Upon awakening, pour the water into the toilet and flush it with a banishing prayer. Never make the mistake of drinking the water or leaving it sitting around. Dispose of it immediately after waking.

Sleep with your head in the East: Many recognize the West as the direction in which the heads of the dead are placed to be energetically aligned with the setting Sun. It is not considered a favorable position for the living to sleep.

Ritual of Light: The psychic projection of a strong auric shield of Divine protective white Light around your home, yourself, and loved ones (whether they are in your physical presence or not, and whether or not they are aware of it) can block negative energy and attack. Practice The Light Meditation provided on the dreamuniversal.com website before going to sleep and upon awakening. You can also practice mindful breathing as you visualize a gently cascading waterfall of brilliant white Light emanating from a sphere of Light just above your head. Let it saturate your entire aura with the Love and Protection of The Divine One. Hold this visualization of Light as an egg-shaped envelopment surrounding you. Charge it with an intense prayer of surrender.

Mirroring: Go into deep meditation and psychically surround your body and your home with mirrors facing away from you in every direction. Pray that any negative energies sent to you be deflected and transmuted into the pure white Light of love and healing. Return every trace of the energy to the sender, along with the blessing of The God, that the individual is shown the truth of their behavior and be guided to the path of goodness and healing.

It is a powerfully protective visualization to see your image inside of a mirrored "globe," much like one might find spinning above an 80's style disco dance floor or in a nightclub. The energy of the attack is scattered and reflected back to the sender.

Study Feng Shui: The study of the art of Feng Shui is a preventative measure against negative energies and psychic attack. One of the things you will learn is to place a Bagua mirror above the entrance of your home, reflecting outward, after you have ceremonially blessed it with a prayer to "open the eye" of protection.

Hamsa Prayer

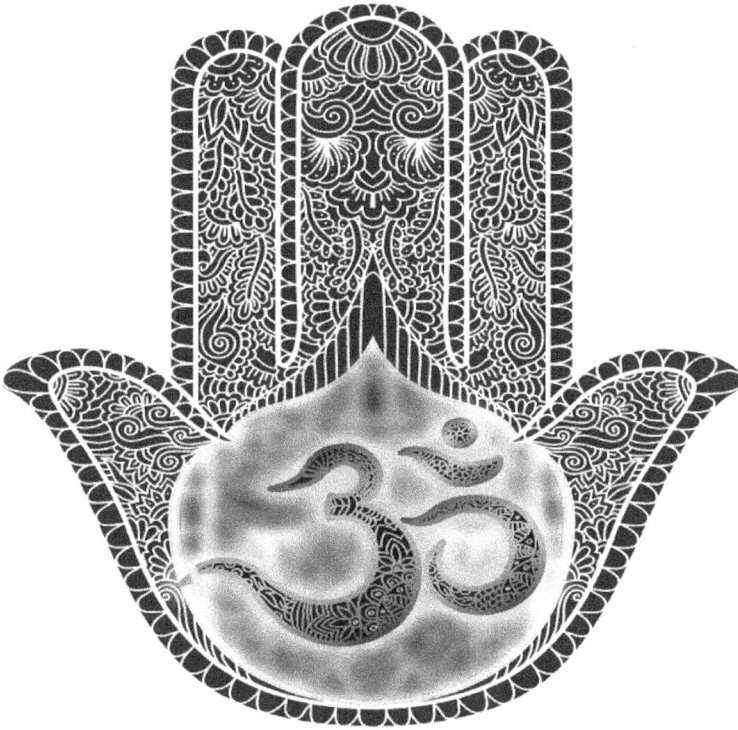

Let no sadness come to this heart
Let no trouble come to these arms
Let no conflict come to these eyes
Let my soul be filled wuth the blessing of joy and peace

Hamsa Prayer: The Hamsa translates from Arabic as "five," symbolizing the five fingers of a hand, illustrated with an open right hand. It is an ancient symbol and talisman, believed by diverse faiths, to manifest spiritual protection, health, good fortune, luck, and happiness, and to ward off the "Evil Eye." It is also known as the Hand of Fatima, the Hand of Mary, the Hand of Miriam, the Hand of the Goddess, and is believed to represent the Hand of God. With gratitude, we receive the gift of mystical wisdom as a guide to make our life experience happy and as free from suffering as possible. It teaches us to cooperate with the flow of the rhythms and rhymes of this gift of existence. It can serve as an intentional reminder and focal point in the day to day meditation called our lives. Many such practices cause us to manage our energies in a manner that does not swim against every current of existence. At the same time, it must be understood that it is The God who protects, not Feng Shui, amulets, images, statues, talismans, and the like. It is believed by some to be a powerful focal point of meditation and remembrance. Before using the Hamsa, understand every detail of its spiritual significance, to determine if you still feel comfortable using it.

Eye of Sophia

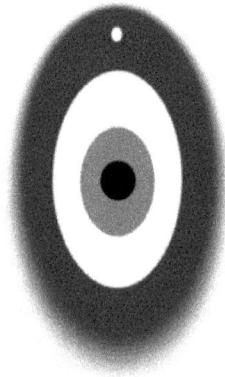

The Eye of Sophia, The Hagia Sophia (Wisdom), also known as a Nazar (meaning "sight, surveillance" in Arabic), is a blue and white, eye-shaped amulet commonly worn as jewelry, displayed in the home, in automobiles, or the workplace. It is regarded as a Feng Shui cure, when activated, to attract blessings and healing energy for protection against the legendary "Evil Eye."

With origins in the Mediterranean, it means "God looking into the soul of the faithful." The Eye represents the Third Eye (Ajna [Sanskrit], Sixth Chakra). This Third Eye of Intuition is a gateway to the inner realms of consciousness. In ancient and modern civilizations, it is believed to symbolize a shield against envy, jealousy, the covetous gaze, witchcraft, and sorcery. Some believe the Eye of Sophia can repel thought-forms, charged with energetic poison that can damage and destroy lives. The malevolent energy of the Evil Eye is considered by some to be capable of delivering a curse against the health and well-being of the target of the "attack," their children, family, property, and happiness, causing misfortune and even death. In some traditions, even an apparently innocent verbal expression of admiration or praise for a possession will cause the owner to give it to you to ward off even subconscious energetic attachments that could bring bad luck and adversity.

The Eye of Sophia is used in conjunction with, not instead of, specific spiritual practices of prayer and chanting in absolute remembrance *that the talisman has no power*. It is the *strength of belief* in Divine Protection that has power. Some people even believe that to ascribe powers of protection to such talismans is an expression of disbelief and disrespect of The God. It is only reasonable to understand that nothing perishable has the power to protect anyone from harm, though it may offer some a comforting reminder of the All-Seeing Eye of the Divine.

Use a solution of ammonia and water to cleanse all mirrors and reflective surfaces (including rear and side-view mirrors in your car, mirrors in your make-up bag or compact, and particularly mirrors in your bedrooms and bathrooms). It is not a good idea to sleep in a room with mirrors and reflective surfaces because they can operate like portals through which invading energies and entities may pass. Cover mirrors when they are not in use, especially in the dark. It is particularly unwise to place a mirror on any outside-facing wall of your home.

Study Martial Arts: The Third, Fifth, and Sixth Chakras are exceptionally vulnerable to psychic attack. They are all primary, specific energetic points of entry. Chi Gong (Qi Gong) or any of the healing and Martial Arts that work with the Chi energy of the complex body system can restore peace of mind and make us more confident in the ability to ward off and become more immune to attack. There are meditation exercises to strengthen the chakras in this text. The study of our energetic body is better classified as a lifestyle choice rather than a protection ritual. A couple of old sayings come to mind; *"It is better to be safe than sorry."* and *"An ounce of prevention is worth a pound of cure."* Our Light body is fortified as its own defense against attack when we make the respect and care it deserves an uncompromising standard for our lives.

Seek swift and amicable resolution to conflict: If you are at odds with someone in your life, it is important to resolve the conflict as swiftly as possible and establish a win/win outcome. An accumulation of negative energy directed specifically at you, either consciously or unconsciously, by someone who believes that you have in some way wronged or hurt them can manifest disastrous consequences in your life. Some believe that the Sun should never set on an argument.

In cultures that are particularly aware of the potentially harmful effects of negative energy, the resolution of a conflict is regarded as very high in priority. In Indigenous Hawaiian culture, there is a ceremony called Ho'oponopono, wherein a Kahuna or wise Shaman will mediate conflicts between partners, family, and friends. They will retreat, usually into nature, and remain there until the negative energy has been healed at its source, no matter how long it takes. This ceremony is designed to dissolve the energy of anger, hatred, and jealousy that can ultimately lead to unbearable suffering.

Most cultures rooted in mystical traditions are very sensitive to the phenomenon of negative thought-forms. A thought-form can take on a Life Force of its own, *attaching* to and creating a magnetic force field around the object of the attacker's intention. These poisonous thought-forms occur as astral garbage polluting the aura and scrambling the energy field, creating mental, emotional, physical, and spiritual illness. These negative thought-forms will have an even stronger effect if there are feelings of guilt or fear to nourish them, especially if the subject really is guilty of intentionally injuring the attacker.

If the person is not guilty and the attack is unjustified or rooted in jealousy, envy, or any other sinful thought form, the attacker surely has no advantage when refuge is sought in The God. Within this sacred refuge, we are covered by an impenetrable cloak of Love and Protection directly proportionate to our faith. The energy of the attack will reverse on the attacker like a boomerang. There are times when the touch of an attacker is Divinely permitted. Too often, only in retrospect are we able to see the wisdom of it being allowed. It is known on an essential level the highest good of the intended victim and all concerned that we might be blinded to in the moment of our inquiry. As we lament over our perception of having been conquered, we cannot see that there is a backdrop of an intricate ethereal mosaic of our fate, our Karma, and our destiny. Maybe it is a test of faith or a lesson to be learned. It does not matter what the reason is for the permission of it, as all of our faith and trust is in The Most High. Our life and our death are all for The Creator.

A spiritual scholar who ritually prays five times a day told me the reason she does it is that evil seeks the opportunity to attack at *least* that many times every day. The use of sincere prayer is one of the most powerful deflectors of attacking energies and entities known. Prayer can speak the language of many religious and cultural belief systems, the common denominator being the belief in The Creator and Divine Protector of all. Harm none and seek refuge in the Protective Light of the Creator, which never sleeps as It watches over us and intervenes in our affairs.

Arguments: Thoughts are things! Energy is real! Energy, whether positive or negative, will remain in a place long after those who created it are gone, affecting anyone who enters. After any type of domestic conflict, intense exchange of communications, injury, shock, death, grief, or violence, observe basic spiritual cleansing protocol to neutralize the intense energy. Residual energy from emotionally charged events must be dispelled to restore positive Chi balance in your home.

Avoid attracting negative entities and energies in the first place: Certain activities are believed to attract spirit activity. Do your spiritual homework. Consider views from diverse perspectives but trust your own gut instincts and higher reasoning. It doesn't matter whether or not someone else thinks certain mystical practices are safe. If you feel the least bit uncomfortable with any particular practice … if it does not feel safe or wholesome to you … don't do it. If you do it and have a bad experience, seek spiritual counsel immediately and don't do it again.

Be careful of certain selections of music: There are musical selections that openly serve as magnets for the attraction of lower astral garbage spirits and entities. Certain recording artists don't attempt to hide their association with demonic forces and entities. Some employ the use of backward masking and planting subliminal messages in their recordings. Some traditions believe that certain types of flute music may conjure spirits. Some also believe that whistling, hammering, and certain types of drum rhythms and chimes can affect spirit activity. I do not seek to start a campaign against specific artists or genres of music but use discretion in your choice of music to avoid attracting negative, unwelcome entities.

Take care in the placement of certain objects in your home or on your body: Some energies can attach to objects that may have been negatively charged by someone or may have been affected by being in the presence of some source of negative energy. It is important to cleanse items that you bring into your environment, particularly if they have been owned, worn, or used by someone else. This can be done in the same manner that you would cleanse the energy in your home or on your person with the sacred cleansing smoke of sage. It is also a consideration in accepting gifts and eating food from people who may mean you harm.

Consumption of animal flesh and blood: It is commonly believed that the consumption of animal flesh and blood can have the effect of attracting negative entities associated with psychic attack. If you have reason to believe that you are under attack, you may want to eliminate animal flesh from your diet, a healthier choice regardless of your spiritual circumstances. If you are going to eat red meat or fowl, it is your choice, and no one has the right to judge you. However, for sound alchemy in mystical work, at least eat kosher or halal meat because the meat does not contain the blood (among other deadly things) found in meat from common industrial processing. The living conditions and the dying conditions of the animals are held to a higher standard. The consumption of pork in any of its many forms is spiritually dangerous for any practitioner of the mystical arts. We simply do not have to kill to eat.

The consumption of alcohol and or consciousness-altering drugs is known to create a portal between planes and could expose you, in a worst-case scenario, to complete possession or attachments of energies and entities. It is senseless to provide the opportunity for something or someone else to slip in during those moments when your astral body begins to slip in and out of the physical body due to inebriation. Entities can enter you and make you do whatever they desire. It is not recommended to frequent establishments that specialize in serving alcohol and catering to intoxicated people in times of a Spiritual Emergency.

Strengthening and cleansing the aura: Maintain a clean and healthy aura. This may be accomplished by cleansing salt baths and a regular discipline of meditation and prayer. Entertaining positive thoughts about yourself and others is important.

Recitation of a prayer that has personal significance to you: The most important thing to remember about spiritual protection is prayer. If you forget everything else that you have learned and remember prayer, you will have nothing to fear. Some use common protection prayers like Psalms 91 from The Bible (KJV), Surahs Al Falaq and Al Nas from The Quran. Chanting and repetitive prayer are most calming to me because it is a manner of *remaining* in prayer rather than engaging in a prayer. I find that it silences the voices of fear-based thoughts.

Ask in prayer and meditation for confirmation: Request in prayer and meditation that it be revealed whether or not there is an attack being waged against you. Ask that the source of the negative energies being directed toward you be unmasked and healed. Ask why this has occurred. Ask for forgiveness if there is any indwelling personal responsibility for it. Ask for guidance with regard to the correct course of action to take and confirmation that the protective measures you intend to set in place will be sufficient to protect you from the attack.

Journal your dreams: Keeping a dream and vision journal is an important yardstick for identifying and monitoring the nature of the energies that you may have attracted around you and how they are affecting your life. You may begin to notice Cause and Effect patterns that offer guidance.

None of the defensive or aggressive measures shared herein will ever surpass the importance of realizing the miracle of our personal, mystical connection with The Creator, The God, through prayer.

The Power of Prayer, Intervention, and Faith

It is tough navigating the unpredictable twists and turns on this road called life. It defies natural instinct and reason to adhere to limiting beliefs of fixed conclusions about just how fluid this mystical Universe really is. Nothing is fixed. Our greatest consolation is to know that we are not our own, whether we know and accept it, or not. We are intrinsically connected to The Creator, God, in a union that is so sacred it cannot be named by our lower plane languages and utterances. We are connected in essence to That Source Consciousness, a Consciousness so unfathomable that it is pure vanity to imagine it is possible to speak Its Holy Name. Prayer should not fall into a category of something to be debated on or argued to dust. The prayers, meditations, and affirmations are our own sovereign choice, based on what makes us feel the strength of our connection. Our essence and That Essence are One.

Our regular affirmations of belief and submission are vital to our spiritual healing in times of fear, loss, and grief. If we waver in our belief of the miraculous Nature of The God, all we need to do is look in the mirror. When we look into our own eyes for that spark of Light that we are, we know that we are looking at a miracle. Prayer is our way of communicating with The God. We validate our love and appreciation for The God and heal our own souls with every word of every prayer and sacred thought. In our prayers and meditations, we strip away the flesh and bone vessel that contains the spirit we are and bare our immortal soul to The God in communion with That Essence.

If our prayers are but mindless verbal recitation, we cheat ourselves out of the experience and comfort of the sacred relationship we have with The God and the truth of our own Divinity and miraculous being. It is worth the time and effort to respect the ritual process of preparing to experience that consecrated holy union.

It is worth the effort to exercise mindfulness in unplugging from the matrix of this system of confusion to connect with a Higher Energy Source, that of the Most High.

It is healing to elevate the intensity of our longing by not just praying but *remaining* in repetitive prayer and chanting. It is well worth the time we take from our busy lives for a departure from the vanity-based drama of the perishable world to rest our weary souls in the loving embrace of Ultimate Reality. As we accept responsibility for our spiritual journey, we must be mindful of the fact that we are not alone. We are intrinsically connected at the core of our being to the Source of all healing. In the face of relentless pursuit by the spirit of despair, with its never-ending effort to capture and collect our souls for fun, we submit in prayer to the Will of the Most High in thought, action, and deed.

So why do we bother to pursue metaphysical studies and practices? I think we may do it for the same reasons we exercise the muscles of our physical body even though it is born perfect, even in spite of any of our perceived imperfections. Our perfection rests in the Loving Eyes of our Creator and has little to do with our or anyone's judgments, opinions, criticisms, or comparisons. Still, we naturally feel compelled to exercise, improve, and groom our already perfect vehicle because that inclination is a natural component of our perfection. However, we are not to bow down to the exercise. We bow down only to The Creator, not to the ritual around our practice.

Prayer is a spiritual exercise. Surrender is the spiritual muscle that results. There, in the spirit of that sacred surrender, is faith … faith beyond evidence, beyond proof. The prayer must be a meditation of surrender. The meditation must be a prayer of surrender. From the killing fields of fear, all we can do is surrender what is left of us to the only Force capable of facilitating our healing. I do not represent any religious or spiritual path over another. The prayers and meditations you choose to engage in are entirely up to you. If the energy of your prayer resonates with the energy of your Higher Self, you will feel it and know. Sometimes the best and most powerful prayer or meditation is simply, *"Thank You."*

At this point, I will refer you to the previous sections of this book, *The Meaning of I AM, Protect the I AM, and I AM Consciousness Rising.* After reading these chapters for an understanding of the I AM, return to this chapter and answer the following questions: Now that I have chosen to distinguish my Eternal True Self from the body-identified, impermanent self, does the True Self really worry about not being able to defend itself? The answer is *NO!* What does the True Self fear? The answer is *NOTHING!* The I AM, our Essence, who witnesses who we think we are … what does it fear? The answer is *NOTHING!*

We grossly underestimate the power and importance of prayer. We live one prayer away from a miracle. It is vital to our spirituality to reconnect daily with the value and importance of prayer. We do not need to ritualize or make an exhibition of prayer. Prayer is a very personal communication between The Creator and creation. There is no right or wrong way to pray. No tradition, culture, or religion has cornered the market on a system of prayer. There is no paraphernalia required to engage in sincere prayer. It is an intensely personal and sovereign practice, each one unique in its own way. A woman who had a Near-Death Experience (NDE) and traveled to the other side shared a touching observation about prayer. She saw prayers rising from the Earth Plane as little spots or bubbles of Light. She was told that the brighter and larger ones were the prayers of mothers for their children.

In matters of Psychic Self-Defense, both the seen and unseen realms are acknowledged as a possible battlefield. Prayer is the shield, the whole armor of The God, the most powerful defense against negative spiritual energies. I have often heard this Bible quote regarding the nature of spiritual warfare and the comfort of knowing that we are not fighting alone.

I will share with you a few of the prayers from many traditions that I found comforting and healing. I encourage you to share prayers that speak to your soul at dreamuniversalmedia.com, to possibly be used in future publications.

Prayer of St. Francis

Lord, make me an instrument of Your peace;

Where there is hatred, let me sow love;

Where there is injury, pardon;

Where there is error, truth;

Where there is doubt, faith;

Where there is despair, hope;

Where there is darkness, light;

and where there is sadness, joy.

Oh, Divine Master, Grant that I may not so much seek

to be consoled as to console;

to be understood as to understand;

to be loved as to love;

for it is in giving that we receive;

It is in pardoning that we are pardoned;

And it is in dying that we are born to Eternal life.

Every prayer is heard. Every prayer is answered. Sometimes the answer is no. Sometimes the silence is a test of faith. In the silence, you may hear the answer spoken to your soul in your own inner voice.

Release Prayer

The Great and Holy Spirit,

Sacred Mother/Father God

the essence of I,___Name___,

am your humble servant

and You are my Beloved

I seek refuge in your Guidance

and surrender my personal will to Thy Will

at this point where the river of my suffering

meet the shoreless sea

of Your Love, Protection,

Compassion, and Mercy

At this time, I stand before You

for guidance in this matter

My soul is burdened

My heart is heavy

and still, my faith

and my gratitude

are stronger than my suffering

I release and surrender my willfulness

asking Your forgiveness

for every moment of

falling into forgetfulness

that only You are my sustenance, my providence

Our connection is Sacred

Our only reality is Our Oneness

I release my attachment to the outcome

I surrender my personal will to Divine Will

Here in the shadow realms of a desolate night

I release and let go as I seek only Your Light

Here in the brokenness of my heart

that beats only for You

that seeks healing only from You

I wait only for You

Ephesians 10 – 12, The Bible (KJV)

Finally, my brethren, be strong in the Lord, and in the power of his might.
Put on the whole armor of God that ye may be able to stand against
the wiles of the devil.
For we wrestle not against flesh and blood, but against principalities, against
powers, against the rulers of the darkness of this world, against
spiritual wickedness in high places.
I share with you prayers from several traditions, offered to me by friends, even
though I believe prayer can be as informal and spontaneous as a conversation with
loved ones.

23rd Psalm, The Bible (KJV)

The Lord is my shepherd
I shall not want
He maketh me to lie down in green pastures
He leadeth me beside the still waters
He restoreth my soul
He leadeth me in the paths of righteousness
for his name's sake
Yeah though I walk through the valley
of the shadow of death
I shall fear no evil for thou art with me
Thy rod and thy staff they comfort me
Thou preparest a table before me
in the presence of mine enemies
Thou anointest my head with oil
My cup runneth over
Surely goodness and mercy shall follow me
all the days of my life
and I will dwell in the house of the Lord
forever.

Psalm 91, The Bible (KJV)

1. He that dwelleth in the secret place of the Most High shall abide under the shadow of the Almighty.
2. I will say of the Lord, He is my refuge and my fortress; my God; in him will I trust.
3. Surely he shall deliver thee from the snare of the fowler, and from the noisome pestilence.
4. He shall cover thee with his feathers, and under his wings shalt thou trust; his truth shall be thy shield and buckler.
5. Thou shalt not be afraid for the terror by night; nor for the arrow that flieth by day.
6. Nor for the pestilence that walketh in darkness; nor for the destruction that wasteth at noonday.
7. A thousand shall fall at thy side, and ten thousand at thy right hand; but it shall not come nigh thee.
8. Only with thine eyes shalt thou behold and see the reward of the wicked.
9. Because thou hast made the Lord, which is my refuge, even the Most High, thy habitation;
10. There shall no evil befall thee, neither shall any plague come nigh thy dwelling.
11. For he shall give his angels charge over thee, to keep thee in all thy ways.
12. They shall bear thee up in their hands, lest thou dash thy foot against a stone.
13. Thou shalt tread upon the lion and adder; the young lion and the dragon shalt thou trample under feet.
14. Because he hath set his love upon me, therefore will I deliver him; I will set him on high, because he hath known my name.
15. He shall call upon me, and I will answer him; I will be with him in trouble; I will deliver him, and honor him.
16. With long life will I satisfy him and shew him my salvation.

The Lord's Prayer

Matthew 6:9-13, The Bible (KJV)

After this manner, therefore, pray ye:

Our Father which art in heaven, Hallowed be thy name.

Thy kingdom come, Thy will be done in earth, as it is in heaven.

Give us this day our daily bread.

And forgive us our debts, as we forgive our debtors.

And lead us not into temptation but deliver us from evil:

For thine is the kingdom, and the power, and the glory, forever.

Amen.

The Phenomenon of Weaponized Prayer

There should be a warning attached to certain prayers … even if they are scriptures from sacred texts. It would not be a good idea to take certain types of prayer into deep meditation with designs upon another or even upon one's self. You incur the Karmic debt of what befalls the target as a result of what constitutes an energetic or spiritual attack. If we have reason to believe someone has wronged us in a way that justifies specific consequences directed using certain powerful prayers, consider that if we are wrong, we have waged spiritual warfare against an innocent person. We will have made ourselves a magnet for the return of the energies sent out, a consequence of the attack. For every cause, there is an effect … a consequence.

I have witnessed what took on the appearance and energy of a murder/manslaughter with the use of sacred scriptures. I observed a very good and decent religious lady throw her hands up in frustration and give up contending with her emotionally abusive mother. She announced it and proceeded with the chanting of specific verses from the sacred texts, and burning petitions inscribed with those verses. Within six weeks, her mother died. She had a medical condition that she could have continued to manage successfully. However, she compulsively began to do everything required to take herself to the grave.

I have experienced a Sleep Paralysis Event, in real time, with a witness and experiencer in the room when it happened. "Good nights" had been exchanged. Lights out. Sweet dreams. A condensation of strange, electrically charged, thick shadowy energy formed like threatening clouds gathering before a terrible storm. The energy of the small room was suddenly consumed by it. Sound shifted to a dense, silent echo with an 'underwater,' other-worldly quality. A death-like stillness filled the room. I was familiar with that feeling … the onset of a Sleep Paralysis Event.

"Oh, no! It's happening again!" Effervescent skin began to go cold, tingly, and numb. The compression began. An invisible cloud of pressure slowly, deliberately descended as every muscle in my body began to lose strength. Breathing became shallow and constricted as a dying person must struggle for a few last breaths of life as the pressure of death pushes the weakened Life Force out of my chest, one shallow breath at a time. My body was gradually weakening, and I knew that soon I would not be able to move, to call out for help, to save my life. Panic ensued. One tear rolled down the side of my face. It felt cold … cold as death's final touch. Shallow breath struggled through strangled fading whispers, "Help me! … a spastic cry struggling against fear's firm grip … "Help me! I can't … move." I knew it was already too late for me … to break the grip of this invisible assassin.

Through this convergence of dimensions and realities, quaking within me, portals opened, pulling me into the dark void that had filled the room, swallowing me whole. I was able to gather enough strength to cry out, barely audible, the hollow whimper of an exhausted baby collapsed in terror. Entities were breathing their presence into the room. My body and my spirit felt airborne and electrically charged. The energy shifted.

I gasped enough air to scream and struggled through another incoherent utterance … barely above a whisper … I pleaded, "Open the door!" I was already prepared to 'let go' of the will to declare, "I'm scared! I can't move! Something is in here … out there." "Open the door, or we won't survive this. What's out there is what is making what's in here happen! Open the door!!! Please, Oh my God, open the door!!! Please!!!!" I was gone full paralysis. With super-hero strength, the door was flung open to expose the agent of the evil energy … seated in piety, on a bar stool outside of the door, in the middle of the night, a "sacred" text lay open in the hands of a demon. Reading, reciting, from the book in a whispered, guttural, raspy chant, he was startled out of a trance state. The spell was broken. The attacking energy lifted. I was alive. I could move. I could breathe. It … whatever that was, was off of my chest. The pressure and the binding released. I could speak. I couldn't believe I was alive. I leaped up and lunged at him. I snatched the book from his grip to see what chapter … what scripture he was reciting from. It was so full of judgment and wrath that there was no room for any consideration of coincidence. It was connected to the attacking energy. It was a deliberate, targeted attack on an innocent person who never deserved that dance with the devil, never deserved to be smothered and left dying, shrouded in a blanket of primordial evil.

That is when I became mindful of the manner in which even a sacred scripture can be used with the intention of manipulating or causing harm to someone. If scriptures are directed out of anger and judgment rather than the energy of pure and unconditional Love, great harm can result. What happens when things like right, wrong, good, and evil get to be defined by monsters? These electrically charged frequencies and energies are clearly powerful enough to trigger a Sleep Paralysis Event. In cases involving the manipulative use of scriptures or other systems and methods of prayer … know that it is a boomerang. It will return by Universal Law three times if the intention was not malefic … And three times three if it was intentional. All in life is a circle. Keep your circle clean.

When using prayers and verses from sacred texts, be sure to remain general and objective. One of the greatest prayers any of us can pray is for the healing of another. However, we must be careful to resist playing God and becoming an unsolicited intervention in the lives and personal matters of other people. We must not allow ego to nail us into a coffin of assuming moral superiority in manipulative judgments of the lives of others. Do not direct the concentrated focal point of the energy of prayer in such a manner as to use it as a poison arrow aimed at the hearts of those being held in judgment. Pray all prayers in great humility and surrender to the Will of The Divine One.

Dark Energy and Sleep Paralysis

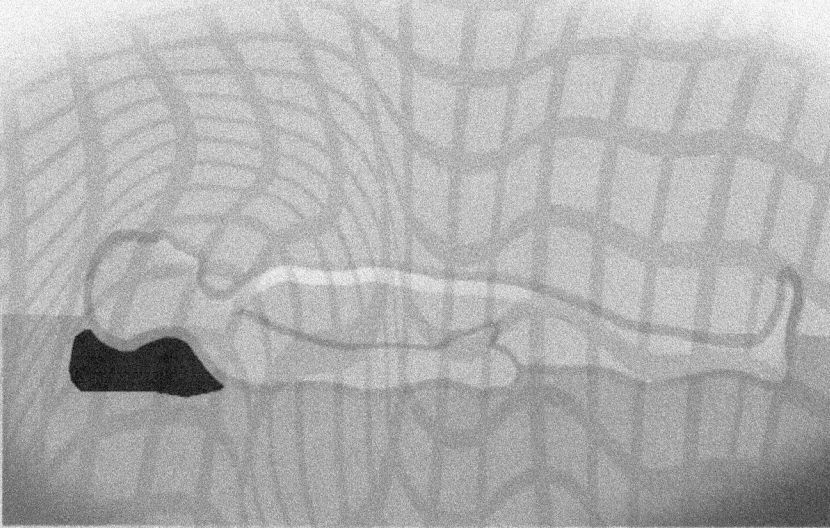

Dark Energy: invisible matter; negative zero-point energy.
Dark Energy precedes the existence of all thoughts, words, concepts, or precepts.

Signs and Symptoms of Weaponized Prayer Attacks:

- Sleep Paralysis Events;

- Nightmares and other sleep disturbances;

- Dizziness, vertigo;

- Major depression, crying, loneliness, fearfulness, abandonment issues; Obsessive Compulsive Disorder (OCD), mood swings, uncontrollable rage;

- Changes in eating habits (loss of appetite, compulsive binge eating, strange cravings);

- Stomach issues (severe chronic indigestion, constipation, diarrhea);

- Pain in the abdominal region;

- Unusual movements in the abdominal region;

- Headaches, hot and cold flashes, tingling and numbness of the skin, muscle cramping and aching;

- Compression and pain in the chest, heart palpitations, shortness of breath;

- Feelings of being followed and surveilled;

- Hearing voices/whispers from no apparent source;

- Ringing in the ears (tinnitus);

- Seeing shadows with no apparent source;

- Seeing apparitions, flashes of light, and/or shadows in peripheral vision;

- Having thoughts that are not your own (Thought Implants);

- Fixations on someone or something, rumination, forgetfulness, brain fog;

- Loss of interest in previously enjoyed activities;

- Malfunctioning vehicles, electronics, and lighting;

- Frequent accidents and mishaps;

- Reversal of fortune, series of "coincidentally" unfortunate events;

- Changes in the behavior of family, friends, and pets;

- Unusual behavior of strangers;

- Strange, symbolic presentations of birds (ravens, owls, predatory birds), insects, and animals;

- Unusual attachments and aversions;

- Seeing and/or smelling cigarette or cigar smoke from no apparent source.

How Weaponized Prayer Works:

- The target is the focal point of the attacker's attention and directed energies;

- The desire is to manipulate the Free Will of the victim;

- Judgment Call – solicitation of spiritual intervention in passing judgment;

- Declarations of Karmic debt and creation of a "binding" to that agenda;

- Manipulative desire, envy, covetousness, jealousy, hatred, lust, sloth, greed;

- Candle Magick – burning candles charged with manipulative intentions;

- Writing and burning of petitions with the intention to manipulate or control;

- Use of alchemically coordinated incense, oils, etc., to attract manipulated results;

- Spellcasting – seeking by occult means to influence the lives of others;

- Conjuring – intentional projection of psychic energy;

- Petitioning or bargaining with saints, angels, demons, entities, and energies;

- Projection of thought-forms with manipulative intention;

- Energy vampirism – targeting emotions to drain the Life Force of the victim;

- Ritual work using either sacred or unholy scriptures with malefic intention;

- Prayers from *any* tradition or belief system to compel the Free Will of others;

- Intentional chanting of compelling repetitive prayers or commands;

- Use of negative or manipulative affirmations to target the victim;

- Sigil Magick – use of symbols as a "seal" or signature to compel outcomes;

- Sex Magick – use of sexual energies to fortify a manipulative intention;

- Binding Rituals – spiritual work performed to suppress, control, or compel;

- Ritual/Ceremonial prayer work aimed at eroding the Free Will of the target;

- Using pictures, personal belongings, or information of the victim to harness energy for attack;

- Visualizations summoning the Law of Attraction for manipulative purposes;

- Use of charms, incantations, and images to reinforce willful projections;

- Compelling malefic spirits, jinn, entities, and energies to perform interventions;

- A manipulative, willful prayer that ends with "Amen!"

Note that much of the above (certainly with the exception of obvious malefic intent to do harm) could be practiced with the highest of intentions in the most innocent of all Light. Some say that what determines the difference is INTENTION. My observations have instructed me that what determines the difference is the OUTCOME. Our inflicted desires upon the lives of others can produce a negative, even tragic outcome. How does that differ from negative witchcraft and other paths that are held in judgment for the same, or parallel practices? Live and let live.

What Makes Weaponized Prayer Work?

- The possibility that this event was fated and "allowed";

- Fear inspired by threats and bullying by the attacker;

- Fear overwhelms the target;

- The weak spiritual belief system of the victim;

- The weak spiritual practice of the victim;

- Denial and flawed mystical belief system of the victim;

- Confidence of the attacker;

- Target succumbs to the effects of manipulative forces;

- Target's acceptance of projections of guilt;

- Actual guilt (All you have to be is wrong);

- Welcome repentance due to the target feeling worthy of punishment;

- A subliminal, mutually cooperative effort due to the target's surrender;

- Strength of belief in any idea infuses it with power;

- Fatigue, exhaustion, and broken spirit of the victim;

- Compromised physical, mental, psychological condition of target;

- Target not Self-Realized ... knowing the "self" that needs protecting is not real.

What to Do If You are the Victim of Attack Prayers:

- Strengthen your own spiritual practice;

- Continually reaffirm the strength of your relationship with The God of your highest understanding;

- Remain in sincere prayer from your strongest path of spiritual belief;

- Become the prayer you pray through a strong meditation practice;

- Refer to FEARLESS: PSYCHIC SELF-DEFENSE for protocol;

- If you have wronged someone, repent and make peace;

- If someone has wronged you, challenge the strength of your heart to forgive them and seek refuge in Divine Protection and Providence;

- Do not fight false fire with false fire in counter-attack scenarios;

- Limpia (Spiritual Purification) will keep your frequency high by employing methods of cleansing your energy field;

- Affirm that ONLY the Will of Divine is welcome to cross the threshold of the door that opens to your highest level of discernment;

- Remember the Divinity that you are and your sacred relationship with the Absolute. Dwell in the secret place of the Most High. Evil, regardless of what label it chooses to wear, cannot enter there.

The knowledge of Self is the most powerful shield. The realization that we already are all we need to be gives us the strength to rise up in spiritual sovereignty from the ashes of destruction. Sometimes the attacker believes they are going to God as a faithful advocate on your behalf, with "positive" intentions that they truly believe are "saving" your life. Then you blast them with hell-fire and holy water, sage, ammonia, and attacking energy. That causes you to lose your edge. No one wins that war. You are not fighting them. You are becoming them.

Surrender to the Will of the Divine One, stand your spiritual ground, and let them spin in their own webs of indefensible behavior. Of course, you are hurt and angry … because you can feel it. You can feel something quietly, subtly, subliminally tinkering with your subconscious mind. The rewiring of consciousness, no matter how skillfully it is performed, sends up red flag security breach warnings to a Self-Realized being. Shifting realities on beings who are awake and feeling the pressure of seductive hypnosis and conditioning closing in on them will yield predictable results. RAGE will cause the desire to seek the destruction of *whoever* is introducing the divergent reality. Yet, the more awake you are, the deeper your commitment is to *remain* as the True Self … unthreatened by egoic attacks that are aimed at egoic defense systems.

If you are a truly Realized Self, why are the projections of others so threatening to your remembrance of Self? Not everyone is going to like us. But that does not mean there is necessarily anything wrong with us. I offer the wise words of my mother … "I can see why someone wouldn't like you … But what I cannot see is why you *care*." We must not let ego find another rock to hide under. There is only One Love … No "them versus us." What is in them is in you, is in all of us. Send it love, not hate or rejection … forgiveness, not denial or retaliatory aggression. Love that place in the Realized Self that knows that we are One Love … One Prayer … One Intention. Time is not a line … It is a circle … One Circle. We must keep our circle clean.

The Power of Repetitive Prayer

There are effective ways to break free when seized by the spellbinding grip of a Sleep Paralysis event. At the onset of an S.P. event (SPE), the first chill, sensation, vibration, lapse of consciousness, complete loss of muscular control … immediately go to mindfulness of breathing and fervently chant words of power and repetitive prayer mantras. The prayers and mantras you use must specifically empower you. We must conjure the strength we never believed we had. We must acknowledge unseen Light forces and affirm that we are not alone. It may not be possible to chant out loud because of the sensation of paralysis of the vocal cords, but the chanting of our inner voice sends an even more powerful vibration than if we had intoned it out loud.

The chanting of mantras and repetitive prayer dates back to the beginning of time. A mantra can be as simple as a single Word of Power, a vibrational utterance, or a childhood prayer. This sacred practice balances and clears internal and external energies, bringing harmony to mind, body, and spirit. The sensation of this powerful energy results in our consciousness being shaken from the perishable realm into Ultimate Reality, the Eternal Now. All healing occurs there where the arrow becomes one with the mark … the Essence … no beginning … no ending … no Time … where the prayerful ones become the prayer.

Words of power in repetitive prayer and chanting can be used for very specific purposes, including the clearing of the dense emotional fog we call fear. The sound and vibration involved with the chanting of mantras can produce transformation and have a positive healing effect. Sacred sounds, repetitive utterances, mantras, chanting, and prayer date all the way back to the beginning of time. All we know began with the Sacred Om and is sustained by its vibration. It has no beginning or end. It is well worth the effort to study how to engage the power of repetitive prayer, as practiced by so many traditions, on so many spiritual paths. It does not matter what language it is spoken in as long as it is the language of the very soul of our being.

Repetitive prayer should not be a divisive issue. Among the core mystical groups of most spiritual traditions, the root language is ultimately Sacred Silence. What matters is the breath and the heart's intention as they are carried upon the magnificent wings of the most surrendered prayer, whispered into the Ether. These are not the prayers and chanting of beggars with personal agendas and a list of demands. It is the sound of fusion with the Absolute Energy and finding the point of connection within. What matters is our ability to suspend our senses and drop all ego self-identification. What counts is how powerfully we are able to withdraw our attention from all distractions and focus it in such a way as to create change on a cellular level. What resonates with, and as Divine, is the purity of our hearts.

The information shared in this book is not meant to be purely remedial. There must be a wholesome, balanced lifestyle in place to support your practice. It makes no sense to have an elaborate altar, consecrated for healing and holistic well-being, if every door to the temple of the Soul is swinging open to any and every random energy. Much drama would be averted by simply closing and locking the doors in our lives to the mental and emotional triggers that cause us to fall into fear.

Most paths and traditions practice some form of chanting sacred sounds and words of power, each with their own unique method of repetition. Repetitive prayer is often practiced with a string of a prescribed number of prayer beads, or malas, for counting and focusing attention. There are specific "mudras" or hand and body positions associated with certain systems of chanting, meditations, and prayer. Some are practiced with instrumental accompaniment. Drums bring their own level of vibration and frequency. Some practices include spinning, dancing, or swaying rhythmically, while others require stillness of motion. Your best mantra is the mantra of your choice. The best mantra can be as simple as a childhood prayer or even as simple as "Thank You. Thank you for existence." You may feel drawn to a certain mantra or prayer system. Choose with discernment and in-depth knowledge of the meaning of what you are chanting or praying. Repetition of a mantra serves to quiet the over-thinking, reactive mind, inspiring transcendence beyond the origin of thought into pure awareness. To enter the silence of Ultimate Reality is the goal of most meditation disciplines.

You would be ill-advised to engage in most traditional practices without mindfulness regarding the proper respect for their sacredness. A strict protocol must be observed, down to specific subtleties of perfect pronunciation, personal hygiene, and diet. It is worth the effort to study how to perform these very basic but profound healing rituals. This practice is prescribed for times of perceived danger as a powerful shield of protection. Use this knowledge to empower your practice. The choice between the forces of fear and the forces of courage is ours to make. We are given the understanding that they are interdependent, and neither is "good" or "bad" … they just *are*. To see it in the context of a pendulum swinging rather than a balance being kept, we become an enemy of our own spiritual stability. We may find the worst enemy of our happiness in the mirror. That is where the energetic cleansing begins. Removing the magnets that attract spiritual drama will result in a more peaceful life.

One of the simplest of disciplines is the repetitive chanting of AUM/OM. The energy from the vibration engages the Third Eye and has the power to induce a deeply meditative and transcendental state of consciousness, which serves many purposes. The Sanskrit symbol for the Sacred AUM/OM illustrates the Four States of Consciousness. Our spiritual practice strives for the Fourth Level, the transcendent state of the Higher Self. From that perspective, protection from the trauma of spiritual attack is viewed differently. The first question would be, "Who is the 'self/Self' that is under attack?" If the personhood is under attack, the person must be dropped, and the matter must be taken to another realm to be resolved or dissolved. From a transcendental perspective, there is no "self," consequently, no self to be attacked. Once the trappings of the ego self, with its conditioned, subconscious, cultural narratives have been stripped away, the Self that remains knows that it cannot be harmed, damaged, or killed. It knows that it is Timeless, formless, identity-less, label-less, and without agenda or interest in carnal worries rooted in victimhood.

The OM/AUM

TURIYA
(Samadhi)
Transcendental State, Bliss,
Pure Consciousness,
Represented by the silence after Aum

ILLUSION
(Maya)
The World of Illusion
that veils True Awareness,
Prevents us from realizing
The Highest States of Bliss,
Duality

DEEP SLEEP
(Sushupti)
The "M" in auM,
Latent Unconscious

WAKEFUL STATE
(Jagrat)
The "A" in Aum,
The Conscious Mind

DREAM STATE
(Swapna)
The "U" in aUm,
The Subtle Worlds,
The Active Unconscious

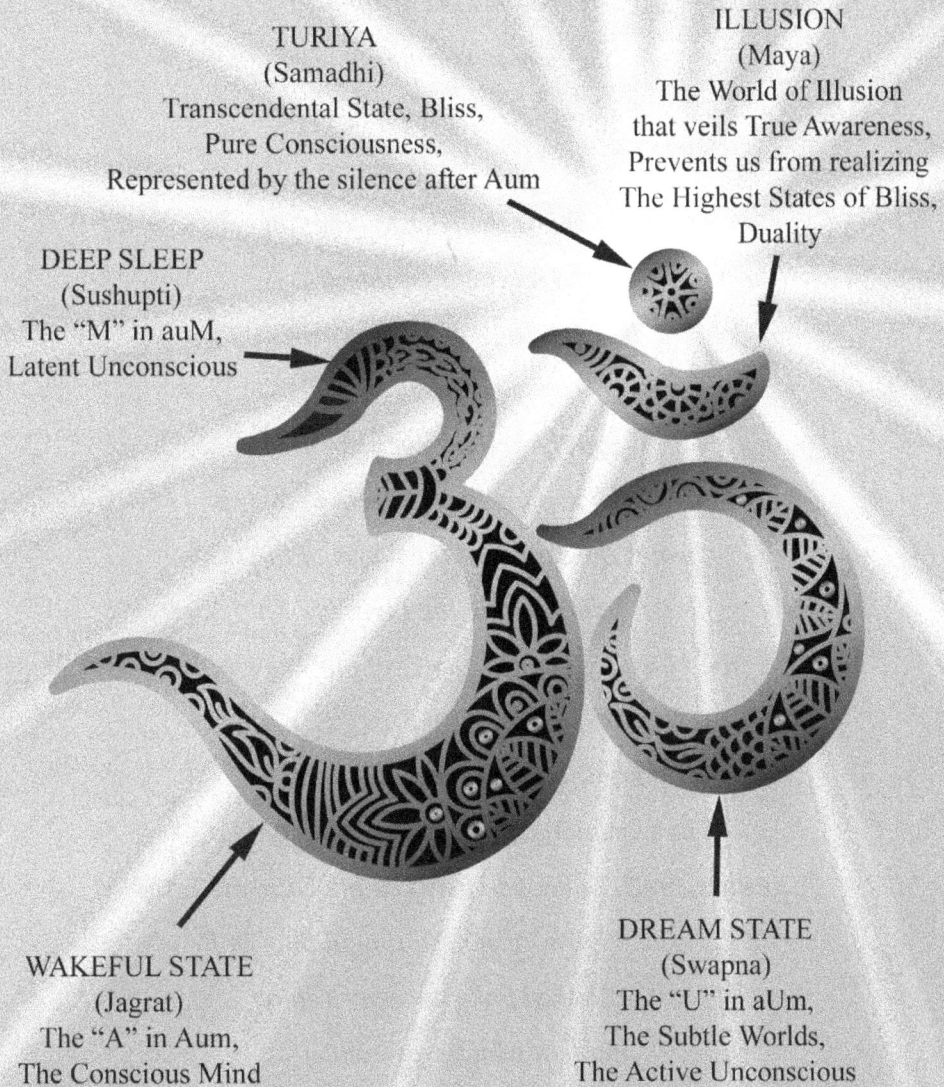

'OM,' 'OHM,' or 'AUM' is the sacred sound of the Universe. The OM symbol
demonstrates the States of Consciousness.

THE SACRED OM/OHM/AUM

This Ancient Mystical Sanskrit Symbol

represents the original

sound vibration

by which The Creator caused

the Universe to evolve

from chaos to order to creation

and all that sustains it.

It speaks of the dream world,

the waking state,

and the veil between them.

AUM, when intoned with teeth touching,

vibrates the skull and the bones of the face

stimulating the Light of

the Third Eye, at the center of our brow line,

the Sixth of our Seven Energy Centers

known as the Chakra System.

The vibration and frequency of the AUM

is the sacred connection between the Ultimate I AM

and The Divinity manifesting in the I in I,

that Sacred link between Creator

and that which was created.

It is the voice of the Contained calling out

from within the container of our physical form

singing the song of its liberation.

The container can either be a prison

incarcerating our Essence

or it can be the sacred garment

that compliments and adorns It.

The vibration of the AUM,

at the Fifth Chakra

in the area of the throat,

can be the medium

through which It is freed.

Sacred wisdom in wordless Holy language

through the representative visual art

of its evocative calligraphy

can cause the symbol of the AUM

to become a catalytic connection

that seeds the mystical Essence.

This sacred symbol is consistent with the three Sanskrit sounds

A U M representing various fundamental triads believed to be a vibration

of the spoken Essence of the Universe.

It is uttered as a mantra

in meditation, affirmations, and blessings.

Let us meditate every day.

We meditate upon The Divine Essence.

Do unto others as we would have them do unto us.

One God

One Love

One Breath

Born of the Eternal AUM

of and into

The Light of the Creator our souls merge

as members of the same body of Eternal Light.

Let us join in this Universal dream.

We will once again
dream together.
Together we will awaken,
our lives transformed
to emit our own frequency
and stop living in reference to
and under the influence of
discordant frequencies
that distort our perception of our own reality.

Like the AUM, I am imperishable.
I choose a life that confirms this truth in every moment.
The Timeless tone of the sacred AUM is my meditation.
I must never forget who I am.
I remember I am that space
I share with no one.
I am
beyond time
beyond you and me
I am That AUM.

States of Consciousness

State 1 – Waking (Jagrat)

- The "A" in OM (A-U-M);
- Conscious Awareness;
- Time/Space Continuum;
- Personal "I";
- Body/mind identification;
- External World;
- Covered by the Veil of Maya (Illusory World);

State 2 – Dreaming (Svapna)

- The "U" in OM (A-U-M);
- Still in Time/Space, but mutable, unstable, fluctuating, shifting, changeable, wavering, compared to Waking State;
- Inward-directed energy, but still under external influences;
- The mind is free to create and experience ethereal realities with quieted senses, Parallel waking realities in the union of the seer/seen, subject/object relationship;

State 3 – Deep Sleep (Susupti)

- The "M" in OM (A-U-M);
- Outside of Time/Space Continuum;
- Outside of body/mind identity consciousness;
- Inside the dreaming of Dreamtime World;

- We are aware of having been in this state only after we have returned to full consciousness;
- The experience of this state is required for our revitalization and to sustain our holistic well-being;
- Undifferentiated awareness, State of Deep Sleep, unconscious, oblivious;

State 4 – Transcendental (Turiya)

- Experiential knowledge of what the sages identify as Oneness with Divinity;
- The consciousness has merged with The Supreme Consciousness, Source, The God;
- The experience of merging with, or absorption into Pure Consciousness when the experiencer merges with the Absolute.
- It is beyond Time or Space.
- There is no duality.
- The Supreme Consciousness;
- It is the *silence* that follows OM (A-U-M);
- It is called The Fourth State;
- The direct experience of what the sages call the Fourth State is Eternal, unlike the other three states that come and go in it;
- It is the underlying, transcendent reality behind all three states of consciousness;
- It is a state of consciousness that extends beyond the context of a meditation practice or experience and spontaneously presents as a state called "flow" to a quiet mind;
- Turiya is obtainable in stages of Samadhi;
- The "Bliss" State is the bliss of the experience of the True Self;

The Turiya State can be induced. It is said that Sri Ramana Maharshi, an enlightened master, The Sage of Arunachala, would awaken this Transcendent State of Consciousness in spiritual seekers through his silent presence and a pensive gaze. It is not uncommon to experience such states in a Vipassana Meditation 10-day retreat at some point during the course. It is a common state to experience in some Yoga meditations and practices, in various levels of Samadhi, the Yogic Deep Sleep, Thoughtless State of consciousness.

5 – The Veil (Maya)

- The world of illusion;
- The world of names and forms;
- The world of masks of false identity;
- Duality;
- Seeks to conceal the True Self;
- Strong investment in keeping the veil intact, as a desert mirage ceases to claim attention once it is named and the True Self is revealed.

Beyond States – Turiyatita

Turiyatita is the "Stateless" State, beyond the Fourth State of Consciousness, called Turiya. As Turiya is the Witness, Turiyatita dissolves into all that is witnessed, and all that is beyond witnessing. In the pure Unity of its absorption it disappears into Oneness with Divinity … The Absolute … beyond form … beyond formlessness … Beyond. Turiyatita is the foundational, pervasive presence behind each of the other states. Each of the States is Impermanent as they come and they go. Turiya/Turiyatita is the only permanent State .... the only one of them that is real.

For Chanting (repetition) and Zikr (Dthkr) (remembrance), the number of beads, the number of rotations, the culture, the language, and the tradition of the mantra will differ from person to person. It is important to remember that beads cannot protect us. Protection is within us, at our most essential level. Our protection is the realization of our relationship with Divinity. This is not an act of enforced personal will. It is an act of surrender in Oneness with The God.

The Power of HU

HU

HU whispered into
my namelessness
HU are you ... ancient soul?
beyond breath
beyond death
HU are you ... ancient soul?
beyond the merge
beyond the purge
Do you know HU I AM?

Otherness disappears into oneness
Within disappears into without
Torn from what I once called me
now a paralyzed wave
adrift on a shoreless sea
beyond the agony
beyond the ecstasy
beyond belief
beyond hypocrisy
beyond the "I"
beyond the "me"

HU are you ... ancient soul?
There is no distinction
between the light within
and the light without
There is no distinction
They will not cancel you out
There is no distinction
Between faint whispers
and piercing screams
between piety
and blasphemy

HU are you ... ancient soul?
You are not disappearing
There is no distinction
between music and silence
Holy Water and tears

agony and ecstasy
courage and fear
There is no distinction between us
HU are you ... ancient soul?
You are the limitless wave
I am the limitless sea
The ache of the longing
is the remembrance of me
Do you know who I AM?

The intonement of HU is believed to be the True Nameless Name of The God, one that no path or traveler on it can claim ownership of. It is a mystical, vibratory expression of a oneness that is beyond language, beyond the comprehension of this mundane plane of names and forms. It refers to the Supreme Being beyond the Unknowable Plane of Zero Point Negative Existence. From time immemorial, the ancient ones have conjured many names from many languages, traditions, and cultures. In the wake of that noise was the Silence of the mystics, as it was in the beginning. But they knew there was always Something there ... Some Unknowable Something ... Beyond the thought of form, beyond the imagination of Absolute Immeasurable Potential.

The first manifestation of the Breath ... the Vibration, the Frequency, the Ultimate Cause of everything, known and Unknown. HU is the breath, the Voice, the Sacred innermost Spirit, and the song of all things. Creation dissolves all identity in the infinite ocean of stillness and harmonizes in the silent song of surrender to The HU. All of creation exhales the last breath of longing, with the dreams and illusions of separation annihilated and surrendered into the Oneness of HU.

The HU mantra is the spiritual *Source* as well as the *Completion* of all sound, all words, all being. The keeper of the secret of sound guards the mystery of creation. Timeless revelation has spun Light and shadow worlds in and out of healing the excruciating pangs of suffering, impermanence, attachment, and aversion. From obscurity to illumination, through the manifest and unmanifest, mortal and Eternal … through the HU, we find the healing of perishable creation in the Realms of the Infinite. Sound vibration charges and cleans all seven bodies and their energy points, activates the Solar Plexus, and recharges the central nervous system as it balances and aligns the chakras. This mantra is a life-sustaining tool for reducing anxiety, insomnia, fear, and depression, focusing on connecting the body and the soul with the Oneness of Hu.

- The HU is chanted similarly to the OM (AUM) as "Huuuuuuu … ";

- HU is the emanation of the Abstract Plane, meaning unlimited sound;

- HU creates an absorption into the Oneness of Ultimate Reality;

- It symbolizes Union with The God;

- All sound is based on HU;

- HU is the mantra of Silence;

- It harmonizes negative frequencies, chakras, energy points, and energetic bodies;

- The vibrations of HU are too subtle to be perceptible to the physical ears or eyes;

- HU activates the non-physical aspect of the sense of hearing;

- Heavenly Emanation of the Essential Aspect of Breath;

- The sound of the Source of all sources;

- All sounds have their uniqueness until they all finally become HU;

- HU is known as Abstract Sound, Primordial Sound, referring to its Authorless Nature;

- It collapses all distinctions, dualities, and constructs;

- It collapses all distinctions of concepts and precepts;

- It collapses the time barriers of past, present, and future;

- It collapses distinctions between physical inner space and outer space. It is in, it is out, it is around, and it is about;

- It is a door/portal/vortex of Energy that dissolves the ego and increases inner Light;

- HU collapses all realms into the Unknowable;

- It allows the True Self to effortlessly transcend all planes of existence, freed from all the limitations of mundane reality;

- Transcendence through the HU mantra can approach and exceed states of rapture;

- One may enter a state of extreme intoxication, manifesting as symptoms such as trance state, i.e., fixed stare, dilated pupils, dreamy facial expression, blissful glow, expressions that radiate otherworldly joy, and ecstasy;

- HU can inspire experiences of the unseen worlds in the form of receiving intuitions, visions, and revelations. Impressions of Divine Wisdom may be imparted in experiences with the Holy Spirit;

- One may experience a release from pain, anxiety, worries, fear, and sorrow as the soul feels freed from the imprisonment of the senses and the physical body;

- It kills fear, anger, sadness, depression, ego, hate, arrogance, and jealousy;

- The HU mantra can keep others from controlling you;

- It is a powerful tool of Manifestation;

- Sound and vibration of HU are the source of inner revelation;

- The mystics of all traditions know that sound vibration has a peculiar effect on every aspect of Universal existence;

- The mystery of HU is revealed to the mystic;

- When the abstract sound is audible, all other sounds become indistinct to the mystic;

- Yogis and ascetics experience HU through Breath, as is experienced in song, the shankha conch shell, ney flute, reed flute, and didgeridoo. It leads to the awakening of the inner life and connection with the inner tone.

APPENDIX FIVE

THE ARCHETYPE OF
THE INTERCEDING SPIRIT
(THE HOLY SPIRIT)

FACELESS: The Sacred Relationship

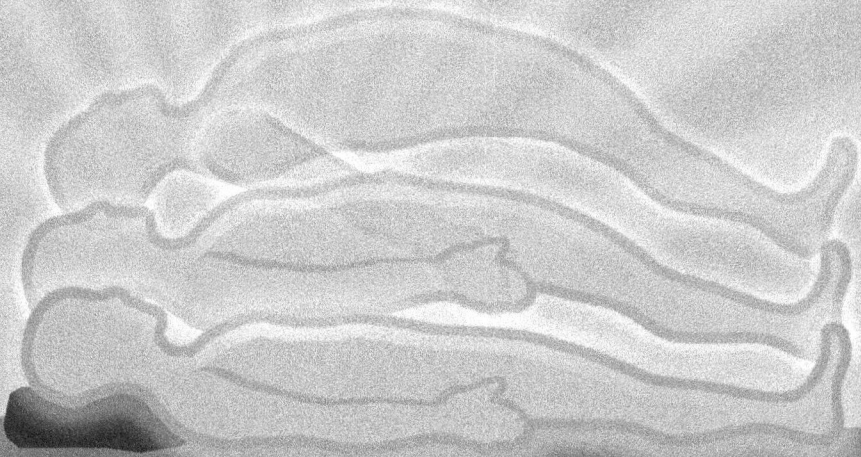

This section is an excerpt from my book FACELESS: THE SACRED RELATIONSHIP, a mystical journey behind the masks of the archetypal faces of the energies that permeate our lives. It is shared here as an in-depth overview and character analysis of a phenomenal energy that defies introduction or description. I share this, not as an archetype or a personality. But as the Refuge in Whom we trust our souls. In such an overview of the influences "spirits" of varied descriptions can have on our lives … The Holy Spirit is the Ultimate, Most Powerful, and Relevant force and influence on the subject of Psychic Self-Defense.

THE INTERCEDING HOLY SPIRIT
Planetary Association – Preceded planets
Ruled by the Fifth Element – Light Akasha
Soul Star Chakra

As an archetype, in this text, the term Interceding Spirit (Holy Spirit) is not used in a "religious" context. It refers to a mystery that can only be called The Nameless, from a metaphysical perspective. A person who is in no way religious is just as available to the experience of this mysterious phenomenon as a person who rests firmly in the belief in The God and the spiritual hierarchy of their religion of choice. A nontheistic or atheistic person can just as easily become caught up in the throes of experiencing an array of diverse manifestations triggered by the power of the Holy Spirit. Regardless of their belief or non-belief system, one can appear to be triggered to exhibit apparently involuntary expressions, many no longer being in sovereign control of their 'person.'

Many religions, cultures, mystical paths, and belief systems seek to "own" exclusive rights to the access of the Holy Spirit, calling it by many names. Attempts at "ownership" are sometimes done through subtle, subconscious, subliminal references that are a part of our societal and spiritual conditioning. It is accomplished through media, tradition, culture, subliminal seduction, hegemony, thought-form implants, ethereal/energetic projections, and other control mechanisms designed to manipulate mass consciousness. It is done through the whispered language of subconscious programming, boxes and containers of identity, labels worn like toe tags, and the viral hallucination of ownership of something that is NOT ownable. Perhaps these divisive manipulations are what has caused sayings like "the opiate of the masses" to be used in reference to these collective thought-form bubbles. These interpretations seek to establish, from the perspective of their own specific brand of hypnosis, that they, each in their own special way, are the "chosen ones." So many are waiting for a Chariot of some sort to swing low, scoop them up, and sweep them away, leaving behind everyone else who believe, think, and live their lives differently. That is all an element of the hypnosis. *However*, just behind this elaborately crafted veil of illusion, there is another version of "the collective" … The "Inclusive Collective," who, each in their own special way, *know* that we are *all* the chosen ones … each in our own special way.

If the Holy Spirit can *only* be experienced in a religious context, how do you explain phenomenal interventions in the lives of atheists or so-called non-believers, completely without solicitation and unsupported by any particular belief system? Some, after having had "the experience," transcended religious references to explain what had happened to them. Many have categorized it as "Unknowable." There are marked, undeniable similarities among the reports of those who have succumbed to it or interacted with it. Bottom line, the experience of these interventions *transcend* religion, culture, race, ethnicity, personality, form, gender, Space and Time. It can only be classified as a *miracle* of the Unknowable Realm.

This Unconceivable Energetic Force is an element of The Absolute, The Ultimate, the Incomprehensible. A Force such as that cannot be an *object*. Some want to know or reason, "Is it male? Is it female? Is it neither, or is it both?" It is considered by many traditions or systems of belief to be beyond gender and human characteristics. Its Essence is insulted by being degraded to references of personhood that seek to reduce its presence to body parts, human features, and physical characteristics. It is inappropriate to attempt to assign it human appearances based on our own conditioning and finite understanding, even though it has been reported to have taken on a human appearance for its own time and purposes.

The Holy Spirit is not a person. It is a Spirit, but it is NOT a common spirit, as in references to jinn, ghosts, poltergeists, hauntings, or even angelic or elemental presences. It is The Inbreathing of Oneness with the Light and Essence of The Creator and the Out Breath of that Sacred Connection.

Across every mystical path and tradition (mostly in a religious context), characteristics of the Holy Spirit are consistently referred to, and described in many ways:

- It is a non-physical presence;

- It is made of Light or Self-illuminating triple darkness of dark matter/energy;

- It has no fixed form;

- It exists beyond Time and Space;

- It is memetic in nature, capable of shapeshifting apparitions;

- This Spirit can be experienced as Yin, Feminine and Receptive or Yang, Masculine and Interpenetrating, and has no fixed gender;

- The Hebrew language *Ruach ha-Kodesh*, as well as the Arabic translation *Ruh al-Qudus* *(Ruach)* and *(Ruh),* are *feminine* references; and speak of the Divine aspect of prophecy and wisdom. Writers in these languages commonly use maternal images when speaking of the Holy Spirit;

- The Christian Trinity manifests as The Father, Son, and Holy Spirit, commonly depicted as a winged dove and as tongues of fire, holding that these are three aspects among the many manifestations of the One God;

- In the Catholic Church, the Holy Spirit is often referred to in English as "He," yet maintained that the established gender reference of each respective language should be upheld. Masculine gender references are common, yet understood to be *figurative* in reference to the personifications used when speaking of aspects and attributes of The God, being that The God is Spirit and spirit has no fixed gender;

- Some paths of Christian belief teach that the Holy Spirit is of a feminine energy. Both feminine nouns and verbs, as well as feminine analogies, are thought to be used by The Bible to describe the Spirit of God;

- It is a manifestation of the Spirit of the Christ;

- It is a manifestation of the Spirit of the Mother of the Christ;

- It is often described as a Feminine energy;

- It is a manifestation of the Divine Feminine;

- The Bahai faith refers to it as the *"Most Great Spirit,"* the bounty of God;

- It is the vital or animating force in all living things and creatures;

- It has an "in-dwelling" quality;

- In many literal translations, it is the *Breath of the God*;

- It is an aspect of Divine Grace;

- It has a viral quality, as though one may *transmit it* or *catch it*;

- It is capable of triggering or activating a spiritual awakening;

- It is an interpenetrating or occupying force, as in being *filled with it or full of it*;

- It is a conductive force, as one being made to *channel it*;

- It is a sentient force, as one being *touched by it*;

- It is a conduit in a manner that suggests the transmission of diverse energies;

- It could cause one to be affected by it in some discernible way;

- It is completely beyond our linear understanding and expectations;

- It is completely beyond our concepts of Cause and Effect.

Elemental Qualities of the Interceding Spirit:

- *Fire Element:* It can be electrical in nature. There is an electrical current that associates its manifestations with the fire element, strong enough to literally knock a human down to the ground by invisible contact. Therefore, the Holy Spirit is understood to manifest as a destructive, fiery force in the context of a cleansing, purging, sanctification, purification, or as an act of judgment. It can also refer to the fiery energy called Kundalini, surging up through the spinal column, from the 1st through the 7th Chakra. It is associated with fire as an element, in reference to being baptized by it, impassioned by it, or given it as a refined force in the context of prophecy and healing.

- *Water Element:* There are common references on many spiritual and mystical paths to being "baptized in the Holy Spirit" and being immersed or submerged in it. In this reference, the Holy Spirit and the water element are used synonymously. To be plunged beneath the water and surface reborn symbolizes a strong force and source of great power to create change on an essential level. It also refers to bathing, washing, cleansing, and initiation of a process of purification. Associations with the water element extend to references of being "filled with it," as one would speak of filling an empty vessel with water, signifying replenishment or renewal. The references, "Water is a "type" of the

Spirit of God" and "Water of Life," represent the Holy Spirit. In a reference, "I will pour out my Spirit," the water element speaks of the Holy Spirit.

- *Air Element:* The Holy Spirit is directly associated with breath, a breeze, a gust, a burst, or a torrent of wind. It can occur as having no apparent cause or source, a Force or phenomenon that 'touches' or makes a form of contact, creating a spontaneous effect. A forceful breath expelled from the mouth carrying sacred words, for the purpose of anointing, blessing, charging, or cleansing is also a manifestation of it. It also means *Life,* as in *Breath of Life.* It is a manifestation of *air in motion,* like a *strong driving wind.* Air, like spirit, is invisible, but it can be perceived by normal senses. It can be heard. It can be felt. It can be seen through the manifestations of its effects. Breath when referencing communications can take on many forms. Spirit can communicate or speak through diverse mediums. Messages, revelations, and even prophecy can be transmitted through something that someone says at a particular moment, whether they are communicating directly to you or not. These uncanny communications can travel by means of the airwaves, such as over the internet, television, radio, or through telepathic transmission directly to the mind.

- *Earth Element:* Most are familiar with the fact that demons have been known to operate in a form of what we identify as a "possession," with the ability to "take over" every aspect of a person's being. They may have the ability to speak, see, and hear through them, using their faculties. They are known to be able to impose or implant thoughts upon the mind, and command actions, without the knowledge or ability of the host to control what is happening. Outside of an extremely religious context, people don't talk as much about the energetic antithesis of such a phenomenon … The Holy Ghost/Spirit. In accounts that would be labeled miraculous, it has also been described of the Holy Spirit to be able to "take over" and compel a person who has been "touched" by it, or "filled" with it, to perform incredible manifestations of extraordinary or supernatural power. It has been described as an unknowable dynamistic Force that can appear either as personal or impersonal, and fill a person in a way similar to a fluid, permeating their entire presence.

- *Ether Element*: The Holy Spirit is associated with spiritual and mystical manifestations, a Presence in all major religions, and has been known to create manifestations in the lives of people who are atheists or completely indifferent to anything mystical in context. These events can occur by means of miraculous, spontaneous remissions in physical ailments, some of which may have been terminal, through a touch or energetic directive into the "human energy field" or aura.

It is believed to be able to travel in the auric field, in direct contact with the physical body, in such a way as to sustain it, protect it, and connect it with "higher" energies and forces. This Holy Ether or Akasha, occupying the Heart Chakra, is the full experience of the Omnipresent, Imperishable, and Unknowable, Ultimate Creative Force of all Being. From Ether, the revealer of all forms and names, all emerged. We do not have to be able to understand it or name it. Its existence is inarguable.

The Zeal Point Chakra - located in the back of the head at the base of the skull (the medulla oblongata) between the 2nd and 3rd cervical vertebrae. It is referred to as the "Mouth of God" and has a direct correlation to the energies of the Holy Spirit. The High-frequency conscious mind that masters expression of spiritual power through the voice.

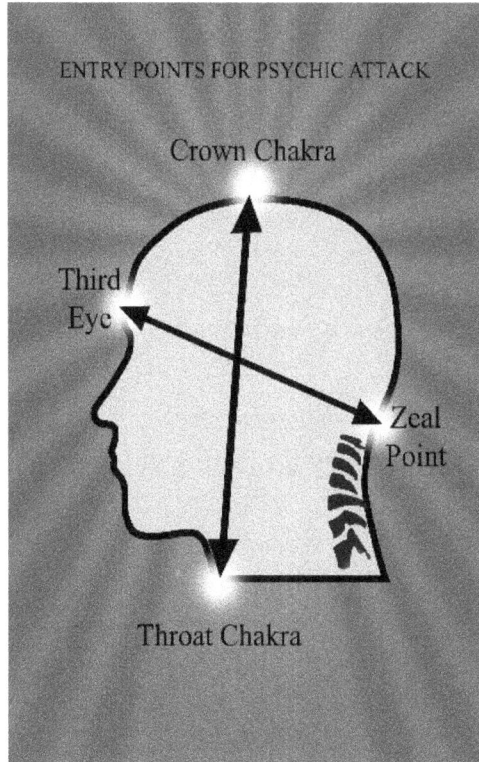

The Soul Star Chakra – the first of the Transpersonal Chakras (The Seat of the Soul), located just above *The Crown Chakra*, the gateway of the energy flow into the body. Point of surrender to Divinity, the Holy Spirit, as our inner and guiding Light; where Transcendent Love and Spirit connect and are channeled into the physical body; Oneness with Divinity; selflessness and compassion; more ethereal, a higher octave of the function of the Crown Chakra, and is less available to egoic energies. The Soul Star Chakra connects us directly to the Cosmos, Ultimate Source, and the Holy Spirit.

The Fifth (Throat) Chakra is located in the throat region. 'Vishuddha' (meaning purification) is the Sanskrit word for the Fifth Chakra. It empowers us to mystically speak or channel Transcendent Truth. It is the crossroad point where the higher consciousness and physical body intersect. This energy vortex, where matter and spirit traverse, is associated with the Holy Spirit, revelation, inspiration, and communication. It is a portal through which high vibrational energies are drawn into both the subtle and physical bodies … the gateway to Divine Light'. The Holy Spirit descends from the realms of pure, formless consciousness occurring as an indiscernible vibration that few can hear, capable of creating form.

When one has had an encounter with this Spirit, diverse manifestations include but are not limited to:

- Ecstatic states of consciousness with reports of feeling dissolved, absorbed by it, disappearing into it, merging with it, being filled with it, becoming one with it;

- Out of Body Experiences (OBE), a feeling of being taken away, out of the body, and returned to the body;

- Doubling over in a "crunch," consistent with being punched in the stomach;

- Quaking, the appearance of a seizure with no physical cause;

- Crying, weeping, laughing uncontrollably for no apparent reason;

- Behaving and appearing inebriated, staggering, and communicating as though in a state of drunkenness. Loss of composure, muted or slurred speech, vacant or dizzied look in the eyes;

- Most report being indelibly "marked" in ways that people who know them consider remarkable. They note changes on every level of their being … some common, some profound in nature;

- Describing the feeling as "good" by comparison to altered states of consciousness induced by alcohol or drugs;

- Complete loss of consciousness, fainting, falling out as though struck down by some unseen force. This phenomenon is called being "slain in the Spirit";

- Speaking or singing in tongues (unknown languages), a state called "glossolalia." Incoherent or prophetic outbursts for no apparent reason;

- Full body chills, goosebumps, tingling (feelings of effervescence), shivering, stiffening of the body;

- Spontaneous frenetic dancing, spinning, rapid whirling, giggling, hopping or jumping, rolling, running, unusual dancing;

- Prophetic visions and utterances, with or without mental images or words;

- The feeling of having been shown in words and imagery a "story," accompanied by the feeling of 'living in it, or often from an observer's perspective;

- Reacting like touching an electrical wire or cable. A fragile human frame being touched by that kind of energy is like a full-body shock.

MANIFESTATIONS include, but are not limited to:

- Distinct changes in the experiencer's character:
  - Their behavior;
  - Their disposition or attitude;
  - Their temperament;
  - Their sense of detachment from worldly affairs and concerns;
  - A shift of their striving or ambitions;
  - Their choice in associations;
  - The way they dress;
  - Their choices in music and entertainment;
  - Their choices in reading and studies;
  - The way they spend their money;

- Their eating habits;

- Their manner in handling personal relationships;

- Their relationships with their children and other family members;

- Their empathic concern for the poor and suffering;

- Their preoccupation with ways of ending the suffering of others;

- Their opposition to the oppression of self and others;

- Their habits, drinking, smoking, drugs, and sexual behavior;

- Their business practices;

- The way they treat others;

- The way they require themselves to be treated;

- Their indifferent reaction to their own personal suffering or joy;

- Unusual abilities to see into the spirit world;

- Unusual abilities to interpret dreams;

- Unusual abilities to create or compose (channel) art, music, poetry, and prose;

- Intercessory prayer (on behalf of others).

- Charismatic gifts:

- Words of wisdom;

- Words of knowledge;

- Increased faith;

- The gift of healing;

- The gift of miracles;

- Prophecy;

- Discernment of spirits;

o Speaking in tongues;

o Interpretation of tongues.

These evidential manifestations cannot be reduced to the laws we recite of common cause and effect. The "Cause" is invisible to humans, yet visible "Effects" are witnessed. Rarely do you hear reports of people taking 'personal' credit for the incredible manifestation of the Holy Spirit. I am sure that a fear of being cut off would accompany any egoic claims of being the personal source of such power. The source of these gifts typically defies reason and is consistently attributed to the realm of Spirit.

- Grace:

  o will fight for you;

  o will intervene in your personal affairs;

  o will grow your faith;

  o will grow your understanding;

  o will touch you;

  o will comfort you;

  o will heal you, and heal others through you.

The Spirit of Intercession is the manifest belief that the Holy Spirit is the ethereal guide, the Spirit of Absolute Grace, the Gift that intervenes in our affairs, in our state of love and surrender … or not. There are many who are far from being pious that report having been visited or touched by this mysterious Spirit, who have done absolutely nothing, by our judgment, to qualify. Some experiencers report that with the "electrical current" or "spark" of this touch, a state of "dissolving," suspension of the senses, a spontaneous spiritual awakening occurs. This often occurs after having fallen into hopelessness and helplessness to change the circumstances of their life. A mark is indelibly carved into the heart of one who has surrendered his or her personal will by the touch of the Holy Spirit.

The reason I refer to the archetype of the Holy Spirit as the "Interceding Spirit" is because I, as we all do, understand that in this life … Things go wrong. We can be made to feel powerless in the face of the whole ground being snatched from under our feet, finding ourselves left to deal with vulgar and uncouth opponents, apparently alone with no hope. Things go wrong in ways that appear they are not survivable. Yet, there are accounts of miracles that have occurred that defy explanation. There are testimonials and witnesses of a power, a force, beyond religious context, dogma, or understanding, that has miraculously intervened in the affairs of people's lives, often in a very personal way. Leaving a specific signature behind, there was a declaration of order established, a balance, and fairness restored. It is done by drawing from and being a conduit of the transmission of an Energy from the Highest Realms of Ultimate Transcendence, and *beyond* that, into the Absolutely Unknowable. It is believed to be the "Active" Force, Essential Spirit of The God, demonstrably projecting, as an Energy, through, to, and into anyone, any place, and at any time, just by Willing it, according to Divine Will. True accounts have defied reasonable explanation. For those who disbelieve, no proof is possible. For the latter, only direct experience could carry even a grain of proof.

The Holy Spirit is sometimes experienced as a Feminine or Yin energy. As her attribute, the manifestation of the Divine Feminine, she, in all of her creative, nurturing energy, is experiencing an incredible betrayal of her spirit. In the wake of her usurped power, she now attends an ill-conceived perpetual ceremony of the crowning of the "King." She stands in the ruins of her peaceful rulership, replaced by toxic masculine principles, imagery, and energies. Her tears flow in rivers. She sighs in resignation. In the face of the audacity of it all, she stands as the principle of the primordial womb. That is what perplexes the self-exalting, egoic traditional masculine principals, in denial of the nature of the non-dual True Self. In sacred scriptures, there are consistent references to Divinity as "We" in the context of gender. How could it be any other way?

God is used too often as a reference to an authoritative male Deity (with basic human characteristics and body parts) that dwells outside of one's self … that controls, surveils, rewards, and punishes, and requires a fear-based, rather than a love-based relationship. How could such a Force to be reckoned with be named and painted with the graffiti of personhood? How can any claim ownership of that which cannot be owned … only experienced?

If one's sad reality is completely anchored in contextual concepts of Cause and Effect, one will never understand the workings, the beauty of effects that occur with no 'apparent' cause. The gifts of the Holy Spirit are often given as a reward without evidently deserving it, a Grace, a Blessing … just because.

The Holy Spirit is beyond petition, beyond an altar, beyond prayer, beyond belief, beyond surrender, beyond perception … beyond the spiritual power structures of this plane of existence. The conspiracy of her complete disempowerment was accomplished by toxic masculine values that took control of industries that would influence and condition the world to disrespect her. And, for whatever reasons, even women fall under that spell and participate in their own spiritual dethroning. Within her womb, all creation found form, through her love it was born. At what point do the two opposite polarities of The Holy Spirit separate and become individuated hostile entities, operating in a conflicted sovereign way, no longer interdependent upon one another … each seeking to eclipse the Light of the other?

When the clouds of that shadow war descended, so did a collective forgetfulness … devouring the Light of beings that were trusted to be the portal, the womb into which the spirit is given to take form, issued onto this plane of experiencing. She was given to be the nest of its nurturing, the "channel," conduit, intermediary, the transitional vessel between the Realm of Divinity of the Spirit World in the realm of physical manifestation … whether she ever gives physical birth or not. She now rises up from the ashes of having been reduced to a caricature of a wicked imagination after having ultimately given up and reduced herself to that absurd level … if only in her own mind.

The "Divine Feminine" archetype is not a "person"ality steeped in "person"hood. This energy is not being presented as some "personal" concept of an in-dwelling or supportive entity. It is commonly believed in many spiritual and mystical traditions that there will be a "return" or a "revisiting" of the Holy Spirit to the "Mother Earth" to right wrongs and injustices experienced by the collective, bringing consequences and reckoning to the perpetrators of these inequities. The Nameless Secret, The Source of Transcendent Love, will heal and restore the well-being of this troubled world.

Whenever righteousness wanes
and unrighteousness increases,
I send myself forth.
For the protection of the good and for the destruction of evil,

and for the establishment of righteousness,
I come into being age after age.

~ Bhagavad Gita 4.7 –8 ~

References to the Holy Spirit are often used synonymously with The God, but not in a way as to establish associations with the Divine One. It is more acknowledged as a fusion of the Attributes of the One. The Unknowable One is beyond name, gender, translation, tongues, and utterances we use to describe it. For it to have a name, someone would have had to have been present at its birth to give it that name. How could that be? It is Birthless, Deathless, Faceless, Timeless, Limitless, Nameless, Selfless … Self-contained of every name, every attribute, and capable of every form, yet, beyond any mundane qualities, beyond all belief systems, philosophies, doctrines, or religions.

The compassionate voice of the Divine Feminine may petition, "Forgive them Holy Mother/Father, for they know not what they do." The energetic manifestations of Divine Feminine … These are our mothers, our companions, our daughters, our sisters, our teachers, our friends, our intermediary source. She symbolizes the Yin … dark matter, the dark energy of creation, from the plane of non-being, the self-illuminating triple darkness of the womb that birthed these beings into the manifest realm. The compassionate voice of the Divine Masculine may petition, "Forgive them Holy Mother/Father, for they know not what they do." The Ethereal manifestation of Divine Masculine … These are our fathers, our companions, our sons, our brothers, our teachers, our friends, our intermediary source. He symbolizes the Yang … emerging Light, the energy of creation, from the plane of non-being, the self-illuminating triple darkness of the womb that commanded these beings into the manifest realm.

We are not total opposites. We are not bags of body parts seeking to define the entirety of our being by physical attributes. We are energy, vibration, and frequency clothed in matter. Our existence occurs as two sides of the same coin … Indivisible. Each side contains the spirit of the other. But look closer. A coin does not have two sides, it has three sides. The third side is the energetic circumference that declares an interdependent oneness. We must meet on the third side, in the realm of the union of our peripheral reality as counterparts of the vehicle of existence, if we want to avert the dire consequences of gender-based wars. These bodies are our vehicles, not our weapons against one another. We are Light. We must accept ourselves as Light, energy, and pure consciousness on the third side, the paradox.

Engaging in a relationship with any aspect of The Holy Spirit archetype begins with the awareness of its sacred nature and its relevance in regard to the well-being of the planet and its beings. Generally, and with regard to relationships, this energy transcends identification as a mere "archetype." We must expand our perceptions and become one with the Spirit and allow it to guide and protect us, and fill us full of its Light. When hope is gone, when all is lost, the spirit of renewal rises up and shines out of the eyes of the formerly hopeless, who found Her voice in their heart.

A whisper arises from the threshold of the Realm of Turiya … "You are not alone. You cannot do this on your own. You were never *required* to do this on your own. You have no "own." You are my own, and I am your own. Grace exists as you. Be confirmed in that!" whispers the Deliverer and Origin of Grace.

I have been a seeker and I still am,
but I stopped asking the books and the stars.
I started listening to the teaching of my Soul.

~ Rumi~

The Holy Spirit is an Intervening Spirit of Truth and is partial, unlike impartial spirits, entities, and energies that might be called upon to defend or protect you, expecting favors or offerings in return, unbeknownst to you.

APPENDIX SIX

Meditation is the Bridge Between Worlds of Consciousness

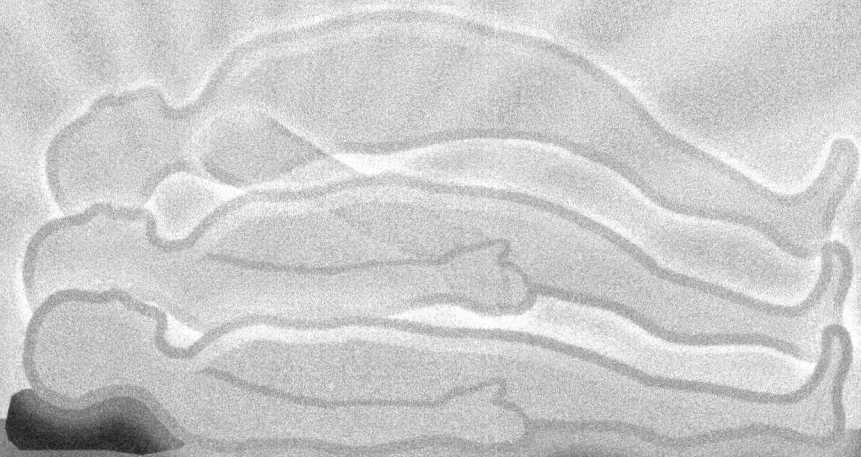

Meditation is the Bridge Between Worlds of Consciousness

Knowing when and how to step out of our own way and venture beyond linear intellect into the world of the mystic is something that cannot be easily taught. Nor is it something that needs to be taught or necessarily sought after. Most of us naturally have a strong resistance to willingly surrendering control of any aspect of our consciousness, that thread of control we think we have over our lives. At some point, or not, with study and practice, that spark of mysticism can ignite the fire of spiritual awakening. It can happen spontaneously, or not. We all have the capacity to experience an expansion of consciousness, and most have a choice. In general practice, the least we can expect to experience in a Mystical Meditation practice is a relaxed and peaceful state of mind, a retreat from the chaos and stress of our lives.

The practice of meditation has been known to trigger unpredictable and often phenomenal experiences. After entering a meditative state, some people experience the distraction of hearing a voice, or voices, in continual monologue or dialogue. The goal of serious meditation is to quiet the endless, mindless chatter of the ghosts that stalk our subconscious world. Much of it is self-generated. Some may have visceral experiences that occur much like a Lucid Dream, with uncanny links to outer reality as with the phenomenon of Sleep Paralysis.

In the practice of meditation, many will enter a semi-trance state and begin to perceive information that is subject to visionary interpretation. To tap into all that is available, we must be fearless enough to journey to the planes of consciousness where dreams occur. These realms are much like our own, parallel to our own, differing in perspective, density, and frequency. The transcendent qualities of the Astral Plane allow that *any* and *every*thing can catalyze the opening of a portal into a deep meditative state, even without our intention. The clouds, the waves upon the water, the sand, the rocks, and any random stimuli can cause us to be drawn into a meditative trance. There are many ways to accomplish this objective. One of the most effective is to set aside time, if no more than ten to fifteen minutes a day, to dedicate to a daily ritual of embracing stillness and silence. Even deeper and more refined realms are attainable through prayer. Sharing the insights of our meditations will become an effective meditation done in the spirit of prayer. That is why maintaining a daily journal is encouraged.

Many subtle techniques can be used to put ourselves into Dreamtime within moments. For the best results, the practitioner's goal is to experience a shift in perspective about our linear views of Time and Space. This requires a conscious shift of attention from the external to the internal Transcendent Planes. It requires us to turn within and redefine reality to include Dreamtime, at the crossroads where vertical and horizontal realities meet. In preparation to safely make this shift, we must first draw around ourselves a strong, protective force field of Transcendent Light with prayer and visualization.

A simple but powerful exercise can help to provide an energetic defense shield in a matter of moments with a subtle shift of awareness. Envision yourself comforted by the Pure, Radiant White Light of Divine Protection as a shield and barrier to any presence of harmful intent. Visualize yourself encapsulated in an egg-shaped body of Light, which extends several feet from the physical body. Nothing penetrates this powerful barrier except that which is Divinely Ordained with Permission to do so. Prayer and remembrance of The God as our Protector empowers these visualizations.

Light Sphere of Protection

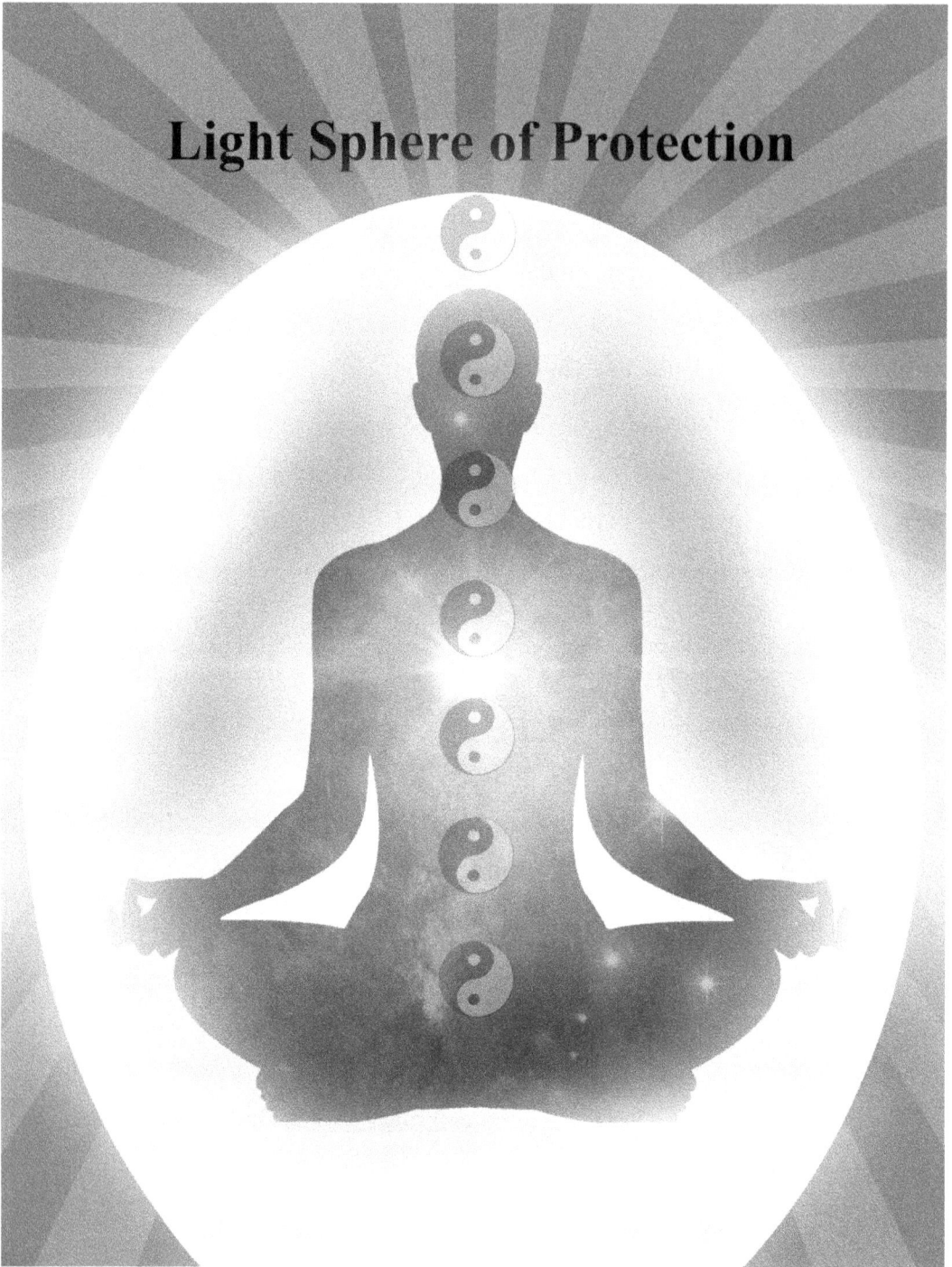

Our most formidable enemy in the assaults against our psyche is the torment of our own fears. To see things as they really are is the most powerful weapon we have. With time, it will become a comfortable lifestyle that will provide sound spiritual security for us, as we walk through many dimensions, across the bridge between dreams, and learn more about the costumes and faces of this world that all of us hide behind.

The Sacred Self

The Sacred Self is the holistic presentation we bring into prayer, meditation, ritual, and any sacred spiritual practice. Through a sense of Oneness with the Sacred Self and the Divine Oneness, we are able to experience the Realm of Timelessness. Observe the basic rules of physical and spiritual hygiene when performing meditation and prayer ritual. Some methods include performing ablution, a ritual cleansing as prescribed according to many traditions before spiritual work, and prayer. "Cleanliness is next to Godliness" is not an empty cliché calling out to meaningless ritual. A purification bath of sea salt and baking soda will amply prepare you for intense meditation, cleansing the aura of astral garbage. Soak for about twenty minutes. In the preparation of the bath, as you pray or chant your mantra aloud, run your hands through the water, projecting the energy of your prayers into the water in a stirring motion.

Anoint a white candle with olive oil and prayer. Place the candle in a fire-safe location that is easy to view from the tub to provide a pleasant ambiance and a powerful focal point for concentration. Certain oils enhance this cleansing ritual, such as rosemary, rose, and lavender. Engage in your choice of affirmations, visualization, intense prayer, or a guided meditation. Do not use a recording of a guided meditation unless you have listened to it first, in its entirety, in a fully conscious state. Determine that you completely understand and are in agreement with every single word of the meditation.

Many read or chant verses from Holy Scriptures. Some engage in prayers that take on the form of personal conversations with The God, with the understanding that is exactly what they are. I have experienced a quickening of frequency and energy when I ran a slow stream of water from the shower while meditating in the tub. The cleansing of the aura and sacred workspace to prepare for meditation and prayer is accomplished by "smudging," using smoke charged with prayer and positive intention as a clearing of discordant energies. You can burn a "smudge stick" of sage or burn cedar, sweetgrass, or Palo Santo. Light your sage wand, in prayer, and fan the smoke with your hand or feathers, using your right hand. Pay specific attention to the top of the head (Crown Chakra) Third Eye or Sixth Chakra, (between and just above the brow line), the nape of the neck, the throat, the heart, and the Solar Plexus area, all the way to the bottom of the feet and back up to the Crown Chakra. The smoke represents the rising of the spirit of the prayer to the Great Spirit, the Creator, for spiritual cleansing and protection.

This ritual cleansing should be performed in a manner consistent with your chosen tradition of prayer while visualizing the aura being cleansed of negative energies. In addition to cleansing yourself, take the time to cleanse your meditation area and the entire house with frankincense, myrrh, sweet grass, salt, lime, lavender, and sage, prior to spiritual work. What you use, when, how, and why will become intuitive choices as you delve deeper into your studies.

Basic Guidelines for Meditation

It is best to avoid meditation when tired, sick, angry, extremely depressed, or in a general state of extreme fatigue. Your unstable, ungrounded energy may compromise your meditation experience. Remember that gloomy moods can alter the quality of your meditation. It would be advisable to pray your strongest prayer before entering into a meditative state.

Before engaging in any meditation: Observe the recommended basic protocol regarding personal hygiene and be attentive to the cleanliness and ambiance of your setting.

Take particular care in the maintenance of a clean, healthy aura. The human aura can be negatively affected by the energy you expose yourself to. Thoughts are things. We are all being constantly bombarded with negative thought-forms, energies, and vibrations from our environment, as well as the negativity that we generate from within ourselves. The electromagnetic force field around the physical body requires maintenance to keep it cleansed of the garbage that so easily attaches to it and drains our positive energy. An accumulation of this negative energy can make us walking magnets for bad experiences and compromised health. An unhealthy aura is a breeding ground for spiritual, mental, emotional, and physical disease.

Prepare a quiet place for prayer and meditation. There should be no television, radio, electronic devices, or distracting conversation. The telephone should be turned off, along with anything else that could startle or distract you. It is recommended that you remove watches and ticking clocks from your sacred space. Be conscious of excessive exposure to electromagnetic currents for their ability to scramble your frequency.

Keep the lighting warm and avoid fluorescent lights. Avoid meditating in complete darkness and never meditate under fluorescent or CFL (compact fluorescent lighting.) They can alter your moods, disrupt your auric field, and cause you to become disoriented. They produce dead orgone (cosmic Life Force) energy that can compromise your immune system and make you sick. Dead orgone energy from fluorescent lighting can be blocked by safely using a decorative cloth covering as shading, to lessen exposure to its harmful effects. A single white candle can be a relaxing focal point.

Evoke the protective White Light of Divine Spirit to envelop the essence of every manifestation of your being. The deepest and most profound meditations are entered into in a prayerful state of mind. The feeling of safety and security will enable you to relax, knowing that you are cloaked in Divine protection. Know that the Light that protects us, is the Light that we are. We emanated from that Transendent Light.

Sit in a private, quiet, comfortable place with soft lighting where you will not be disturbed. Assume an erect, comfortable posture. Facing the East is best, energetically. Touch your tongue to the roof of your mouth and clench the buttocks to effectively channel the flow of energy. Touch your thumb to the middle finger of your hands, rest them, palms up, on your thighs/knees. If you are not physically able to sit in a full or modified Lotus position, be mindful of your posture and sit up in a comfortable chair. A style of meditation called Yoga Nidra is practiced lying down. There are as many styles and techniques as there are amazing meditation instructors and practitioners.

Be mindful of your breathing. Use your breath as a focal point in your meditations. As a way of staying focused and raising your vibration, the chanting of a mantra sacred to you helps to facilitate cleansing and protection. Be mindful of the mantra that you choose to chant. Make sure that if it is in a language that you do not understand, get the literal translation and study it before you continue your practice. I have witnessed people chanting up their worst nightmares because of a misguided meditation practice and a carelessly chosen mantra. One of the greatest mantras is simply *Thank You*. Chant it and become Conscious gratitude, living under Ultimate Grace. I do not recommend any particular mudra (hand, finger, posture positions) to perform the meditations in this book. I use a basic tip of the index finger touching the tip of the thumb, palms up, resting on the knees, upright modified lotus position. Many variations of that will work. It is worth the effort to research and experiment with the mudras that are best for your preferred system of meditation. It is not a cursory study, but it is a rewarding one that is certainly worth the effort.

Don't eat, drink, smoke, chew gum, or participate in idle chatter while engaged in spiritual work. This behavior is distracting and vulgar. You are cultivating your ability to focus and concentrate, and you do not want to engage in gross and disruptive behaviors. That does not show a proper level of respect for yourself or the sacredness of spiritual practice. These guidelines fall under the category of common manners.

No alcohol or drugs. Do not meditate under the influence of any form of intoxicant! Even after meditation, it is not wise to fall under the influence of any intoxicating substance. You may not be grounded enough to maintain complete control of your energies. Do not ingest any substance that would alter your consciousness before, during, or after meditating. This absolutely includes consciousness-altering pharmaceutical drugs. Consult the medical practitioner who prescribed your medication and ask if there are risks that are relevant to a meditation practice. Any substance that causes impairment can attract energies and entities that are better left crouching in the distance, far, far away. Depending upon the depth of your trance or dream state, there are times during sleep and meditation when you are, as pure conscious awareness, drifting out of the physical body. That is risky enough without adding intoxicants that distort the effects and experience of meditation to the equation. It can result in adding increased and dangerous detachment between the physical and non-physical bodies.

Meditating while intoxicated is as dangerous as driving drunk. You may provide a willing host for some random discarnate being wandering through the lower Astral Planes, anxious to seize a form as you drift out of a drunk or drugged body. It may not even be personal. If you know you are experiencing unwelcome spiritual or psychic phenomena, the worst thing you can do is choose not to face it sober. That is why I recommend the study of Psychic Self-Defense techniques for protection, whether you are engaged in a mystical practice such as meditation or not. My book, FEARLESS: PSYCHIC SELF-DEFENSE, Transcend the Fear of Spiritual Warfare, was written based on several decades of in-depth study and personal experience. It provides for well-informed understanding of deeper levels of mystical practice.

It is not advisable to go into deep meditation on a full stomach, though there are no hard and fast rules on this one. Eating a heavy meal before meditation and spiritual practice inhibits the ability to focus and concentrate because of our grounded energy. A full stomach can dull the senses and interfere with the discernment of subtle communications.

Never go into a meditation without a prayer of total submission to the Will of The God and a spirit of gratitude and humility. Given certain necessary conditions, you can spontaneously link into a current of Timeless information, past, present, and future, that can direct and assist you in life. Ask for guidance and protection.

Journal changes in your sleep patterns. This is not Law, but you may notice your dream patterns changing as you begin to open the doors of forgotten chambers of your subconscious mind through meditation. Studying and practicing a discipline of meditation can trigger spontaneous releases of memory, connecting you to other frequencies and realities. The act of meditating is so powerfully charged with cosmic energy that welcome or unwelcome drama may become attracted to your Dreamtime world. Many tried, and true ancient and modern practices will keep you in charge of the company you keep, whether you are awake or asleep.

A Note of Caution:

The studies in this text are for informational purposes only and are not intended to diagnose, treat, cure, or prevent any disease. If you are experiencing symptoms of diagnosed or undiagnosed emotional or mental illness, clinical depression, thoughts of harming yourself or others, or seized by overwhelming health issues that would impair judgment, attempting certain types of meditation, may not be advised, as it may cause these feelings to intensify. You are encouraged to consult a licensed therapist or medical professional.

Journaling

Keeping a written journal is important. Technology can track and record our "doings" reliably. But how do we track our "beings" in such a way that we would not worry that our very soul was being surveilled? We do not express ourselves the way we used to. Now with a spell check, auto-correct and tight margins that weigh and measure our "published" material against the vision of the monitoring eyes of judgment.

Pen and notebook in hand, we must journal outside of the framework of all of our *doings*. How often do we stop and quietly reflect on how and who we are *being*? How often do we have that conversation with ourselves? How often should we engage in Self-Inquiry, beginning with the meditation, Who am I? We must inquire of ourselves … *beyond* rank identifications, *beyond* personhood, parenthood, gender, religion, race, nationality, and career … *Who* am I being? Who am I *really*? How am I *being* as a force on a mission in this self-created reality?"

Self-Inquiry is vital to our being. We must concern ourselves with our *being* at *least* as much as we concern ourselves with our *doing*. The written journal of our contemplations and inquiry into the Source of our being gives us dots to connect when we revisit our journal entries. Journaling gives us connecting bridges to build from a shapeshifting tapestry of our experiencing the illusory realms of Maya (the impermanent, material world) to our transcendence of it, and back.

The question, "Who am I?" is the beginning of a powerful conversation toward Self-Realization. If we are to defend ourselves against attacks that we perceive to be traveling through invisible realms of influence, how can we do that if we don't even know who we really are? Who is the "I" that we defend? Is it the ceaselessly morphing, carnal being staring back at us from the mirrors of life from the cradle to the grave? Can we trust that "I" in the mirror that is perpetually changing in predictable and unpredictable ways as we helplessly witness? Generally, that is the "I" a psychic attacker targets. If you have a thorough knowledge of Self, any attacker is confused as they stare at the "I" they can see, only to find that the unseen stares back. It is a confident awareness that knows, even though it cannot be seen, it is a powerful witness who is being observed by the "Ultimate I," that Sees, Knows, and Protects.

In matters that require Psychic Self-Defense, it enhances our spiritual practice to keep a journal or diary and designate specific times to consult it. Make a meditation of that consultation. Review it periodically to chart your progress toward accomplishing the spiritual goals you have set for yourself. If messages and information you receive in a meditation draw a complete blank and make no sense to you, by all means, record that in your journal. The meaning will unfold in its own time. Track related events using your journal. A journal is an excellent way of monitoring subtle nuances of multi-layered meanings that memory cannot be trusted to preserve. That will facilitate the decoding of cryptic communications from Spirit that tend to expand in clarity over time.

You will notice as you begin to establish a healthy relationship with the practice of Self-Inquiry that your dreams will begin to change dramatically. You will go into deeper REM states than you ever imagined possible. You will receive communications and profound insights in your dreams. There is nothing to fear if spiritual protection through prayer is practiced, respecting the Sacred Relationship between Creator and creation.

It is very important to record your dreams in your journal immediately upon awakening. If there was anything particularly disturbing about your dream, and you wish to determine its meaning, go into prayer, meditation, and even fasting. Always consult a medical professional before fasting. Do not take vain "demands" into prayer, meditation, or fasting. That is disrespectful of this sacred process. Be patient. No prayer goes unanswered. Answers will come, and guidance will be given. When you receive the understanding you seek, record this information in your journal. Pay close attention to the gradual unfolding of the meaning. Refer back to your notes to expand on your interpretations often.

Keep your journal under password, lock, and key. I trust that no one would be so invasive as to violate anyone in this manner. It would be better to avoid journaling on a computer. Your journal will contain very personal information that you may not want to share with *anyone*.

Go to dreamuniversalmedia.com to print out the cover page to your
DREAMCATCHER JOURNAL/SLEEPLESS and as many copies
of the questionnaire as required.

APPENDIX SEVEN

The Light Meditation

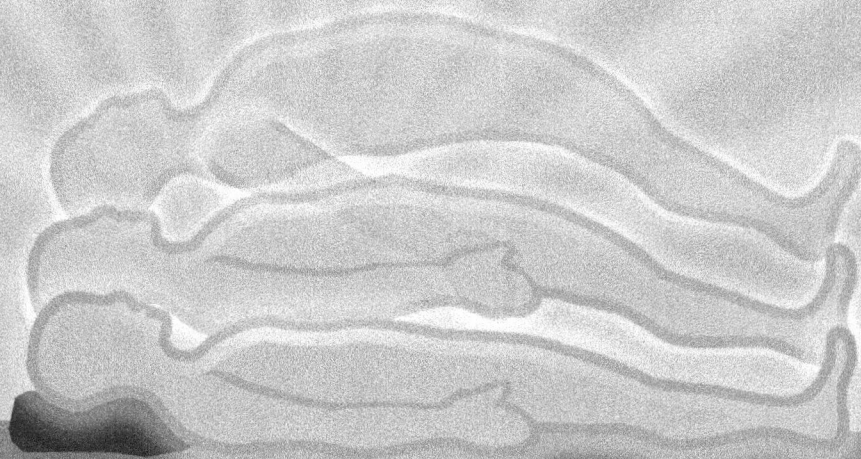

THE LIGHT
MEDITATION

I AM PROTECTED
AS ETERNAL LIGHT

The Light Meditation should be performed before engaging in any spiritual ritual work or meditation. It is designed to cleanse and activate the energies of our Chakra System to facilitate balance, harmony, and protection. It is a useful meditation that can be practiced daily with your prayer of choice for energy maintenance and as a spiritual cleansing and shield. This guided audio meditation is available as a download on the dreamuniversalmedia.com website. The transcript of the Light Meditation is presented here for your perusal to assure that you are aware of and aligned with all aspects of its content.

THE LIGHT MEDITATION
TRANSCRIPT

I am seated in a comfortable position

facing the direction of the rising Sun

My back is straight

My feet are touching the floor

My hands rest palms up

I close my eyes

My mind's eye envisions

a single white candle that I light

with the intention of inner illumination

from my most profound depths

extending to the Origin of my existence

the Focal Point of Ultimate Light

From this comfortable seated position … I breathe

I AM the OBSERVER and WITNESS of my breath

as it touches the middle of my upper lip

I observe the sensations for qualities

such as heat, coolness, moisture, dryness

I observe … undistracted by these sensations

I go within.

I slip between the invisible pockets of silence

between my inhaled and exhaled breath

My attention goes to the sensation of my breath

as it flows across the center groove of my upper lip

The focus of my awareness moves to my Solar Plexus

the 3rd Chakra

At its most profound point, there is an ethereal SILVER CORD

anchored in my physical reality

to ground me, to guide me

back to the starting point of my journey if I should need it

A pinpoint of Light pulsates

to the rhythm of my heartbeat

and radiates from that focal point of Light

expanding to extend to, and beyond my entire body

enveloping me in this pure, radiant, protective Light

extending beyond me to envelop this room

extending beyond this room to envelop this entire building

this entire city and far beyond

seeking and connecting

to its Point of Origin.

I inhale through my nostrils

I exhale through my mouth

I inhale LIGHT

I exhale FEAR

I cup my hands over my mouth

to collect sacred breath laced with golden Light and positive intention

I inhale Light and become it

I exhale fear and rebuke it

The silver cord that extends

from my navel area at the CORE of my being

dispels all fear as my consciousness drifts

It will guide me back

to my comfort zone

and starting point

whenever I choose

I cup my hands over my mouth

to collect the breath of my earnest petition

right hand over the left

good over evil

knowing one defines the other.

In my working breath

are words of power

and utterances of commandments

a release

a surrender

of all that is of Maya

all that is temporary

I release my attachment to the CHANGEFUL

I embrace only the UNCHANGING

INCLUDING the so-called "self"

of my own lower perceptions

I embrace all that I really am

BREATH, AWARENESS, CONSCIOUSNESS

INTO THE STILLNESS THAT I AM

I suspend my senses

I shut down

I open up

Calm and focused breath

occurs in natural rhythms

I inhale through my nostrils

I exhale through my mouth

I inhale LIGHT and become it

I exhale FEAR and rebuke it

I inhale golden Light

I cup my hands over my mouth

to collect my breath

laced with THIS golden Light and focused intention

I use it to dispel and cleanse unwelcome energies.

It is charged with the intention of attracting the healing that I desire

With this sacred Light Breath

I wash MY HANDS

then MY FACE

of all carnal witnessing and unsavory desires

I cleanse MY NOSE of the scent of the shadow worlds …

MY EYES … of all they have seen of suffering

I cleanse MY THIRD EYE … 6th Chakra

located between my eyebrows

of all it has observed of lower vibrations

MY EARS … of the filth they have heard

I cleanse MY INNER AND OUTER VOICE at the throat level,

the energy vortex of my 5th Chakra

I cleanse thought-forms, both spoken and silenced, that traveled

on wings of words that injure like bullets and blades

I HEAL that with this sacred breath of radiant Golden Light

I cleanse MY CROWN, 7th Chakra at the top of my head

of all that has ever sought to come between my Higher Self and my Source

the Source of all … The Ultimate Reality

With this sacred Light Breath

I move my attention down to the back of MY NECK

I cleanse and seal this entry point of whispered suggestions

from the lower planes of consciousness

seeking a home … seeking manifestation

through MY mind and spirit

I cleanse my feet of every step they strayed

from the path of my Enlightenment

with Golden Light

of Sacred Breath

My footsteps are guided

My path is protected

My journey is blessed

I inhale LIGHT and become it

I exhale FEAR and rebuke it

Hands cupped over my mouth,

right hand over the left,

I collect this Sacred Breath in my hands

I hold it to MY HEART

HEALING CLEANSING ENERGY OF GOLDEN LIGHT

enters MY HEART at my 4th Chakra

whirling, spinning, yielding in surrender

to my connection to Divinity

I accept that I am healed by this Breath of Light

I cleanse myself of the PAIN I have suffered that seeks to break me

I cleanse myself of emotional attachments to joy

that seek to ADDICT me and CONTROL me

I am not my emotions

I am not my past

I am not my future

I am not my mind

I AM MORE THAN THIS

I break through the mirror of illusion

I forsake the lies that seek to define me

as less than an Eternal being of Divine Essence

I inhale through my nostrils

I exhale through my mouth

I inhale LIGHT and become it

I exhale FEAR and rebuke it

I inhale Light

I cup my hands over my mouth to collect

breath laced with golden Light and positive intention

My mantra is

Thank You

My mantra is
Thank You

With this golden breath, I shield my Solar Plexus
from all energies that may seek to enter uninvited, unwelcome,
with their urges and weaknesses, cravings and clinging,
anger and unforgiveness, seeking to eclipse my will
with its self-serving obsessions and uncontrollable
desires and projections, seeking to make me believe they are my own

Sacred breath is the BRIDGE between the many selves that I am
from the lower to the upper realms of consciousness
With it, I have cleansed and sealed this space that I am
I do not stand alone as its gatekeeper
I am protected from creation
That Which created me sustains me

I inhale through my nostrils
exhale through my mouth
I inhale Light and become it
I exhale fear and rebuke it
I inhale Light
I cup my hands over my mouth to collect
breath laced with golden Light and positive intention

With this breath, I shield my 2nd Chakra
located in the area of my lower abdomen
the seat of all desire, attachment, and aversion
With this sacred breath of pure Golden Light

I suspend my senses

I cleanse the lower energetic, sensual,

carnal aspects of my being and heal them in the Eternal Now

The cleansing breath of Golden Light subdues the raging fire of my Root Chakra

the 1st Chakra - Sacral Chakra

sending this creative energy rising into the Golden Light

of the manifestation of my authority over my own animalistic nature

This primal fuel energizes all of the other chakras as it gently rises,

Uncoiled Golden Light of purification

Rising

Up,

Up,

Up through the 2nd Chakra below the navel

Cleansing … Releasing negative energies

Up,

Up,

Up the Spine through the spiraling vortex of the 3rd Chakra

Spinning beautiful waves of Golden Light

gently rushing up this life enabling thread of creation's energy

Releasing … Cleansing … Healing … Illuminating

With Golden waves of Light energy

sweeping clean all residue ... all debris

All attachment … All aversion … all longing for all else

but The Beloved … The Divine One

My mantra is

Thank You

My mantra is

Thank You

CLEANSING LIGHT gently rises through the 4TH Chakra … MY HEART …

healing it from the senseless acts of emotional savagery it has suffered …

Loving it for all of the Love it is capable of … trusting it with my life.

I close my body down

I am not my body

I am not my mind

I am not my emotions

I AM MORE THAN THAT

I suspend my senses

I break the mirror of illusion

I meditate on the Light that I AM

the Light of the Eternal I AM

I have manifested on this plane

from the realm of the Divine One

I have expressed myself as my desire

for this Sacred Journey

from the angelic realm

the realm of the guides,

the realm of the Sacred

the abode of the prophets,

the mystics, the messengers, and servants

of the Most High GOD

Breath and Light are One

The Light of my Core Being

is One with the Core Point of Light

expressed out of triple darkness,

the Consciousness, the Love of the Ultimate I AM,

the Unknowable One, the Limitless One,

Whose name is best expressed by SILENCE.

My most sacred mantra is

Thank You

Beautiful energy has gathered in my HEART Chakra …

the Temple of my Beloved

the Temple of the Divine One

In Love … Golden Light energy continues to rise … powerfully … subtly

Up through my 5th Chakra at my throat

Up through my 6th Chakra, my Third Eye

Reaching the 7th Crown Chakra

GOLDEN ENERGY collected at the top of my head

connecting with my strongest PRAYER

Connecting with my strongest prayer

Connecting with my strongest prayer

I pray

I pray for protection from all unwelcome,

Uninvited energies

(silence during prayer)

Shhhhhhhhh

I accept this cloak of protection

enveloping the entire form of my body

physical and formless

cleansing my aura, purifying my intentions,

closing out all that is not of this protective Light

A pinpoint of Light pulsates to the rhythm of my heartbeat

and radiates from that focal point of Light

expanding to extend to and beyond my entire body

enveloping me in pure, radiant Light

extending beyond me to envelop this room

extending beyond this room to envelop this entire building

this entire city and far beyond … seeking and connecting

with all beings at the Point of Origin … PURE CONSCIOUSNESS

I breathe from my core

from the most profound center of my being

I cleanse myself with Sacred Breath

Golden Breath has become a solid SHIELD of PROTECTION

Waves of beautiful Golden Light

sweep up and over and around me

all the way up and over and around me

swirling up and over and around me

THE LIGHT IS MY SHIELD

It is my Comforter

I have always been THAT LIGHT

My mantra is

Thank You

My mantra is

Thank You

I return from the silence … the stillness

grounded in my humble, energetic abode

anchored in the SAFETY I have affirmed

the PROTECTION I have affirmed

the LOVE I have affirmed

the FREEDOM I have affirmed

Released from guilt … released from shame

Released from judgment

If I have ventured out far enough to have trouble returning

I follow the silver cord extended from my navel

back to the state of consciousness that is awake and alert

aware, fully focused, and grounded

no longer corrupted by false identity and conditioning

The energy of this freedom washes over me in shimmering waves of assurance that

I am a being of Eternal Light … connected to all of creation

essentially connected to the Creator of all and I AFFIRM …

That which created me is sufficient to protect me!

I AM ONE WITH THAT!

The Light Meditation is available as an audio download at Dreamuniversalmedia.com. Please see the instructions in the chapter "Meditation Download Instructions" at the back of this book. It can also be found at dreamuniversalmedia@youtube.com

Epilogue

"Every Angel is a Jinn. But Not Every Jinn is an Angel"

This research on Sleep Paralysis has taken an unexpected turn into a dimension of consciousness that I have found to be spiritually compromising. The jinn … They say to The God, "I will come at them from the front and from the back, I will ambush Your new creation … all the way to the hellfire." They do not want for us to have knowledge of them. We cannot see them, but they can see us. It all started with … *"just to be thorough"* … I took on, as a part of my research project on Sleep Paralysis, a search for the accounts of acts of *benevolent* jinn. Every expert that I consulted on the subject has relayed to me that the jinn are not *all* evil. In spite of a mischievous nature, there are those who are not only capable of, but CHOOSE to "bow down" to Good, serving the Light, The God, and the Will of The God.

I pondered on their behalf … "Did we force them into subconscious territories of the mind, so they get us in our dreams?" When certain parallels and so-called coincidences led me to "jinn," my least favorite subject … I just wanted to back off because I have a chip on my shoulder about it. I didn't want to think about it. I didn't want to talk about it. I didn't want to write about it. I certainly didn't believe that I would find myself standing at a precarious crossroad of opposing physical and non-physical forces, in the middle of a war of complex dualities rising up in the collective consciousness. In the event of a Complex Sleep Paralysis "attack," I have never stopped to ask, "Are you, or are you not, a benevolent jinn?"

Is there any doubt as to the intention or the benevolence of an entity that has snatched you out of your body and is drawing the very Life Force from your being? That's why they are called "attacks!" How could we consider calling a jinn, or any other being, "benevolent" if they demonstrate an intention of terrifying us, paralyzing us, and making us feel they are sucking out our soul through straws of hatred and envy? This whisper is not one of nursery rhymes, superhero movies, and video games to play. The nature of this ancient hatred is not easy to understand. The level of their hatred is beyond our comprehension. We cannot defend ourselves against that which we do not understand.

This existential evil manifests in the hearts of people. Their primary objective is breaking our heart, spirit, and our faith, creating chaos and hatred, poisoning everything good of our existence. If this energy of fear finds a place to land in your heart, you are gone. Only Divine Will can expel it. Now the collective heart of the world is in a battle for survival. No matter what it is, you think you see … behind that is a reality, beings that can … not only *change*, but *shift*, into their own ever-present counterparts and companions, or YOURS … and turn *you* into a monster … a monster capable of monstrous deeds. They *choose* to shift between manifestations. That does not mean that they have to. They have Free Will like we do. We should have common sense enough not to stop and interview them about their intentions, mid-attack. We have the Free Will to either choose or succumb to their hypnosis and oppression. Free Will is a blessing and a gift, as long as we remember we were given the Free Will, even to choose our own demise.

It is hard … It should be impossible even to imagine the level of hatred I am speaking of. Even though these behaviors may appear irrational, in the extremity of their cruelty and causation of violent and abysmal suffering … the true emotions behind these attacks must be examined and understood. Imagine the plight of being the new baby of a family that becomes the object of extreme and vile contempt, conciliating for safety, vulnerable to the wrath of jealous, abusive sibling rivalry. This struggle is known and understood by any parent of more than one child. A conflict among siblings is generally overseen and intervened in by the parents of the children. The older child or children may take on the role of "bully," claiming seniority, in some cases to the ultimate danger of the 'new arrival' who is defenseless against the older, stronger, jealous sibling(s). Generally, a set of rules are set in place to protect the object of their relentless attacks.

Competitive for attention, they are angry because they feel replaced. They are jealous of having to share space, attention, and affection. They wake up every day and go to sleep every night with the same agenda, whether or not they are provoked. Being inclined to have a particularly mischievous nature, the rivalry turns to war, particularly when there is a perception of favoritism. As time progresses, the new arrival is advised of ways to protect, defend, and coexist while staying out of harm's way ... yet it is the parent(s) that enforce/s the means to assure the safety of the fledgling. The defenseless child/children will scramble for the capability of sovereign protection. The more they are aware of the parent's role in securing them while, and even after, they learn to protect themselves, the safer they are. That is some serious drama without bringing into the equation the loosh/aliment factor, the voracious appetite, not to mention the difference in species. Maybe that was not a good analogy. That's honestly all I could think of until I got to the part that the energy of that baby is sustenance to the older ones. This is the point at which the family movie turns into a horror film.

I'm reaching here! Okay, in the atmosphere of enmity, I offer that the best way to win a war is not to declare one. The best way to defeat an enemy is to not have one. The most powerful enemy we will ever face is the one staring back at us in the mirror. If we conquer that one, the conquest of all of the lesser ones is imminent. Our victory is claimed in the development of our evolving spiritual strength in the face of the trials and tribulations of our existence. Our purpose is known. Our fate is known. Our Love creates the 'becoming' of a Covenant of Divine Protection. Our triumph is to RISE up out of the duality of our existence into the Oneness with the Divine One, Creator of all that is. We are more than a fear/hate-based agenda. We are more than conquerors. We are the intersection of where the river meets and merges with the sea … the alchemy of the union of the Loved and the Beloved … the Union in Divinity.

This book began as a book about Sleep Paralysis. I have gathered more information to share than I ever went in search of. ***And this is where it ends.*** Though I found it to be a fascinating study, my recommendation is that we seek, with a greater passion, to educate ourselves about the miracle of our relationship with and as Divinity … rather than fixating on our relationship with the potential of pure evil. We unleash our full potential to become a higher frequency that speaks Life into the song, the breath, the Light of Yin and Yang, respecting the Cause and Effect of all creation.

It is not my position to question or consider the nature of jinn feelings. The mysteries of their creation can only be known by THAT Which created all things. My only position is to know, love, and understand my relationship with That Which created it all. If what I am studying has openly declared itself the open enemy of the purest love I have ever known, it is not my job to seek redemption but to pray for the mercy of the Creator for all of creation.

The day *always* comes when we get swallowed into the icy, death stare of the very negation of our existence … our humanity, along with THAT Which Created it … and we *choose*. Then we *become* the manifestation of the choice *we* make. We will choose between forces of good and apparent evil. We are not alone. We are guided and protected by That from which all things mystical arose, That from which the ability to create arose, That from which the ability to shapeshift arose … That which commissioned an army of **beings of the Angelic** Realm around us, among us, and within us, to protect us and guide us into remembering who we are and our relationship with Divinity. We chant the mantra HU in remembrance of that sacred relationship, connecting with it through a sound current that transcends all Earthly languages. HU is a Third person, gender-neutral pronoun that transcends the personification of Divinity or attribution of a "grammatical gender" referring to the Divine One. HU refers to the Divine Breath … The Subtlest Essence of the Holy Mother/Father God Presence. HU represents Union with the Absolute, the Most High, Nameless, God Presence.

That is where the story begins, with the Ultimate existential question, "Who are you?" Are you the body-mind identified ghost, cowering in the corner, afraid of the boogie man? Or are you the Self-Realized spark, becoming the Ultimate Flame of Illumination.

So, the closing paragraphs of this book were to be about …

Look at my "ME":

- What my thorough research turned up;
- What scary woo-woo stories I have to tell you;
- This is fascinating!;
- This is deep!;
- What happened to me;
- What happened to them;
- How thoroughly I researched it;
- How detailed my findings were;
- How terrifying it was;
- How I won;
- How I had been attack-free for years;
- How, by implementing my advice, others had been attack-free for years;
- How smart, strong, intelligent, spiritual, and knowledgeable I AM;

- When I AM is nothing. I am nothing … nothing but an energy field filled with Light and shadows trying to maintain a viable frequency, like everybody else;
- Not the one who makes passes for the enemies of everything good;
- Not the apologist for it or redeemer of it;
- Not the one who is so well-studied and experienced in these phenomena to claim that I now have sovereign courage in the face of this dark goo of bitter evil;
- Not the one who is looking into this ancient darkness for the "love and light" in it (new-age style) or the redemption of it;
- Not the one who is inspired more by hate than love;
- Not even the one who judges it;
- Only the one who turns away from it as "not the choice made by the reality of my being";
- Only the one who bows before THAT, that I AM … giving praise and thanks to the Most High, in gratitude for the purpose of this life I was given … by only THAT … protected by only THAT;
- The current of our faith is stronger than the current of their rage.

What actually happened … Every area of my life was attacked on every level. My world turned into a horror movie. I stared into the abyss. It stared back at me as if to say, "Oh, so you don't respect the translation of our name … "The Hidden Ones!" You want to research … Okay! So now, research this!" I got an astral beat-down. I got it that the message was to "back off." My reality shapeshifted, and everything and everyone in it was used as a weapon, formed and fashioned against me. Fixed became fluid, vaporous, invisible … form became shadow. That drove my research to a chilling experiential level. I looked into the eyes of "family" and "friends" and saw strangers looking back at me. The experience inspired my new book and accompanying guided audio meditation, SELFLESS: TURIYA-Beyond the Dark Night of the Soul. Some of it, I don't

337

believe I will ever get over. My healing required the help of gifted spiritual professionals. I plan a retreat into the mountains of South America for a Soul Retrieval. That will be another book or documentary, perhaps … one I may produce myself. I removed a section of my research from this book into another publication named *The Hidden Ones*, that will not be available for commercial sale. It does not particularly address Sleep Paralysis. It more addresses complex hyperdimensional entity interference issues. It is not for entertainment purposes, nor is it advisable for casual curiosity-based research. It is for direct experiencers and can be made available to those in specific need of that type of healing. So, let's get back to the things we *can* change.

What would our lives be like if we chose to come undone over the appearance of every one of the countless phenomena in this vast creation? We have to know when to stop with our minds and proceed on our faith in the face of no evidence or proof. We have to know when to stop choosing to swim against the current of fearful denial. I tried to stick to the "white light, high-frequency, good energy, clean chakra" vibe. I wanted to stay there, in lotus position. Then, it turned stalker and was shockingly revealed to me, again and again, in loathing and repugnance in the eyes and snarling voices of others, in a host of undeniable ways. Then, I started seeing it everywhere … this vaporous subtlety, this formless wisp of being … of seemingly no apparent consequence. I clearly was not going to be allowed to tread water at the shallow end of the pool of shadows.

Spinning on a thought form of war with jinn, we must make sure we don't find the monsters we perceive to be under our beds, living in our heads, in our hearts, waging war with our very souls, and everything good in our lives. The anger, the pain, and the fury of that rejection, is clearly so profound that I don't believe our psyches are able to process that kind of emotional information. So, these beings want *us* to feel *that*. Our greatest enemy will always be our own fear and our own lack of knowledge of our True Self. The True Self that we are, has a direct connection to, and relationship with, the Source of all creation, as the sovereign wave that collapses back into the vast ocean from which it rose and caused itself to be named, then transcends back into namelessness. There is only one way to manage the fear, complete *SURRENDER* to Divine Will or be dissolved into the acid of our own fear, rage, and lack of faith. Cultivate the innate Love for and of the Creator to vanquish the demon called fear.

AGAIN, this started out being about Sleep Paralysis. I had enough of the dismissiveness and the ignorance of an inconvenient reality. Astral entities are real. Denying their existence will not make them go away, it will only make us look as foolish as they see humanity as being. It is caused by many things. I hope my research gives you as much insight into this phenomenon as it gave me.

I am among the multitude who have felt tormented by this mysterious phenomenon and the origin of it. I stared into the darkness of that abyss and felt *nothing* staring back but the electrical energy of a hatred so malignant it was unbearable. I have experienced the feeling that I have stared quite deeply into its eye. But I witnessed that as a person. I asked my I AM to witness from a non-personal perspective, and my findings were easier to bear but chilling and sobering. I felt suspicious of what could be perceived as my seeking a pass, an understanding of, perhaps redemption for them (the jinn.) Instead, there was bewilderment and shock, even pain, for having felt this foreboding energy. I tried to imagine how *awful* the feeling of being rejected by The God, feeling discarded, and being "cast out" for a new creation that was somehow "better." What I cannot even try to imagine, though, is standing up and saying, "No, I am better than them ... I am made of fire, and they are made of clay. I would rather go make hell and preside over that than be in this now dysfunctional family, not only tolerating but bowing down to my inferiors!" ... or something to that effect.

They *cannot* love us. We *cannot* seek that love from them (form or formless), any more than we seek it in the flesh, rather than the Divinity, of one another. Yes, there is benevolence and purpose to be found in all of creation. Do we really understand enough about creation to feel we have the authority to declare any part of it a mistake? One level of benevolence could be found in the obliteration of another. It depends on the face in the mirror. In the instant the smoke of that perspective passed over the depth of my consciousness, something happened to me. I stared into it, the self-illuminating triple darkness of zero-point negative existence. But what I saw staring back at me was a hatred so profound, it had the power to take *me* back to zero-point negative existence and simply uncreate me. It was not human. I would put a LOL behind that if I were on social media chatting about it. Because no-body, no-thing, has that authority over my existence other than THAT which declared it to be so. All other declarations are OF the void, AS the void, FROM the void, and That which can only exist as That.

Pablo Neruda's profound quote is appropriate *right here, right now.* *"Let us forget with generosity those who cannot love us."* I am sure that extends to all king and queendoms, regardless of form or formlessness … not just the jinn. I share this in full disclosure and remembrance of the evil I have seen. I have also known the Highest Love. It is undramatic and often gets lost between the cracks of mythology and folklore. It is sufficient to heal me from this hatred. Even in the face of what appears to be the opposite of, or other than *hatred*, the word "shapeshifters" becomes an important one to understand.

What must we ever even expect of a "shapeshifter" … wavering in all that is Sacred? From the void of their being, they feed on our love, our passion, and our connection to the Source, Divinity. If we want to see our greatest enemy … look for the jinn within, the jinn in the mirror, the jinn looking out of our Third Eye, projecting the energy of their contempt upon our inner and outer realities, poisoning everything in our energy field. Destroyers of innocence, of families, of faith, of health, of livelihoods, throwing around phantom manifestations, assuming familiar forms, conjurers of abysmal hopelessness, health, and well-being for entertainment purposes only … and will rise up inside of you and assume your form. Their parasitic energy manipulates our emotions to breaking points we never imagined we could be pushed to … particularly evoking fear.

Read my book FEARLESS: PSYCHIC SELF-DEFENSE, Transcend the Fear of Spiritual Warfare. We must not fear them because they feed on the energy of it. The extent to which we fear demonstrates our faith and belief in Divine Providence. How powerful are they really if you can say *"Hu"* and it diffuses and dissolves their every effort? Of their temptations and seductions, whatever it is we *think* we see that evokes a modicum of desire from the hell of attachment and craving … *All we actually see is a mirage.* When it is time to pay the piper, the price to pay is too unbearable to even think about. Even in the worst-case scenarios of the appearance of the victory of our enemies prevailing over us and reducing our lives to the nightmares of their imposed realities … We affirm: Our Life and our Death are all for The God. We affirm … Surrendered, is this gift … my life … I bow, I place it before The God, not out of fear of evil, but love for THAT!

At our core, there is something that does not belong to us, a Soul. It was never truly separated from its Source, except in the delusion of our own perception of an individuated carnal life experience. We cannot sell it or give it away. It cannot be stolen or conquered. It is not a "wavering" love. It is at the epicenter of a constant and unwavering Namaste kind of energy … the purest expression of Love. Namaste translates from Sanskrit to English as "The Divine in me sees and bows down to the Divine in you." This is spoken as a blessing and a deeply respectful greeting. We must not bow to flesh and form, power and might, fear and hopelessness. Bow down only to That Which created and preceded form, That

Which we are sealed from even the true knowledge of. It is beyond Light. It is beyond Shadow. It is beyond our capacity to fathom. It is beyond Unknowable.

So, my position on this, now that I am certain that the world is a whole lot stranger than I ever imagined … I'm going to let what created this phenomenon sort it out, for I am no one, merely another phenomenon that flashed in the pan of life. The purpose this book grew into was to announce and share that I had finally conquered these mysterious, invisible bullies. Well, I did not. I approached it all wrong. All I could think was banish, destroy, protect, defend, defeat … when the strongest, bravest, sanest, most real thing I can do if I am not enjoying their company is to be so much more of everything they hate … Light. Instead of making a life out of cursing their darkness, I increase my Light … I AM Light. So, when I find myself seized by the unknown … I chant, pray, meditate, and affirm in answer to my Self-Inquiry … Who am I?

Our energy is better spent studying the Love of The God,
than the fear-based study of self-declared and natural enemies of THAT!

Becoming One with Sacred Space
as Pure Consciousness

Let us engage in Self-Inquiry as a meditation of Sri Ramana Maharshi. In matters of Psychic Self-Defense, we must be fully aware of who it is that we defend. We ask, "Who am I, really?" That is our meditation. Through this basic act of surrender and humility, we never lose sight of who we really are without attachment, without aversion, without judgment. As we engage an ongoing study of the amazing mysteries of the art of Psychic Self-Defense, we affirm that we cannot defend what we cannot understand. We must explore the ever-evolving aspects of ourselves and hold that journey as sacred. Know that the journey is *within* that safe place that cannot be touched by anything or anyone. In and as that awareness, we are invulnerable. In, and as that awareness, our hearts were never broken; our dreams were never stolen; no person, no thing has ever touched who we really are. Delicately kissed by morning's dew, we are a rose whose fragrance is its only reality … not the thorns or the savagery with which it was violently torn away from the bush home it knew. We are that dew, that rose, that fragrance, that thorn, and the savage reaper. We are all of that. We are the Sun that shined upon that rose. We are the Moon that watches it sleep. We are the Earth and water that nourished its life. We are the blooming and the withering. We are the seed. We are the root and the fruit … and it is *all* good. We are the air upon which its fragrance rides into awareness of all who can feel it. We are all of that.

The phenomena associated with spiritual warfare is nothing more than that … *phenomena*. It does not exist without *us* as its host. It is pure thought-form, so who is the thinker? Who accepts this thought-form and gives it a home of manifestation? What will it be after it has found no home in our consciousness? If it is a discarnate spirit, who does it stalk when we have become unavailable in our personhood, after our realization of the formless being that we really are? If it is a wicked energy, where does it land after we do not give it our permission to use our lives like a theme park full of rides? If it raises its ugly head as a domino effect change of fortune that sends our lives toppling around our feet, why was it *allowed* to visit us? Are we alone in our struggle with the plights of the human form? Is this "Watcher or Observer" able to intervene in our affairs and protect us from attack? Is That All-knowing Awareness observing as the wisdom of allowing certain experiences to bleed through the duality of our perceptions of *right and wrong*, *fair and unfair*, to touch us in an apparently awful way? Are we able to see only in the rear-view mirror that we have been led to our highest good? So, if elements of an attack are allowed, does this mean that evil has triumphed over good? The Ultimate Victor is the Ultimate I AM. In that Field of Consciousness, all things are known. There are no dualities. There is no time, no past, no future … only the NOW. Every cause that is set in place is seen at the same moment as its effect.

If we, from the perspective of the I AM, find ourselves under attack, do we have reason to succumb to fear? If That Which Witnesses us is sufficient to protect us, why do we need to study Psychic Self-Defense? We study because we seek to transcend this illusion because we are That which we study. There is nothing to do. There is nothing to become. We are That. We are That which appears to be nothing, knowing it is, therefore, everything … as a drop of rain that becomes the ocean.

There will always be the appearance of chaos in the world. It is the dance of existence keeping its own balance. Let no one make you believe that because there is evil in the world, love is not eclipsing it with our every breath, our every smile. Life is good, even now. All of those things we have always wanted to do, we'd better do them, as the I AM. Stay there. Remain in the NOW. Love life! All that we have endeavored to attain from external sources will be discovered within our own essence as we stand up, Self-Realized, in the I AM of our being. We have nothing to fear and every reason to rejoice in our liberation. Every time we close our eyes and go within, we are carving out our sacred space in this chaotic world. As we manage a lifestyle around living from that quiet, safe, peaceful place, we win. What is the prize? The prize is The Ultimate I AM realized in our hearts.

I regret sounding preachy. I am not the expert in these matters, except for the fact that I have experienced these things that we study, and there is a level of expertise derived from experience. This experiencing caused me to initiate a lifetime commitment to this study with the longing to share it with others. There is something Divine about us. We are That Sacred Space.

ABOUT THE AUTHOR
JAI (Jāy)

With early beginnings as a published songwriter, JAI's passion has remained her poetry. She has been published in the Los Angeles Sentinel, SIC Magazine, Talisman Magazine, UCLA's NOMMO Magazine, Point of Light, The Drumming Between Us, and African Voices. Her publications by *Dream Universal Media* are listed below. *Dream Universal Media* specializes in literature, audio, and video recordings, specifically designed to heal and elevate the consciousness of mind, body, and spirit through Mystical Meditation.

JAI is a student and teacher of metaphysical sciences and many mystical healing traditions, including Tibetan, Hawaiian, Native American, African, Caribbean, Eastern, Chinese, and Japanese, all of which inspired her work. JAI continues to teach, publish, and write.

THE TIMELESS NOW: HEALING FROM GRIEF AND LOSS
Mystical Meditation-The Sacred Law of Impermanence

FEARLESS: PSYCHIC SELF-DEFENSE – Transcend the Fear of Spiritual Warfare

SLEEPLESS: Transcend the Fear of Sleep Paralysis

SELFLESS: TURIYA – Beyond the Dark Night of the Soul

FACELESS: THE SACRED RELATIONSHIP

LIMITLESS: MADE OF LIGHT – Your Companion Reference Book for FACELESS

NAMELESS: A Poetic Journey to The Higher Self

I AM NOT A POET ANYMORE

SANDBOXES

DREAM UNIVERSAL JOURNAL

AUDIO and VIDEO MEDITATIONS INCLUDE:

The Light Meditation
I Die to My Ego Self Meditation
Stone Meditation
Turiya Meditation

JAI (Jāy), literally means "Victory" in Sanskrit, representing the Spirit of this sacred journey. Look for more at *dreamuniversalmedia.com* and the Facebook Group: SLEEPLESS: Transcend the Fear of Sleep Paralysis.

Meditation Download Instructions

To download the audio meditation included in this book, go to Dreamuniversalmedia.com and select the OUR PRODUCTS page, then select the Audio Meditations section and follow the instructions.

Works Cited

A Course in Miracles. Foundation for Inner Peace, 1985.

"Vipassana Meditation." *International Meditation Centres |Home*, www.internationalmeditationcentre.org/global/index.html.

Gibran, Khalil, AL-AJNIHA AL-MUTAKASSIRA, 1912
(The Broken Wings, English Translation)

Kahlil Gibran, The Wanderer, 1932
Alfred A Knopf, New York, New York

Gibran, Kahlil. *The Prophet*. New York: Knopf, 1952. Print.

Rumi, Jalal Al-Din, and Coleman Barks. *The Essential Rumi*. San Francisco, CA: Harper, 1995. Print.

Rumi, Jalal Al-Din, and William C. Chittick. *The Sufi Path of Love: The Spiritual Teachings of Rumi*. Albany: State U of New York, 1983. Print.

Recommended Reading

A Course in Miracles

Hazrat Inayat Rehmat Khan; The Soul's Journey

Idries Shah; The Sufis

Nisargadatta Maharaj; I Am That

Paramhansa Yogananda; Autobiography of a Yogi (Self-

  RealizationFellowship)

Sri Ramana Maharshi; Who Am I?

Thich Nhat Hanh: The Pocket Thich Nhat Hanh

Sayagyi U Ba Khin; What is Vipassana Meditation

Rupert Spira: Being Aware of Being Aware

Sun Tzu and John Minford; The Art of War

C.W. Leadbeater. Man, Visible and Invisible. The Theosophical
Publishing House
First Edition 1902

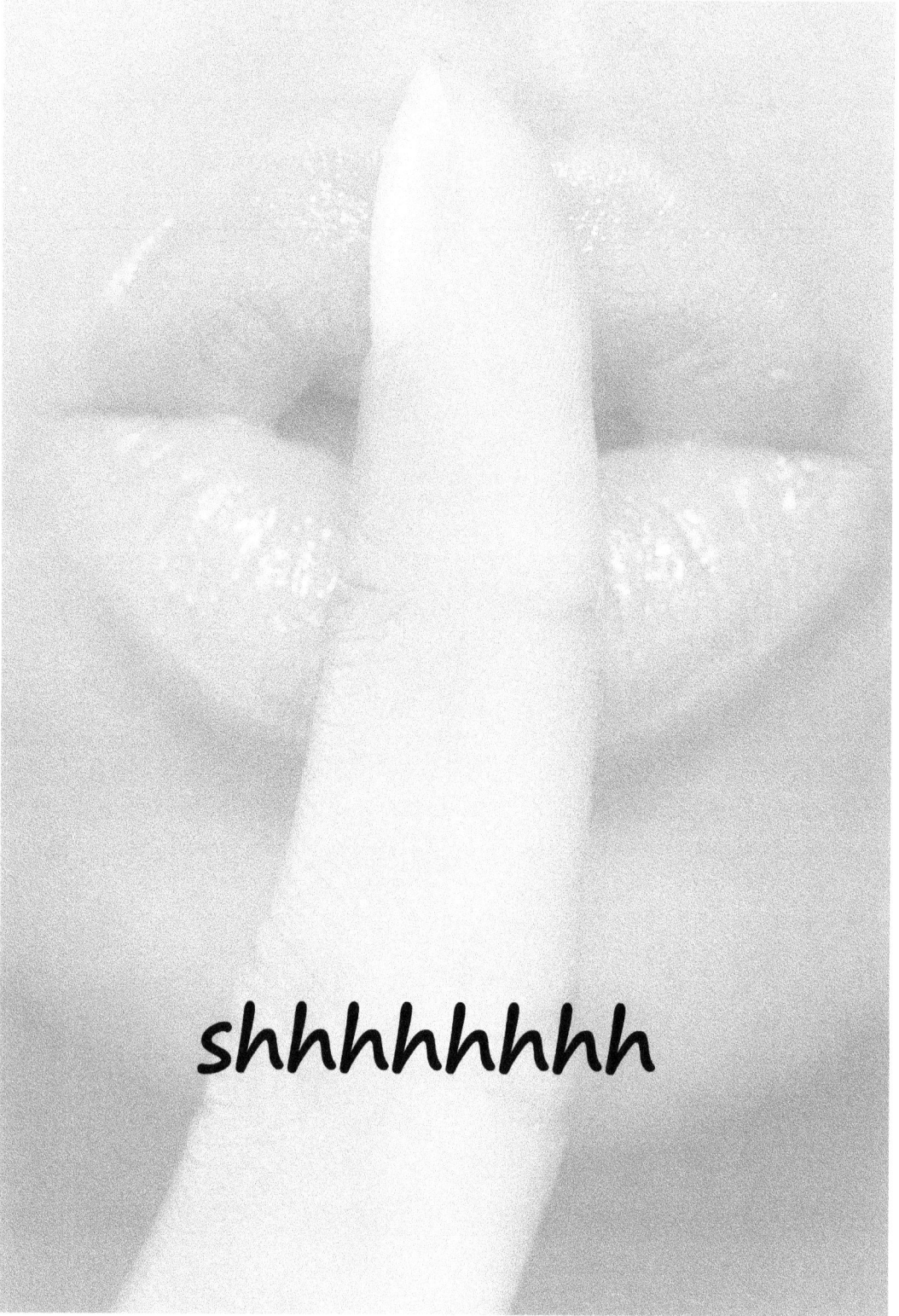

shhhhhhh

www.ingramcontent.com/pod-product-compliance
Lightning Source LLC
Chambersburg PA
CBHW080548090426
42735CB00016B/3185